THE ABUNDANT LIFE
BIBLE
AMPLIFIER

SAMUEL

OTHER BOOKS AVAILABLE IN THIS SERIES

Exodus   Jon L. Dybdahl
God Creates a People

Matthew   George R. Knight
The Gospel of the Kingdom

John   Jon Paulien
Jesus Gives Life to a New Generation

Timothy & Titus   Charles E. Bradford
Counsels to Young Pastors for Struggling Churches

Hebrews   William G. Johnsson
Full Assurance for Christians Today

Peter & Jude   Robert M. Johnston
Living in Dangerous Times

ALDEN THOMPSON

THE ABUNDANT LIFE
BIBLE
AMPLIFIER

SAMUEL

**From the Danger of Chaos
to the Danger of Power**

GEORGE R. KNIGHT
General Editor

Pacific Press Publishing Association
Boise, Idaho
Oshawa, Ontario, Canada

Edited by B. Russell Holt
Designed by Tim Larson
Typeset in 11/14 Janson Text

Copyright © 1995 by
Pacific Press Publishing Association
Printed in the United States of America
All Rights Reserved

Unless otherwise mentioned, all Bible quotations in this book are from the New International Version, and all emphasis in Bible quotations is supplied by the author.

Thompson, Alden L. (Alden Lloyd)
    1 and 2 Samuel : from the danger of chaos to the danger of power / Alden Thompson.
        p.   cm. — (The Abundant life Bible amplifier)
    Includes bibliographical references.
    Spine title: Bible amplifier 1 and 2 Samuel.
    ISBN 0-8163-1265-6 (alk. paper). — ISBN 0-8163-1266-4 (pbk. : alk. paper)
    1. Bible. O.T. Samuel—Criticism, interpretation, etc.
I. Title. II. Title: Bible amplifier 1 and 2 Samuel III. Series.
BS1325.2.T48 1995
222'.406—dc20   95-19880
                                             CIP

95 96 97 98 99 • 5 4 3 2 1

CONTENTS

General Preface 9
Author's Preface 11
How to Use This Book 13
Introduction to the Books of 1 and 2 Samuel 17
List of Works Cited 29

**Part I: Samuel: No King and Seldom a Word From the LORD
(1 Sam. 1–7)**
1. A Holy Man Grows Up in an Unholy Time (1 Sam. 1–3) 35
2. The Ark: Worthless Charm, Holy Terror (1 Sam. 4–7) 55

**Part II: Samuel and Saul: The LORD Gives; the LORD Takes Away
(1 Sam. 8–15)**
3. Evil Request, High Hopes (1 Sam. 8–12) 77
4. The LORD Was Grieved That He Made Saul King 101
(1 Sam. 13–15)

**Part III: Saul and David: Who Is the LORD's Anointed?
(1 Sam. 16-31; 2 Sam. 1)**
5. From Faithful Servant to Hunted Foe—Part 1 123
(1 Sam. 16:1–18:9)
6. From Faithful Servant to Hunted Foe—Part 2 143
(1 Sam. 18–23)
7. When Both Men Know the Score (1 Sam. 24–2 Sam. 1) 161

Part IV: David: To the Summit and Back (2 Sam. 2–12)
8. Taking Charge in Israel (2 Sam. 2–6) 187
9. From Heaven to Hell (2 Sam. 7–12) 209

Part V: David: Wounded King in Decline (2 Sam. 13–24)

10. Rape and Revenge, Revolt and Return—Part 1 237
(2 Sam. 13–17)

11. Rape and Revenge, Revolt and Return—Part 2 261
        (2 Sam. 18–20)
12. Falling Into the Hands of a Merciful LORD 283
        (2 Sam. 21–24)

DEDICATION

To Karin, Krista, and Steve

GENERAL PREFACE

The Abundant Life Bible Amplifier series is aimed at helping readers understand the Bible better. Rather than merely offering comments on or about the Bible, each volume seeks to enable people to study their Bibles with fuller understanding.

To accomplish that task, scholars who are also proven communicators have been selected to author each volume. The basic idea underlying this combination is that scholarship and the ability to communicate on a popular level are compatible skills.

While the Bible Amplifier is written with the needs and abilities of laypeople in mind, it will also prove helpful to pastors and teachers. Beyond individual readers, the series will be useful in church study groups and as guides to enrich participation in the weekly prayer meeting.

Rather than focusing on the details of each verse, the Bible Amplifier series seeks to give readers an understanding of the themes and patterns of each biblical book as a whole and how each passage fits into that context. As a result, the series does not seek to solve all the problems or answer all the questions that may be related to a given text. In the process of accomplishing the goal for the series, both inductive and explanatory methodologies are used.

Each volume in this series presents its author's understanding of the biblical book being studied. As such, it does not necessarily represent the "official" position of the Seventh-day Adventist Church.

It should be noted that the Bible Amplifier series utilizes the New International Version of the Bible as its basic text. *Every reader should read the "How to Use This Book" section to get the fullest benefit from the Bible Amplifier study volumes.*

Dr. Alden Thompson, professor of biblical studies at Walla Walla College, holds a doctoral degree from the University of Edinburgh in Scotland. In addition to his work at Walla Walla, where he has also served as Vice President for Academic Administration, Thompson has served as a pastor in California and as an exchange teacher at Marienhohe Seminary in Germany. His previous books include *Responsibility for Evil in the Theodicy of IV Ezra*, *Who's Afraid of the Old Testament God?*, and *Inspiration: Hard Questions, Honest Answers*.

George R. Knight
Berrien Springs, Michigan

When I agreed to write on 1 and 2 Samuel for the Bible Amplifier series, I could not have predicted that my reaction to the completed work could be captured so well by those terse words in Ecclesiastes 5:2: "God is in heaven and you are on earth, so let your words be few."

The purpose of the Bible Amplifier series has forced me to see 1 and 2 Samuel, not as just a collection of stories, but as a message from God to His people in crisis. Jerusalem and its temple were in ruins; the king was in exile. "Let me tell you how it happened and why," says the author of these books.

So I have learned much about sin, punishment, and revenge; about hope and despair; about the dangers of chaos and the dangers of power; and about the human craving for salvation. Chronicles covers the same ground as Samuel, but with a much more buoyant step. The fact that the Chronicler never once mentions David's great sin against Uriah, Bathsheba, and God is just one clue to the vastly different purpose that drove the two inspired writers.

As a result of working through 1 and 2 Samuel this time, I have revised several of my earlier convictions. But the revision that stands out most clearly is largely an intensification of an old conviction, namely, that in comparison with the models in the Old Testament, the revelation of God in Jesus Christ represents a quantum leap toward His ideal kingdom. Jesus was, and is, the Son of David, but David, His forebear, barely glimpsed Him from afar. Surprisingly, such a perspective has enhanced my appreciation for both Testaments. Somehow, I suspect that is what God intended all along.

My prayer is that the reader will be open to the message that has touched my life in these books. With a certain awe, I find myself drawn to the words of David in the last chapter of 2 Samuel: "Let us fall into the hands of the LORD,* for his mercy is great; but do not let me fall into the hands of men" (2 Sam. 24:14).

Alden Thompson
College Place, Washington

*Most English translations of the Old Testament have adopted the Jewish tradition of using the word *Lord*, written in small capital letters, in place of *Yahweh*, the personal name by which God made Himself known to Israel. That practice is followed throughout this volume.

How to Use This Book

The Abundant Life Amplifier series treats each major portion of each Bible book in five main sections.

The first section is called "Getting Into the Word." The purpose of this section is to encourage readers to study their own Bibles. For that reason, the text of the Bible has not been printed in the volumes in this series.

You will get the most out of your study if you work through the exercises in each of the "Getting Into the Word" sections. This will not only aid you in learning more about the Bible but will also increase your skill in using Bible tools and in asking (and answering) meaningful questions about the Bible.

It will be helpful if you write out the answers and keep them in a notebook or file folder for each biblical book. Writing out your thoughts will enhance your understanding. The benefit derived from such study, of course, will be proportionate to the amount of effort expended.

The "Getting Into the Word" sections assume that the reader has certain minimal tools available. Among these are a concordance and a Bible with maps and marginal cross-references. If you don't have a New International Version of the Bible, we recommend that you obtain one for use with this series, since all the Bible Amplifier authors are using the NIV as their basic text. For the same reason, your best choice of a concordance is the *NIV Exhaustive Concordance,* edited by E. W. Goodrick and J. R. Kohlenberger. Strong's *Exhaustive Concordance of the Bible* and Young's *Analytical Concordance to the Bible* are also useful. However, even if all you have is Cruden's *Concordance*, you will be able to do all of the "Getting Into the Word" exercises and most of the "Researching the Word" exercises.

The "Getting Into the Word" sections also assume that the reader has a Bible dictionary. The *Seventh-day Adventist Bible Dictionary* is quite helpful, but those interested in greater depth may want to acquire the four-volume *International Standard Bible Encyclopedia* (1974-1988 edition) or the six-volume *Anchor Bible Dictionary*.

The second section in the treatment of the biblical passages is called "Exploring the Word." The purpose of this section is to discuss the major themes in each biblical book. Thus the comments will typically deal with fairly large portions of Scripture (often an entire chapter) rather than providing a verse-by-verse treatment, such as is found in the *Seventh-day Adventist Bible Commentary*. In fact, many verses and perhaps whole passages in some biblical books may be treated minimally or passed over altogether.

Another thing that should be noted is that the purpose of the "Exploring the Word" sections is not to respond to all the problems or answer all the questions that might arise in each passage. Rather, as stated above, the "Exploring the Word" sections are to develop the Bible writers' major themes. In the process, the author of each volume will bring the best of modern scholarship into the discussion and thus enrich the reader's understanding of the biblical passage at hand. The "Exploring the Word" sections will also develop and provide insight into many of the issues first raised in the "Getting Into the Word" exercises.

The third section in the treatment of the biblical passages is "Applying the Word." This section is aimed at bringing the lessons of each passage into daily life. Once again, you may want to write out a response to these questions and keep them in your notebook or file folder on the biblical book being studied.

The fourth section, "Researching the Word," is for those students who want to delve more deeply into the Bible passage under study or into the history behind it. It is recognized that not everyone will have the research tools for this section. Those expecting to use the research sections should have an exhaustive Bible concordance, the *Seventh-day Adventist Bible Commentary*, a good Bible dictionary, and a Bible atlas. It will also be helpful to have several versions of the Bible.

The final component in each chapter of this book will be a list of recommendations for "Further Study of the Word." While most readers will not have all of these works, many of them may be available in local libraries. Others can be purchased through your local book dealer. It is assumed that many users of this series will already own the seven-volume *Seventh-day Adventist Bible Commentary* and the one-volume *Seventh-day Adventist Bible Dictionary*.

In closing, it should be noted that while a reader will learn much about the Bible from a *reading* of the books in the Bible Amplifier series, he or she will gain infinitely more by *studying* the Bible in connection with that reading.

The Books of 1 and 2 Samuel

One of the best ways to begin studying a book of the Bible is to read it straight through from beginning to end, prayerfully and thoughtfully seeking to grasp an outline picture of the whole. In the case of 1 and 2 Samuel, the two books are so closely linked to each other that they should be treated as one. The following suggestions will help you focus your thinking as you read.

1. Quick read. Read through 1 and 2 Samuel quickly (at one sitting, if you can), making a list of the contents by chapter. Make your labels brief and functional, something that will help you identify each chapter and its contents at a glance. A modern version with paragraph divisions generally will be helpful. Which version you use is not crucial (you actually may want to have several different ones handy for purposes of comparison). But since the Bible Amplifier series is based on the New International Version (NIV), you will find it useful to have a copy of the NIV available as we proceed.

2. Key themes. Now go back and read the two books through again, making brief notes on the following items as you go:

Kingship. How do the key actors (Samuel, Saul, David, the people, God) relate to the idea of having a king in Israel? It's a roller-coaster ride. But note the pros and cons.

God's will and human freedom. Though the LORD is Master of the universe, He has granted human beings the freedom to rebel and the freedom to obey. How does God's lordship of the universe affect human freedom? Does it limit it? Enable it? Or both? Note key incidents; high points and low points; examples of remarkable harmony or jarring discord.

Troubling customs or passages. Briefly identify events, phrases, or points in the narrative that you find puzzling or unsettling.

Special blessings. List those stories, incidents, or verses that touch your soul in helpful and encouraging ways.

3. Patterns. Now go back over your notes, and look for patterns, both in the text of Scripture and in your own thinking. Can you construct an outline of the books based on major points of transition or shifts in emphasis?

More Than Just Good Stories

The books of 1 and 2 Samuel are full of good stories about well-known Bible characters—faithful Samuel, tragic Saul, passionate David. But we are dealing with much more than just a collection of good stories about dominant Bible personalities. These books are part of the larger drama of God's active and persistent involvement with His reluctant people as He leads them toward His kingdom.

Kingdom, you say? Whose kingdom? That's a good question. Indeed, it is *the* question the books themselves pose for us: Does God want a kingdom on earth with a real human king? If so, then who will be the king? And who decides?

Your own careful reading of 1 and 2 Samuel can enhance your understanding of the books. Though many of the stories are familiar, the way you look at them and the questions you ask will determine the kind of blessing and the quality of insights that come as a result of your study.

Also crucial is the spirit in which you approach God's Word. Praying before you begin and maintaining an attitude of prayer while you study will enable you to hear God's Word in these books that otherwise reek of human passion and violent deeds. And I don't mean prayer as a substitute for thinking, but prayer to help you think more clearly as you seek to be faithful to God and His Word. As a result, rich treasures will be yours as you explore the world of Samuel, Saul, and David.

The Place of 1 and 2 Samuel in the Bible

The books of 1 and 2 Samuel say nothing about the books' author or authors. But that does not affect their status as God's Word or as part of the Hebrew Bible and ours.

Our English Bibles follow the Greek Old Testament (called the Septuagint and also known by the abbreviation LXX) in placing 1 and 2 Samuel with the other history books of the Old Testament. Indeed, the Septuagint puts 1 and 2 Samuel together with 1 and 2 Kings under a common title: 1, 2, 3, and 4 Kingdoms. That's an accurate description, too, for the four books tell us all about the monarchy, from its founding under Samuel to its tragic end at the destruction of Jerusalem in 586 B.C.

The Hebrew Bible, however, offers a different slant. In the first place, Samuel and Kings were only two books instead of four until the fifteenth and sixteenth centuries of the Christian era. At that point, apparently under the influence of the Greek and Latin Bibles, Hebrew Bibles also began dividing the books into 1 and 2 Samuel and 1 and 2 Kings.

Even more interesting, however, is the Hebrew Bible's use of the label "prophecy" for what we usually call history. Thus 1 and 2 Samuel together form one of the four "former prophets"—Joshua, Judges, Samuel, and Kings. To our way of thinking, the four "latter prophets"—Isaiah, Jeremiah, Ezekiel, and "the Twelve" (the minor prophets viewed as one book)—are more deserving of the prophetic label. But here we have something to learn from the Hebrew mind, for the history of God's people is not just facts, figures, names, and events. It is a powerful carrier of the prophetic vision. God is present and active in the history of His people. And the telling of that history is God's story, too, not just the story of Israel.

Thus we are quite justified in sifting the stories of Samuel, Saul, and David in search of God's message for His people then and for

His people now. We will glimpse the prophetic vision, hear the prophetic critique. And that becomes all the more interesting when we recognize that these "former prophets" most likely were not written in the form we have them until after the experiment with the monarchy had gone up in the flames that devoured Jerusalem.

To say, however, that 1 and 2 Samuel were not actually "written" until after the destruction of Jerusalem in 586 B.C., does not mean that the basic content of the books appeared in written form for the first time at that point. Though Scripture does not tell us much about how the Bible writers produced their books, we should note what little they do tell us. At the anointing of Saul, for example, Samuel wrote down "the regulations of the kingship" in a scroll and deposited it "before the LORD" (1 Sam. 10:25). And at the death of Saul, David's lament is said to have been recorded in the Book of Jashar (2 Sam. 1:18). Though neither of those sources has survived until our day, these incidental references do suggest that the unnamed author of 1 and 2 Samuel did not rely wholly on memory or on visions. He went to the library and the official archives and did his homework.

From Kings and Chronicles, we have some idea of what might have been available. The "annals" of Solomon are mentioned in 1 Kings 11:41; the "records" of Samuel, Nathan, and Gad are noted in 1 Chronicles 29:29; Nathan's "records" are noted again in 2 Chronicles 9:29, along with the "prophecy" of Ahijah the Shilonite and the "visions" of Iddo the seer.

What this means, then, is that careful listening will enable us to hear echoes of two stories, the "original" one, recorded by Samuel and David or their contemporaries, and the "finished" one, which reveals in more subtle ways the concerns of the prophets as they gazed on the ruins of Jerusalem.

1 and 2 Samuel As a Commentary on the Tragedy of the Monarchy

The narrative that runs from Joshua to the end of Kings seems to be a deliberate, real-life illustration of the punishment and reward system laid down so bluntly in the blessings and cursings of Deuteronomy 28. Moses had told the people that if they and their children would obey the LORD great blessings would be theirs. If they chose to rebel, however, the curse of the LORD would be their lot. In the sad record of disasters and rebellions that punctuate Israel's history from start to finish, one can almost see the stain of prophetic tears as the tragedy unfolds, the story of God's people and their kings stumbling along together toward national disaster. The curses of Deuteronomy came upon Israel because the people and their kings rebelled against God and disobeyed His commands.

While the punishment-reward pattern may not be as obvious in the books of Samuel as it is in the books of Joshua, Judges, or 1 and 2 Kings, the sins of kings and prophets are still described with remarkable, warts-and-all candor, contrasting sharply with the glowing accounts of David and Solomon in 1 and 2 Chronicles.

Why the difference? Do Bible writers have the right to shape their stories positively or negatively through selective use of sources? Indeed they do, and it's more than a right. Under the guidance of the Holy Spirit, it is a responsibility. An example from Ellen White's devotional classic *Steps to Christ* illustrates the point. In the very first chapter, "God's Love for Man," she quotes Exodus 34:6, 7 to affirm God's loving character: "The Lord, The Lord God, merciful and gracious, long-suffering, and abundant in goodness and truth, keeping mercy for thousands, forgiving iniquity and transgression and sin." At that, she stops, choosing not to quote the somber conclusion, "and that will by no means clear the guilty; visiting the iniquity of the fathers upon the children . . ." (White, *Steps to Christ*, 10). Why omit those strong words? Because this is a message of encouragement. The heavy words are for occasions that call for rebuke.

To draw the parallel with the Old Testament, Chronicles is the "encouraging" word, a last word of hope at the end of the Hebrew Bible, given at a time when God's people had almost given up. The books of Samuel and Kings, by contrast, give the prophetic word of rebuke, intended to jar Israel awake to the consequences of her sin. The rebuke may not always be explicit in the story. But the telling of the story has a way of delivering its own rebuke, and all the more powerfully because it comes as a story.

Recognizing, then, that the inspired writer is shaping a particular story for a particular purpose, we look more directly at key structural elements and important themes in 1 and 2 Samuel.

The Structure of the Books

The structure of 1 and 2 Samuel falls naturally into place around Samuel, Saul, and David, the three personalities who dominate the story:

1. 1 Sam. 1–7.   Samuel, prophet and judge.
2. 1 Sam. 8–15.   Samuel, friend and foe of Saul.
3. 1 Sam. 16–31.   David and Saul in conflict.
4. 2 Sam. 1–12.   David on the rise until he falls.
5. 2 Sam. 13–24.   David in decline in the wake of his sin.

In many ways, tragedy is etched in the lives of each of the key figures. But God is still present to guide, rebuke, and encourage. In their relationship to each other, to the people, and to God, these dominant characters reveal the key themes and motifs of the two books.

Themes and Motifs

Four themes or motifs are prominent in 1 and 2 Samuel. But one towers over the others: kingship. The other three motifs (obedience, providence, and divine sovereignty), as noted below, simply interpret the human and the divine response to the question of who will be lord and master of Israel.

1. Kingship: From the Danger of Chaos to the Danger of Power. Superficially, the story in 1 and 2 Samuel might appear as God's condescension to the people's rebellious request for a king. Though Saul, the first king, fails, David, the second one, succeeds, and everyone lives happily ever after. . . .

Well, not quite ever after. And close reading points to a much more complex picture. Was kingship a good idea or not? The strongest negative votes come from Samuel's bitter speeches against king-ship in 1 Samuel 8 and 12 and from the Lord's pointed comment: "It is not you they have rejected, but they have rejected me as their king" (1 Sam. 8:7).

But other voices are more positive. Just as Samuel and the LORD agreed to tolerate kingship, Christians also have made peace with the idea, claiming Jesus as part of the royal Davidic line. The Old Testament itself provides the precedent, for Deuteronomy 17:14-20 assumes that kingship would be a natural and divinely approved de-velopment: "Be sure to appoint over you the king the LORD your God chooses" (vs. 15).

But perhaps the most striking argument in favor of kingship comes from that which immediately precedes 1 and 2 Samuel (in the He-brew Bible), the two chaotic incidents at the end of the book of Judges. Judges 17 and 18 describe how the tribe of Dan took a molten image with them and set up a shrine for it in their new home up north. They even had the audacity to appoint a grandson of Moses as priest (Judg. 18:30). Hard on the heels of that shocking tale is the story of the dismembered concubine, concluded with the memorable lines: "In those days there was no king in Israel: every man did that which was right in his own eyes" (Judg. 21:25, KJV).

Those are the last words in Judges, the ones immediately preced-ing Samuel in the Hebrew Bible, and they would most likely come from someone who had seen the benefits of a strong central govern-ment under the leadership of a good king.

Initially, Samuel continues the tale of woe, revealing that not just Israel's political and civil life was in shambles, but her religion as well. The first "scene" in Samuel shows Elkanah, Hannah, and Samuel desperately attempting to hear the word of the LORD at Shiloh, even as Eli's wicked sons steal the sacrifices of the saints and molest the women who come to worship. The same evil culprits drag the ark off into battle. The Philistines defeat Israel and take the ark home with them as a prize trophy.

The punch line to all this? Israel desperately needs a godly king to put things back together again. That undercurrent is lost in Samuel's angry rhetoric against kingship. But it is part of the story.

At the same time, however, 1 and 2 Samuel proceed to illustrate the terrible truth in Samuel's warning about the results of kingship. Again those results seem muted in the early years of David. But beginning with David's double fault of adultery and murder (from 2 Samuel 11 onward), the shadow side of kingship becomes ever more prominent. The last scene in 2 Samuel depicts the overconfident David setting out to number Israel. Power has indeed overcome chaos, but the ruthlessness of power is now the new threat to God's ideal for His people.

The first two chapters of 1 Kings continue to illustrate the dangers of power. To be sure, one can argue that Solomon's use of power is legitimate and all in the service of God—eliminating Adonijah as a threat to the throne, demoting Abiathar from the priesthood, bringing Joab's blood upon his own head, and cleverly setting the trap for Shimei so that his blood comes back on his own head too, an indirect reward for cursing the Lord's anointing. It's all very proper—but all too clinical, chillingly so. Our worst fears, so to speak, are realized as Solomon proceeds to show how even the wisest man on earth can use power to destroy himself and the kingdom.

Thus framed, the books of Samuel reveal how the very power that overcomes the danger of chaos develops into a new kind of danger all its own, the danger of power. Yet God is still the master of history. One who delivers His people from destructive chaos cannot allow abuse of power in His name. Indeed, as the history of the monarchy continues with Rehoboam and his successors, one is tempted to see a massive illustration of that famous Old Testament dictum: "Your blood be upon your own head." The final chapter of 2 Kings is also the final chapter of the monarchy, and it is not a pretty scene. Jerusalem lies in ruins, and her last king is an exile in Babylon.

Was the monarchy a good idea? That is a very good question. It haunts every page of 1 and 2 Samuel.

2. Obedience: The Human Response to the LORD's Commands. Though the Sinai covenant is not prominent in 1 and 2 Samuel, at least not in an explicit way, echoes of the Egyptian bondage and Israel's deliverance continually remind the reader of Israel's heritage and obligations. The house of Eli received its commission in Egypt (1 Sam. 2:27, 28); the Philistines knew the story of the plagues (1 Sam. 4:8); Samuel recounted the exodus history when Saul was confirmed as king (1 Sam. 12); the Amalekites were marked for extinction because they had mistreated Israel during the wilderness sojourn (1 Sam. 15:2); David and Nathan, too, interpret David's plans in light of the exodus experience (2 Sam. 7:6, 23).

How should Israel and her leaders respond to this God who delivered them from bondage in Egypt? With obedience. Even promises that were to endure "forever" could be canceled through disobedience. The most explicit example was the failure of the house of Eli: "I promised that your house and your father's house would minister before me forever," was the word from the LORD. "But now the LORD declares: 'Far be it from me! Those who honor me I will honor, but those who despise me will be disdained' " (1 Sam. 2:30).

Saul, too, failed because of disobedience. His sentence, delivered by an anguished Samuel, has echoed down through the centuries: "To obey is better than sacrifice" (1 Sam. 15:22). The LORD seems to have been much more long-suffering with David's sins. Indeed, His promise to David might seem to be ironclad, for with reference to David's offspring, the LORD had promised: "When he does wrong, I will punish him with the rod of men, with floggings inflicted by men. But my love will never be taken away from him, as I took it away from Saul, whom I removed from before you. Your house and your kingdom will endure forever before me; your throne will be established forever" (2 Sam. 7:14-16).

But forever does not mean forever when human beings persist in rebellion against the LORD. The house of Eli had learned that lesson the hard way. Would Israel and the house of David learn, too, before it was too late? No. Thus the books of 1 and 2 Samuel document the early stages of the death march that would end in the flames that destroyed both Jerusalem and the Davidic monarchy. Yes, obedience matters.

3. Divine Providence: God's Intervention in Human Affairs. Even though the ideas of providence and divine sovereignty easily overlap, I have listed them separately, using the word *sovereignty* for God's continuing lordship in the universe and *providence* for His special intervention in our human world. Both concepts play a key part in 1 and 2 Samuel.

Right from the first, the LORD's providential intervention is evident. He had closed the womb of Hannah (1 Sam. 1:5) but then "remembered her" (vs. 19), not only in the conception and birth of Samuel (vs. 20), but in the gift of additional children as well (1 Sam. 2:21). The LORD also had a direct hand in selecting David as the new king from among Jesse's sons (1 Sam. 16:7-12). But perhaps the most tantalizing instances of providence are noted both by the rejected-but-still-anointed Saul and by the newly anointed David, when they recognized that "the LORD" had "delivered" Saul into David's hand—yet David refused to harm the anointed king (1 Sam. 24:18; 26:23). It was as though providence were putting David to the test.

4. Divine Sovereignty: The LORD Is Lord of History. If the books of Samuel overflow with human violence, God is still seen as Master of all. At the beginning of the two books, Hannah makes that point in her song of praise after she delivers young Samuel to the temple: "It is not by strength that one prevails; those who oppose the LORD will be shattered. He will thunder against them from heaven; the LORD will judge the ends of the earth" (1 Sam. 2:9, 10). In the psalm at the end of 2 Samuel, David makes the same point: "As for God, his way is perfect; the word of the LORD is flawless. He is a shield for all who take refuge in him. For who is God besides the LORD? And who is the Rock except our God?" (2 Sam. 22:31, 32). Hannah praises God's power in prospect, David in retrospect, but both sing of Him who is Lord of all.

In the closing narrative, the same truth comes out in more poignant circumstances after David had foolishly numbered his people. The LORD came to David to make it clear that He, not David, was Master in Israel. David confessed his sin and pleaded for mercy. The last word in the books of Samuel shows that the LORD was still God in Israel and that He would heal the illness of His people: "Then the LORD answered prayer in behalf of the land, and the plague on Israel was stopped" (2 Sam. 24:25).

As we turn now to a more systematic study of the books of 1 and 2 Samuel, we will watch for the signs of God's presence amidst the tangle of human passions and desires. How can God's will best be realized on earth? In the books of 1 and 2 Samuel, we will watch God's people struggle with that question as they stand at the crossroads and choose. But they do not stand alone. God goes with them, even when their choices are not His ideal. They pay a terrible price for sin. But as David himself cried out, "Let us fall into the hands of the LORD, for his mercy is great; but do not let me fall into the hands of men" (2 Sam. 24:14).

Outline of 1 and 2 Samuel

   I.   Samuel: No king and seldom a word from the LORD
        (1 Sam. 1–7)
      A. A holy man grows up in an unholy time (1 Sam. 1–3)
      B. The ark: worthless charm, holy terror (1 Sam. 4–7)
  II. Samuel and Saul: The LORD gives, the LORD takes away
        (1 Sam. 8–15)
      A. Evil request, high hopes (1 Sam. 8–12)
      B. The LORD was grieved that He made Saul king
         (1 Sam. 13–15)
 III. Saul and David: Who is the LORD's anointed?
        (1 Sam. 16–31; 2 Sam. 1)
      A. From faithful servant to hunted foe (1 Sam. 16–23)
      B. When both men know the score (1 Sam. 24– 2 Sam. 1)
  IV. David: To the summit and back (2 Sam. 2–12)
      A. Taking charge in Israel (2 Sam. 2–6)
      B. From heaven to hell (2 Sam. 7–12)
   V. David: Wounded king in decline (2 Sam. 13–24)
      A. Rape and revenge, revolt and return (2 Sam. 13–20)
      B. Falling into the hands of a merciful LORD
        (2 Sam. 21–24)

LIST OF WORKS CITED

Anderson, A. A. *2 Samuel.* Word Biblical Commentary. Vol. 11. Dallas: Word, 1989.

Baldwin, Joyce. *1 & 2 Samuel.* Tyndale Old Testament Commentaries. Downers Grove, Ill.: InterVarsity, 1988.

Beuken, W. A. M. "I Samuel 28: The Prophet as 'Hammer of Witches.' " *Journal for the Study of the Old Testament* 6 (February 1978), 3-17.

Brueggemann, Walter. "Samuel, Book of, 1-2: Narrative and Theology." In *The Anchor Bible Dictionary.* Vol. 5, edited by David Noel Freedman. New York: Doubleday, 1992.

Buttrick, George Arthur, and Keith Crim, eds. *The Interpreter's Dictionary of the Bible.* 4 vols. plus supplement. Nashville: Abingdon, 1962, 1976.

Cullmann, Oscar. "Immortality of the Soul or Resurrection of the Dead?" The Ingersoll Lecture for 1955. In *Immortality and Resurrection,* edited by Krister Stendahl. New York: Macmillan, 1965.

Douglas, J. D., ed. *New Bible Dictionary.* 2d ed. Wheaton, Ill.: Tyndale, 1982.

Dybdahl, Jon. *Old Testament Grace.* Boise, Idaho: Pacific Press, 1990.

Flanagan, James W. "Samuel, Book of, 1-2: Text, Composition, and Content." In *The Anchor Bible Dictionary.* Vol. 5, edited by David Noel Freedman. New York: Doubleday, 1992.

France, R. T. "Messiah." Article in *New Bible Dictionary.* 2d ed., edited by J. D. Douglas. Wheaton, Ill.: Tyndale, 1982.

Freedman, David Noel, ed. *The Anchor Bible Dictionary.* 6 vols. New York: Doubleday, 1992.

Froom, LeRoy Edwin. *The Conditionalist Faith of Our Fathers.* 2 vols. Hagerstown, Md.: Review and Herald, 1965.

Frymer-Kensky, Tikva. "Sex and Sexuality." In *The Anchor Bible Dictionary.* Vol. 5, edited by David Noel Freedman. New York:

Doubleday, 1992.

Fudge, Edward. *The Fire That Consumes.* Fallbrook, Calif: Verdict, 1982; Carlisle: Paternoster Press, 1994.

Ginzberg, Louis. *The Legends of the Jews.* Vol. 4, *Bible Times and Characters From Joshua to Esther;* Vol. 6, *Notes to Volumes III and IV: From Moses in the Wilderness to Esther.* Translated from the German. Philadelphia: Jewish Publication Society, 1968 (first published in 1913 [Vol. 4] and 1928 [Vol. 6]).

Glueck, Nelson. *Hesed in the Bible.* Cincinnati: Hebrew Union College Press, 1967.

Gunn, David. *The Fate of King Saul.* Journal for the Study of the Old Testament Supplement Series. Vol. 14. Sheffield, England: JSOT, 1984.

_____. *The Story of King David.* Journal for the Study of the Old Testament Supplement Series. Vol. 6. Sheffield, England: JSOT, 1978.

Hertzberg, Hans Wilhelm. *I & II Samuel.* Old Testament Library. Translated by John Bowden from the 1960 German edition. Philadelphia: Westminster, 1964

Horn, Siegfried H. *Seventh-day Adventist Bible Dictionary.* Rev. ed. Commentary Reference Series. Vol. 8. Hagerstown, Md.: Review and Herald, 1979.

Klein, Ralph. *1 Samuel.* Word Biblical Commentary. Vol. 10. Waco, Tex.: Word, 1983.

Kuitert, H. M. *I Have My Doubts: How to Become a Christian Without Being a Fundamentalist.* Translated by John Bowden from the original 1992 Dutch edition. Valley Forge, Penn.: Trinity Press, 1993.

Maxwell, Arthur S. *The Bible Story.* Vol. 3: *Trials and Triumphs.* Boise, Idaho: Pacific Press, 1954.

McCarter, P. Kyle, Jr. *I Samuel.* Anchor Bible, Vol. 8. GardenCity: Doubleday, 1980.

_____. *II Samuel.* Anchor Bible, Vol. 9. New York: Doubleday, 1984.

Newsome, James D., Jr., ed. *A Synoptic Harmony of Samuel, Kings, and Chronicles.* Grand Rapids, Mich.: Baker, 1986.

Nichol, Francis D., ed. *The Seventh-day Adventist Bible Commentary,*

Vol. 4. Hagerstown, Md.: Review and Herald, 1955.

Payne, J. B. "Prophecy, Prophets." In *New Bible Dictionary.* 2d ed, edited by J. D. Douglas. Wheaton, Ill.: Tyndale, 1982.

Pinnock, Clark H. "The Conditional View." In *Four Views on Hell,* edited by William Crockett. Grand Rapids, Mich.: Zondervan, 1992.

Polzin, Robert. *David and the Deuteronomist: A Literary Study of the Deuteronomic History.* Part Three: *2 Samuel.* Indiana Studies in Biblical Literature. Bloomington: Indiana University Press, 1993 (abbreviated as *David*).

_____. *Samuel and the Deuteronomist: A Literary Study of the Deuteronomic History.* Part Two: *1 Samuel.* Indiana Studies in Biblical Literature. San Francisco: Harper & Row, 1989; Bloomington: Indiana University Press, 1993 (abbreviated as *Samuel*).

Pritchard, James B., ed. *Ancient Near Eastern Texts Relating to the Old Testament.* 3d edition, with Supplement. Princeton, N.J.: Princeton University Press, 1969 (abbreviated as ANET).

Robinson, Gnana. *Let Us Be Like the Nations: A Commentary on the Books of 1 and 2 Samuel.* International Theological Commentary. Grand Rapids, Mich.: Eerdmans, 1993.

Robinson, H. Wheeler. *Corporate Personality in Ancient Israel.* Philadelphia: Fortress, 1964 (first published, 1935).

Rodriguez, Angel M. "Inspiration and the Imprecatory Psalms." *Journal of the Adventist Theological Society* 5:1 (Spring 1994), 40-67.

Snaith, Norman H. *The Distinctive Ideas of the Old Testament.* London: Epworth, 1944.

Stott, John R. W., and David Edwards. *Evangelical Essentials.* Downers Grove, Ill.: InterVarsity, 1988.

Thompson, Alden. *Inspiration: Hard Questions, Honest Answers.* Hagerstown, Md.: Review and Herald, 1991.

_____. "When the Truth Is a Lie. The Ninth Commandment." In *Lyrics of Love: God's Top Ten,* edited by B. Russell Holt. Boise, Idaho: Pacific Press, 1988. Reprint of "Thou Shalt Not Hurt Thy Neighbor with Lies Or with the Truth." *Signs of the Times,* November 1988.

_____. *Who's Afraid of the Old Testament God?* Exeter: Paternoster, 1988; Grand Rapids, Mich.: Zondervan, 1989 (abbreviated as *Who's Afraid?*).

White, Ellen G. *Patriarchs and Prophets.* Boise, Idaho: Pacific Press, 1943 (first published, 1890).

_____. *Steps to Christ.* Hagerstown, Md.: Review and Herald, 1908 (first published, 1892).

Wilkinson, B. G. *Our Authorized Bible Vindicated.* Payson, Ariz.: Leaves-of-Autumn, 1993 (reprint; first published, 1930).

PART ONE

1 Samuel 1–7

Samuel:
No King and Seldom a Word
From the Lord

CHAPTER ONE

A Holy Man Grows Up in an Unholy Time

1 Samuel 1–3

The first chapters of 1 Samuel take us to familiar territory and precious stories we have heard from the cradle. In particular, we hear Hannah's anguished prayer for a son. Even more vivid in our memories is the timid voice of a boy as he finally awakes to the possibility that God wants to speak to him—yes, to him. One could scarcely find more familiar words in Scripture than those put in the mouth of Samuel by the old man Eli: "Speak, LORD; for thy servant heareth" (1 Sam. 3:9, KJV).

Like a giant zoom lens, 1 Samuel 1 to 3 closes in on three dominant personalities: Hannah, Eli, and Samuel. The story is fleshed out with the appearance of faithful Elkanah, haughty Peninnah, and Eli's outrageously wicked sons, Hophni and Phinehas. But as fascinating as the personalities may be in themselves, they are only the carriers of a much more important story: God's plan for His people. So we will ask them not only how things are between themselves and God but also how things stand between Israel and God. For the books of Samuel belong to the story of a holy nation, a reluctant people led by a patient God. Though His purpose for them is glorious, they struggle to see His vision for them. Did they ever grasp it?

These first chapters move us from a time of near-total chaos in the era of the judges toward the establishment of the monarchy. Samuel becomes a key figure in the story as Israel casts jealous eyes on the surrounding culture and yearns to be like the nations around them. The first three chapters of 1 Samuel tell us about the early years of this promised child and the community into which he is born. The day of that other promised child, Baby Jesus, is still some one thousand years away.

■ Getting Into the Word

1 Samuel 1–3

After noting the five points listed below, read through 1 Samuel 1 to 3 to get a feel for the overall story and the relationship between its parts. Then take each of the five points separately, working through the relevant portions of the three chapters and making note of particular verses and special insights that have a bearing on the point. You may want to use a separate sheet of paper for each of the points.

1. *Personalities.* Characterize in a paragraph or two the key personalities that appear in these chapters. In addition to Hannah, Eli, and Samuel, sketch a profile of the lesser characters too: Elkanah, Peninnah, and the two sons of Eli, Hophni and Phinehas. Make a list of character and personality traits as well as the role played by each in Scripture.

2. *Religion.* Both for individuals and for nations, religion is often a key factor in times of transition. Describe the status of public and private religion in these chapters. Compare the status of the official religion with the practice of individuals.

3. *Providence.* Read through 1 Samuel 1 to 3 with an eye open to the record of divine activity. Divide a page in your Samuel notebook into three columns. In the first two columns, make note of those passages that point to these two extremes: (A) those that suggest God's active presence and intervention in human affairs and (B) those that suggest His absence or at least His silence. In the third column, note whether the perceptions given are those of the key personalities themselves, of the author who is telling the story, or both.

4. *Puzzles.* Make a list of words, phrases, customs, or other aspects that you find puzzling or troubling. Keep an eye on your list as you continue your study.

5. *Blessings.* **Underline or copy into your notebook those passages or special insights suggested by Scripture that you find particularly inspiring or helpful in these three chapters.**

■ Exploring the Word

The People at Worship

With the notable exception of Samuel himself, the first three verses of 1 Samuel introduce all the leading personalities of the first seven chapters in the book: Elkanah and his two wives, Hannah and Peninnah; Eli and his two sons, Hophni and Phinehas. At the outset, it is worship that bonds these remarkably diverse people together in a common narrative. Year after year, Elkanah takes his family to the Shiloh sanctuary for worship and sacrifice. Eli's sons are priests there. We are not yet told that they are wicked priests. That will come. But from the first, we do know that the things of God loom large in the author's mind. In contrast with the story of Ruth, which plays itself out in barley field, threshing floor, and at the city gate; and in contrast with the story of Esther, which takes us to the palace of a pagan king and never mentions God or prayer, 1 Samuel takes us immediately to the dwelling place of God on earth, the sacred sanctuary of Israel's God. That is where His people go to meet Him. By focusing on what Scripture tells us about each of these people in their search for God—or in their resistance to Him—we listen for God's message for us today.

Elkanah

Elkanah was a man of consistent and persistent godly habits. "Year after year" he took his family to Shiloh for worship and sacrifice, even though the sons of Eli were priests there (1:3)—wicked priests, as the narrative informs us later (2:12). But godly Elkanah was not so focused on the things of God that he neglected his family. He always shared the sacrificial meal with his whole family and recognized the special needs of the childless Hannah by giving her a double portion (1:5).

But he could not grasp Hannah's agony. Indeed, the words he spoke to comfort her were also a mild rebuke and hinted at his own hurt feelings: "Don't I mean more to you than ten sons?" (vs. 8). No, Elkanah did not understand Hannah's pain.

Nevertheless, he was always a loyal worshiper and a faithful husband, the father of the promised child (vs. 19) and, later, of yet more children by Hannah through the blessing of the LORD (2:20, 21). He graciously granted Hannah's request to miss the annual trek to Shiloh but also took the occasion to remind her of God's special plan for the boy (1:23). While Hannah clearly dominates the narrative, Elkanah is there too, always faithful, always supportive.

From Scripture it is clear that he was a deeply religious man in a virtually godless age. Jewish tradition pushed the contrast even further, declaring him a second Abraham, the only pious man of his generation. From the evidence in Scripture, we would call him a nice man, a godly man—though he paid a dear price for taking more than one wife.

Hannah and Peninnah

The first reference to Elkanah's two wives lists Hannah before Peninnah, implying that she was his first wife. But where Scripture is silent, Jewish tradition fleshes out the narrative, declaring, for example, that just as Abram and Sarai lived childless for ten years in Canaan before Sarai told Abram to father children through Hagar (Gen. 16:1-3), so Elkanah and Hannah lived childless for ten years before Hannah insisted that Elkanah take Peninnah.

While Jewish tradition certainly moved beyond the biblical account to embellish the story, Scripture itself reveals that the tensions between Hannah and Peninnah were very real, paralleling those between Sarai and Hagar (1:6; Gen. 16:4-6). Abram solved his problem by sending Hagar away. Elkanah apparently had no such option. His second wife stayed by, making Hannah's life one of perpetual torment. Yet it was that very anguish that allows us to catch a glimpse of her search for the LORD.

After enduring a communal meal in which she could not share

because of her distress, Hannah went to the sanctuary to pray, apparently within sight of Eli the priest. She was in a mood for bargains, promising that if the LORD would give her a son, she would give him right back again forever (1:11). Eli, the priest with the flawed family, first accused, then blessed her (vss. 14, 17). But his word of blessing does not indicate that he knew the essence of her request.

Deep irony marks the conversation between Eli and Hannah. To this man of God, who could not distinguish prayer from drunkenness, Hannah protested that she was not a wicked woman (vs. 16; literally, a "daughter of Belial"). As Scripture will inform us in 2:12, it was not Hannah who belonged to Belial, but Hophni and Phinehas. Eli's own offspring were "sons of Belial" who did not "know" the LORD. Still, Eli was God's chosen instrument to communicate the word of blessing to Hannah.

A new buoyancy now marked Hannah's life. She ate and worshiped. After they returned home, "the LORD remembered her" (1:19), and her husband, Elkanah, fathered a child. When she and Elkanah came before Eli to dedicate little Samuel to the LORD, Elkanah may have offered the sacrifices, but it was Hannah who spoke up, not in the first person plural, but in the singular (vss. 24-28): "*I* prayed . . . ," "*I* asked . . . ," "*I* give him to the LORD" (1:27, 28). She was also the one who brought a new little robe each year on the family's annual visit to Shiloh (2:19). The last we hear of her is the record of divine response to Eli's wish that the LORD grant them more children to take the place of the child they had given to the LORD: "The LORD was gracious to Hannah; she conceived and gave birth to three sons and two daughters" (vs. 21).

The only trace of bitterness in this otherwise lovely picture of a gentle and gracious Hannah crops up in the psalm recorded as her prayer in 2:1-10. Although stories for children and devotional commentaries often omit or refine the troublesome phrase, "my mouth boasts over my enemies" (vs. 1), it preserves a striking note of realism about human nature. That realism reminds us that the psalms in Scripture do not reflect the ideal experience but constitute an ideal collection of prayers, illuminating every stage of spiritual growth. The gloating over one's enemies as expressed here and in other psalms and prayers in Scripture (e.g., 2 Sam. 22:35-43; Ps. 17:13-15; 18:34-42) is a reminder that sin stains even the lives of those whom the Lord has greatly blessed.

It is worth noting, however, that when this prayer/psalm is seen apart from its present context, it assumes a much more militaristic and national garb. The concluding reference to the king and the LORD's anointed (2:10) explains why it has been seen as a prophecy of David and of the ultimate anointed One, Jesus Christ. Furthermore, 2:1 does not speak of a single feminine enemy (Peninnah), but of plural masculine "enemies"; and when 2:3 talks against proud and arrogant speech, it is addressing a male plural audience. Even the reference to the "barren who has borne seven children" (vs. 5) is an idealization that does not match Hannah's situation, for her children numbered six: Samuel and five more (vs. 21).

Yet however one might interpret the psalm apart from the context, here it is natural to apply it to Hannah's immediate situation, thus accentuating the personal animosity between Hannah and her rival. Interestingly enough, Jewish tradition reveals some uneasiness both with Peninnah's jeers and with Hannah's boasts, even suggesting that Peninnah's intentions may have been laudable, an attempt to bring Hannah to the point of asking God for children. More typical, however, is the heightening of the rivalry, as in the tale based on the line "she who has had many sons pines away" (vs. 5). According to Jewish legend, every time Hannah bore a child, Peninnah lost two of hers, until eight of her ten children had died. Only Hannah's intercessory prayer on her behalf saved the last two.

Christians can recognize the taint of sin in Hannah's prayer without claiming it as God's ideal. We who accept Jesus as our Teacher and Example hear His words in the Sermon on the Mount: "Love your enemies and pray for those who persecute you" (Matt. 5:44). And we hear Him practice what He preached in His prayer for His enemies from the cross: "Father, forgive them, for they do not know what they are doing" (Luke 23:34). But when we fall short of that mark, we can take courage from the fact that Hannah, too, had not yet arrived. The evidence is recorded in Scripture for all to see. Still, she was a powerful and effective instrument in the hand of God. She and Elkanah, in spite of all the turmoil in their home, brought into the world one of God's great men. She dedicated him to the LORD, and he was faithful to that dedication as long as he lived.

Eli

Scripture portrays Eli the priest in tragic and pathetic terms, bracketing every piece of good news about the man with reminders of the evil that dogged his life. His whole story is thus framed, from his first appearance as the father of Hophni and Phinehas (1:3) until his death at the news of the ark's capture by the Philistines (4:18).

Later generations, viewing these stories through the lens of a destroyed Jerusalem and a collapsed monarchy, might even be tempted to see the fate of Eli's house as an early enacted parable, symbolizing the fate of the monarchy itself. In 1:9, where Eli first appears in the narrative itself, the ambiguity of the Hebrew words for "chair" and "temple" could suggest just such a comparison with the monarchy, for those are also the words for "throne" and "palace." Thus while Scripture says that "Eli the priest was sitting on a chair by the doorpost of the LORD's temple," the Hebrew reader at the time of Jerusalem's fall would hear echoes of a royal throne and palace, now just as defunct as the house of Eli itself.

The aged priest suffered from poor eyesight, both spiritual and physical. He saw Hannah praying, but his eyes were blind, for he saw her piety as wicked drunkenness (vss. 12, 13). In effect, his eyes were also closed to the blatant wickedness of his sons (2:22-24). He had it all backward, rebuking a devout woman so that she felt like a "daughter of Belial" but failing to restrain the real "sons of Belial," his own boys. This was Eli, "whose eyes were becoming so weak that he could barely see" (3:2); and just before he died, his "eyes were so set that he could not see" at all (4:15).

In chapter 2, where the critique against Eli's sons is sharpest, he is a man who has lost control of his sacred responsibilities and his future. His sons were making a mockery of the sacred service and abusing those who came to worship (vss. 12-17; 22-25). They would not listen to their father's rebukes (vs. 25). Finally, "a man of God" (vs.

27) announced to Eli that the priesthood would be taken from his family. God intended to appoint "a faithful priest" who would reflect the divine heart and mind (vs. 35). In the well-known temple conversation, first between Samuel and Eli, then finally between Samuel and the LORD, the point of it all was judgment against the house of Eli: "I swore to the house of Eli, 'The guilt of Eli's house will never be atoned for by sacrifice or offering' " (3:14).

But in spite of Eli's monumental failures, in spite of the LORD's sharp rebuke for his failure to discipline his sons (3:13), Scripture imparts a certain gentleness and warmth to the man. Several incidents contribute to the picture. When Hannah pleaded her case against drunkenness, Eli quickly softened and blessed her request. The fact that Hannah and Elkanah were willing to leave their child with Eli also leaves a positive impression. And surely the man must get some credit for the fact that Samuel "continued to grow in stature and in favor with the LORD and with men" (2:26). But probably the most telling element in the positive portrayal of Eli is the scene in the temple, with little Samuel running again and again through the darkened chambers to the old, nearly sightless man. And in spite of the firmness of Eli's command for Samuel to tell him everything that the LORD had said (3:17), his handling of the boy still suggests a gentle grandparent, a gentleness reinforced by his simple resignation to God's will: "He is the LORD; let him do what is good in his eyes" (vs. 18).

On balance, Eli is indeed a tragic figure. We ask, "How could someone so gentle and caring toward the little boy Samuel go so hopelessly wrong with his own boys?" Yet that is the same question that haunts all the devout parents in the world whose children have gone astray. The question goes back as far as Adam and Eve and the tragic conflict between their sons, Cain and Abel. Indeed, it reaches back further yet to God Himself, the Father and Creator of Adam and Eve, and of Lucifer. And so we wonder about cause and effect, about discipline and freedom. At the end of the monarchy, a similar dilemma faced those who knew King Josiah, the godly reformer. After all the good he had done, he died a senseless death in battle against Pharaoh Neco (2 Kings 23:29, 30). Eli's house as a tragic parable of the monarchy is not far from the mark after all.

Sons of Eli: Hophni and Phinehas

The two wicked sons of Eli are never allowed to speak for themselves in Scripture. We get only as close as the priestly servant who demanded raw meat on their behalf: "Hand it over now; if you don't, I'll take it by force" (2:16). But if the inspired author refuses to let us hear the voices of these evil men, he does not hesitate to raise his own voice in judgment: "Eli's sons were wicked men; they had no regard for the LORD" (vs. 12). And he offers plenty of supporting evidence. In addition to the story of the illicit demand for raw meat (vss. 13-17), he tells of their sexual impropriety with the women worshipers and Eli's attempt at a reprimand (vss. 22-25); he records the stinging rebuke to Eli from the "man of God" (vss. 27-36) and the dire pronouncement in the night to young Samuel that no atonement could ever be made for the guilt of Eli's house (3:11-14).

But in at least one instance, the modern reader will likely be uncomfortable with the way 1 Samuel pronounces judgment on the sons of Eli. After recording Eli's futile rebuke of their wickedness, the author explains why they did not respond: "His sons, however, did not listen to their father's rebuke, for it was the LORD's will to put them to death" (2:25). However stark such a judgment may sound, it must be seen against the backdrop of God's remarkable patience in the face of their callous sins. Scripture implies an extended period of wickedness, marked by greed, abuse of power, and sexual immorality. A disinterested observer might even propose that the situation was so vile that God should have intervened earlier. But ours is a patient God, "not wanting anyone to perish" (2 Pet. 3:9). For those who do persist in evil, however, a day of reckoning must come, a day when God sadly declares, "Ephraim is joined to idols; leave him alone!" (Hos. 4:17).

Jewish tradition softens the picture of Eli's sons, Hophni and Phinehas, arguing that the biblical account of their sin against the women who came to worship is misleading—they did nothing worse than delay the women, keeping them from returning promptly to their families. Phinehas is said to have been the more worthy of the two, serving as high priest during his lifetime. His only sin lay in the fact that he made no attempt to turn his brother from evil.

Scripture, however, makes no room for such softening and does not single out one brother as more worthy than the other: "This sin of the young men was very great in the LORD's sight, for they were treating the LORD's offering with contempt" (2:17). The author is keenly aware of the fact that years of unrequited wickedness had cost Israel her sanctuary, her king, and her independence. For him, if the house of Eli symbolized the failure of the monarchy and the nation, the sins of Eli's two sons showed why. Inspiration cannot put a pretty face on that which had brought such devastating calamity on God's people.

Samuel

When the people of Israel decided that they wanted a king so that they could be like the nations around them (8:5), Samuel became the bridge between the charismatic judges and the hereditary monarchy. Though the priesthood had always been hereditary in Israel, "civil" leadership was not, the short-lived attempt of Abimelech, the son of Gideon, to set himself up as king being a notable exception (Judges 9). But because Samuel served as both priest and judge, the lines between charisma and heredity were obscured, allowing him to appoint his own sons as judges (8:1).

Although Samuel anointed both Saul and David as successive kings of Israel, his sharp critique of the people's request for a king leaves the distinct impression that Samuel saw himself as the *true* model for Israel, not Saul or even David. The author of 1 and 2 Samuel, writing from the perspective of a failed monarchy, shared that perspective, subtly idealizing Samuel as the one who was truly a man after God's own heart.

That process of presenting Samuel as the ideal is evident from the first. Samuel's parents are depicted as godly people who persevere against great odds so that they can have a child to present to the LORD. As the story unfolds, it is clear that both his parents and Samuel himself intended to stand firm against the dominant evil of their day and be faith-

ful in their service to God. In spite of the wicked Hophni and Phinehas
who were serving as priests at Shiloh, Elkanah regularly took his family
on an annual pilgrimage to worship and sacrifice at the sanctuary there
(1:3). The mark of Hannah's deep piety is her prayer in the temple, to
which the LORD spoke His blessing through Eli (1:9-17). Finally, Samuel
was born as the promised child, and while he was still very young, his
parents took him to Shiloh, placing him under Eli's care, just as Hannah
had promised (1:19-28).

From that point on, it is easy for the reader to see Samuel grow in
stature and to sense the enhancement of his reputation. Every statement about his remarkable growth and development is sandwiched
between references to the degradation of his day, particularly as reflected in the life and habits of Eli's wicked sons. Note how the structure of the narrative serves to produce this effect:

Good Samuel:	2:11	Samuel ministers before the LORD under Eli's care.
Evil sons:	2:12-17	Eli's sons pervert the sacrificial system.
Good Samuel:	2:18-21	Samuel ministers before the LORD and grows up in His presence.
Evil sons:	2:22-25	Eli's sons ignore his rebukes and continue in their immoral ways.
Good Samuel:	2:26	Samuel grows "in stature and in favor with the LORD and with men."
Evil sons:	2:27-36	"A man of God" rebukes Eli for not controlling his sons.
Good Samuel:	3:1-10	Samuel faithfully ministers in the temple and hears God speak to him.
Evil sons:	3:11-18	God tells Samuel of the coming judgment against Eli and his house.
Good Samuel:	3:19-21	The LORD is with Samuel; all Israel knows he is a prophet; the LORD reveals Himself to Samuel in Shiloh.

Everyone from Dan to Beersheba (3:20) knew that Samuel was
God's man, the child of promise, the one God had selected to lead

Israel. Against all odds and against great wickedness in high places, he not only retained his purity, but "continued to grow in stature and in favor with the LORD and with men" (2:26).

But while Samuel may have been the ideal man after God's own heart, his name preserves a double irony, a reflection of the tension over monarchy that permeates 1 and 2 Samuel. His mother "named him Samuel, saying, 'Because I asked the LORD for him' " (1:20). As commentators have noted, the Hebrew verb for "ask" seems to better explain the origin of the name *Saul* than it does *Samuel*. The name *Samuel* is more readily linked with the Hebrew word meaning "hear" ("heard of God"). But the narrative in these early chapters of 1 Samuel literally bristles with puns on the word "ask" (Saul). As Ralph Klein has said, "Perhaps the reader is to see, in the series of puns on the word Saul, a suggestion that the real leader of Israel is not Saul, the anointed king, but rather the prophet-anointer, who had been asked ('Sauled') of God (1:20) and who had been dedicated ('Sauled') back to God (1:28). Saul was indeed important for Israel, but the *real* Saul was the Saul after God's own heart, whose name was Samuel" (Klein, 9).

If, however, Samuel is portrayed as the ideal man, his life echoes some of the same ironies that haunted the monarchy. Just as Israel wanted a king in order to be like the other nations, so Hannah wanted a son so that she could be like other women. The LORD granted Israel's request; He granted Hannah's request. And while both the monarchy and Samuel's ministry offered remarkable opportunities to Israel, in the end, both faltered. And even in these early chapters, the ideal Samuel does not always stand forth with the robust certainty that one might expect from a mighty man of God. In these first three chapters, we hear the voice of Hannah most of all, then that of Eli, then Elkanah's. We never hear the voices of bitter Peninnah or of Eli's evil sons. And only once do we hear Samuel's voice: "Speak, for your servant is listening" (3:10). Was it just a scribal slip that has Samuel forgetting to include "LORD" in the response given him by Eli? And why should this little boy be so afraid to tell Eli the contents of the vision (vs. 15)? Such references remind us that Samuel was quite an ordinary mortal after all.

Moving beyond the first three chapters, we could note that the story of the ark's capture is told without a single reference to Samuel. And the ark stayed among the Philistines for seven months, again without any reference to Samuel. Even when it returned to Israel, it ended up in the house of Abinadab, staying there for some twenty years (7:2). Where was Samuel? Only when the people themselves "mourned and sought after the LORD" did he reenter the picture (vss. 2, 3). Was this child of promise as weak as the kings who let God's vision slip away into the night? The people could say that Samuel himself had been faithful. Yet his sons "did not walk in his ways" (8:3); somehow, they had taken the sons of Eli for their model rather than their father. Or was their father a flawed model too?

To be sure, all such references are quite subtle compared to the prominent role given Samuel in the major transition to Saul and David. Yet sensitive readers still might ask the same question of Samuel that they ask about the monarchy itself: What was the LORD's will?

Noting the telltale evidence that Samuel, too, had feet of clay, however, cannot obscure the dominant impression left by the first three chapters of 1 Samuel. Whatever critique one might offer of Samuel at the end of his life, it is clear that in his youth he was deeply committed to the service of God. Threading his way through a wicked environment that was intensely hostile to godly living, he grew "in stature and in favor with the LORD and with men" (2:26). Samuel was indeed a holy man growing up in an unholy time.

En Route to Kingship? A Summary

After looking at the key personalities in 1 Samuel 1 to 3 and pondering the events that shaped their lives, we now must grant a hearing to the prophetic voice that told these stories half a millennium later. What would they mean to a Jew exiled in Babylon, to one who had watched the flames devour Jerusalem and who had seen the Davidic king torn from his throne? What would they mean to one who was asking what it meant to worship God at a time when the temple lay in ruins and the ark of the covenant was gone?

Such questions bring us back to the matter of kingship. The author of 1 and 2 Samuel, living at a time when the monarchy was no more, reached back to the time when it was not yet and retold the story of the rise and fall of Israel's kings. In so doing, he posed a whole cluster of pressing questions for his readers to ponder: Who is the leader of God's people, both in heaven and on earth? Why did the monarchy fail? How could both founding and failure be God's will? If the whole enterprise was a mistake, can His people hope for its restoration?

Bound up with the tangible question of monarchy are the more probing issues of human freedom in relationship to divine providence and sovereignty. Does God allow His people the freedom to destroy themselves? If so, is He still their Lord and still Master of the universe? Those were hard questions then; they still are now.

The author of 1 and 2 Samuel addressed those questions, sometimes in a blunt, straightforward manner, though often in subtle and paradoxical ways. Here, in this concluding section of this chapter, we shall revisit 1 Samuel 1 to 3 and note how the author accents the question of kingship in the telling of the story. A more comprehensive account—masterful and provocative, though sometimes overly subtle—can be found in Robert Polzin's *Samuel*, pages 18 to 54.

As suggested earlier, both Samuel and the house of Eli foreshadow the destiny and fate of the monarchy. But the stage is set by Hannah's agonizing desire for a son. Just as Hannah was taunted for her childlessness by her fruitful rival Peninnah, so Israel felt taunted by her Canaanite neighbors because they had kings and she did not. Hannah's plea for a son (1:11) finds its echo in the elders' plea to Samuel: "Appoint a king to lead us, such as all the other nations have" (8:5).

Though Scripture twice says that the LORD had closed Hannah's womb (1:5, 6), He still responded to her anguished plea and granted her request. She had bargained hard for her son, vowing to "give him to the LORD for all the days of his life" (vs. 11). But such vows can be costly. When Jephthah tied a vow to his urgent desire for a victory over Ammon, it cost him his daughter (Judg. 11:30, 31; 35-40). Hannah, too, got what she wanted, but was it really God's will, and did it foreshadow Israel's ill-fated demand for a king?

In response to Israel's request, the LORD told Samuel, "It is not you they have rejected, but they have rejected me as their king" (8:7). Nevertheless, three times He told Samuel to listen to their request and grant them a king (vss. 7, 9, 22). Against the backdrop of a Jerusalem in ruins, the author of 1 Samuel presses the question of whether it really was God's will for Israel to have a king. And just as one senses the divine disappointment in Israel's clamor for royalty, so, also, one hears overtones of divine sadness lurking in Elkanah's reply to his wife: "Hannah, why are you weeping? Why don't you eat? Why are you downhearted? Don't I mean more to you than ten sons?" (1:8).

Two other clusters of symbols in Hannah's experience foreshadow the ambiguities of Israel's request for a king. The first is the scene in the temple in which she appeared to be drunk but wasn't. She also feared that she had been taken for a "wicked woman," literally, "a daughter of Belial" (vs. 16), in the same camp with the wicked sons of Eli, the true "sons of Belial" (2:12). But she was not a wicked woman. Or was she? "Royal" Eli, the man sitting on the chair (throne) by the LORD's temple (palace), told her she would receive her request but gave no indication that he knew what that request was. Did Israel really know what she was asking for when she requested a king? This same "royal" figure of Eli falls off his chair (throne) and dies when he hears that the ark has been captured and that his wicked sons, successors to his "royal" throne, have been killed. All this can be seen as an enacted parable of what really happened to the ark and to the "wicked" monarchy in 586 B.C., when Babylon destroyed Jerusalem.

The second cluster of multifaceted symbols associated with Hannah are found in her psalm of praise in 2:1-10. The first application of the hymn points to Hannah's triumph over Peninnah, her rival. But it also points forward to the monarchy. The last lines promise that the LORD "will give strength to his king and exalt the horn of his anointed" (vs. 10). However, its third application suggests painful reflection on the failed monarchy:

> "The bows of the warriors are broken,
>   but those who stumbled are armed with strength.

Those who were full hire themselves out for food,
> but those who were hungry hunger no more.
She who was barren has borne seven children,
> but she who has had many sons pines away." (2:4, 5).
"He raises the poor from the dust
> and lifts the needy from the ash heap;
he seats them with princes
> and has them inherit a throne of honor" (vss. 4-8).

The last chapter in the history of Israel's monarchy (2 Kings 25) describes the tragic defeat of Israel's warriors. The royal princes, destined for a throne of honor, were killed in the presence of their father, King Zedekiah. Then his eyes were put out, and he was carried off in shackles to Babylon (vs. 7). Instead of the LORD's raising the poor to a place of honor and plenty, the whole land was degraded to poverty, for now only the "poorest people of the land" were left to work the fields (vs. 12). And irony of ironies, the last word in the book tells how the king of Babylon partially restored the exiled king of Judah, Jehoiachin, granting him "a seat of honor higher than those of the other kings who were with him in Babylon" (vs. 28). Jehoiachin removed his prison garb and "ate regularly at the king's table," receiving from the king of Babylon "a regular allowance as long as he lived" (vss. 29, 30). A restored king—but in exile as long as he lived! And there he died.

The LORD had promised that the house of Eli would minister before Him "forever" (1 Sam. 2:30); He extended the same offer to Saul (1 Sam. 13:13) and then to David (2 Sam. 7:16). If the "forever" promises to Eli and Saul had been retracted because of their sins, then the promises to David were likewise subject to a similar fate. That is the somber implication reverberating through the pages of 1 and 2 Samuel.

As discussed earlier, the author's portrayal of a passive Samuel and a kindly but powerless Eli contributes to the ambivalent stance toward monarchy in these early chapters. Just as Hannah will have a son, so the people will have a king; neither Eli nor Samuel can stop them. Was it God's will, or could there be a better way? The cluster of stories to which we turn next, in 1 Samuel 4 to 7, suggests that there is indeed a better way, or at least there was—a life of simple obedience, lived in the presence of God, with no king required. After the collapse of the monarchy, the exiles must ask themselves whether that better way was again God's will for them.

The first three chapters of 1 Samuel affirm that God grants His people remarkable freedom. They may obey or rebel. But regardless of their choice, His providential care remains active, and His sovereignty over the universe is secure. He may close Hannah's womb. But He can open it again. From such a perspective, even the startling judgment on Eli's sons, that "it was the LORD's will to put them to death" (2:25), attests to God's abiding sovereignty. Humans are free to decide for or against their Maker. But the LORD is there to respond, ensuring that righteousness and justice will triumph on earth.

■ Applying the Word

1 Samuel 1-3

1. *Help From the Lord, Help From Human Beings.* **Focusing on Hannah's life as the primary example, list in your notebook the texts that show how she found solace in the LORD when all human helpers seemed to fail. Then list the passages that show how the LORD also used people to strengthen and encourage her. Ask yourself, "Am I more inclined to exclude the help that comes from the LORD or the help that He sends through human beings? Why?"**

2. *When the Church Falls Short of the Mark.* **In what ways and to what extent can I take courage or comfort from the holy habits of Elkanah and Hannah as they sought to be faithful worshipers while so many were evil and unfaithful? (Write out your answer in your Samuel notebook.) Are there any conditions under which I might cease worshiping with the "official" church and with other believers? What would those conditions be? Should I actively support the church even**

when it seems to be drifting into apostasy because of lack of leadership or because of evil leadership? Why or why not? Write out your reflections in a paragraph or two.

3. *Faithful and Faithless Parenting.* What specific things can Christians learn about parenting from the success of Hannah and Elkanah with Samuel? From Eli's failures with Hophni and Phinehas? From Samuel's failures with his boys? Why do you think Scripture never mentions the mother of Hophni and Phinehas or the mother of Samuel's two sons? Discuss in a few sentences how we can know whether parents have failed in their parental skills or whether the children simply have exercised their God-given right to choose their own life.

4. *Hearing God's Call.* Both Samuel and Eli had difficulty recognizing the voice of God in the night. Finally, it became clear that God was calling. In what ways does God speak to me? How can I be sure that I have heard His voice and that I know His will? Would I prefer that the LORD communicate to me in an audible voice in the night? Why or why not? Write down your thoughts in your Samuel notebook.

■ Researching the Word

1. *Providence and Freedom.* Two of the more striking interpretations of "providence" in 1 Samuel 1 to 3 are the statements that the LORD had closed Hannah's womb (1:5, 6) and that Hophni and Phinehas "did not listen to their father's rebuke, for it was the LORD's will to put them to death" (2:25). On the basis of your own study of 1 Samuel 1 to 3, formulate your position on the tension between human freedom and providential intervention in human lives. Even though some may be tempted to see these two passages as suggesting a stingy and arbitrary God, what evidence do you see in these chapters that would suggest a patient and generous God? Check the following sources (and others that may be available to you) to see whether and how various authors

handle the troublesome statements:

A. S. Maxwell, *The Bible Story*, 3:145-154.

E. G. White, *Patriarchs and Prophets*, 569-580.

F. D. Nichol, ed., *Seventh-day Adventist Bible Commentary*, 4:461-467.

Write a paragraph or two summarizing your conclusions.

2. *Messiah*. Hannah's prayer in 1 Samuel 2:1-10 contains the first reference to Israel's king as *messiah* ("anointed one"), a word that comes into Greek as *christ(os)*. Christians, of course, accept Jesus as *the* "anointed One," *the* Davidic king. But the word has a rich Old Testament history. Using a concordance, study the occurrence and meaning of the word in the Old Testament, concentrating on 1 and 2 Samuel, the Psalms, and Isaiah. Make a list in your notebook of the texts you find particularly significant, and note how they illuminate the meanings attached to the words. Then read about *messiah* or *christ* in a good Bible dictionary. The articles in the *Seventh-day Adventist Bible Dictionary* are brief. The article "Messiah" by R. T. France, in the *New Bible Dictionary* (2nd ed.), pages 763-772, gives an excellent and comprehensive survey of both Old Testament and New Testament material from an evangelical perspective.

■ Further Study of the Word:

1. For general insight, see E. G. White, *Patriarchs and Prophets*, 569-580.

2. On the problem of seemingly less-than-Christian sentiments in Old Testament psalms and prayers, see A. Thompson, "What Kind of Prayers Would You Publish If You Were God?" in *Who's Afraid?*, 158-168.

3. For a concise, contemporary evangelical commentary that follows the order of the text, see J. Baldwin's Tyndale Old Testament Commentary, *1 & 2 Samuel*.

4. For a creative interpretation of 1 Samuel as seen from the

perspective of a failed monarchy, see R. Polzin, *Samuel and the Deuteronomist.*

5. For careful textual comments on the underlying Hebrew and Greek (Septuagint) manuscripts of 1 Samuel, see P. K. McCarter's Anchor Bible commentary, *I Samuel* and R. Klein's Word Biblical commentary, *1 Samuel.*

6. For a more theological perspective on 1 Samuel, see H. W. Hertzberg, *I and II Samuel,* and G. Robinson, *Let Us Be Like the Nations.*

7. For traditional Jewish interpretations and references to Jewish sources, see L. Ginzberg, *The Legends of the Jews,* text in vol. 4, notes and references in vol. 6.

CHAPTER TWO

The Ark:
Worthless Charm, Holy Terror

1 Samuel 4–7

*No sooner does Scripture declare that "Samuel's word came to all Israel"
(3:21), than Samuel disappears for three chapters and twenty years. Not until
7:3, when Israel is ready to renew her relationship to the LORD, does he re-
appear. But before that happens, the three chapters in between tell about the ark
of the LORD's covenant—its capture, its exile, and its return by the Philistines.*

*Then chapter 7 reveals that some twenty years after the ark came back
home, God's people awoke to their great danger. With Samuel's help, they put
things right with God, enjoying peace on earth for a short time and a few brief
verses. But it was the lull before the storm. Chapter 8 opens with an elderly
Samuel appointing his wicked sons as judges. The people said they had had
enough and asked for a king "such as all the other nations have" (vs. 5).*

*Our present chapter, then, takes us to the threshold of the monarchy.
And we will again hear two messages: first, a story of Israel's last days
before she asked for a king; second, a prophetic response looking back at
those events from a perspective of a monarchy come and gone, judged wanting by the God whom Israel served.*

■ Getting Into the Word

1 Samuel 4–7

Use the four points below to focus your thinking as you begin your study of 1 Samuel 4 to 7. Then read the chapters
through twice, observing possible links with 1 Samuel 1 to 3.

Using a separate sheet of paper for each topic, jot down in outline form those aspects of the story that pertain to each item.

1. *The Ark: A Danger and a Joy.* A famous incident involving the ark is the one in which Uzzah was struck dead for attempting to steady it when the oxen stumbled. Refresh your memory of that event by reading 2 Samuel 6; then ponder the stories about the ark in 1 Samuel 4 to 6, making three separate lists: (A) events or incidents in which the ark brings a blessing; (B) incidents linking the ark to misfortune; (C) incidents in which the ark by rights should have exerted a powerful influence but instead seemed strangely ordinary and powerless. Prepare a brief list showing how you would program the ark's power if you were selecting incidents in which it might bring blessing, misfortune, or nothing at all.

2. *True Religion and False.* List and briefly describe the passages in which the religious acts or attitudes of the people of Israel are mentioned either in a positive or negative way. Then write a brief paragraph summarizing the role of Israel's religious leaders in these events, indicating whether they were actively or passively involved or simply absent.

3. *The LORD at Work in a Foreign Land.* List the ways in which the LORD worked directly with the pagan Philistines, either for or against them. In a brief paragraph, summarize what this story reveals about God's dealing with people who are not of His fold.

4. *Follow the Map.* Using the maps in your Bible or in a Bible dictionary (the *Seventh-day Adventist Bible Dictionary* has good maps), locate the place names that appear in these chapters. According to 3:20, Samuel was known "from Dan to Beersheba." Compare the location of these places to those mentioned in 7:16, 17, where Samuel ministered directly. In a sentence, summarize what you think the implications are for Samuel's direct influence on religious life throughout Israel.

■ Exploring the Word

The Glory Has Departed (4:1-22)

A military confrontation between Israel and the Philistines catapults the ark to center stage in this section of 1 Samuel. Regardless of whether Israel (Hebrew; NIV) or the Philistines (Greek; NRSV) initiated hostilities, the outcome was painfully clear: the Philistines thrashed Israel, killing four thousand men.

Back in camp, the elders of Israel asked the obvious question: "Why did the LORD let it happen?" But Scripture doesn't hint at anything like serious heart-searching. A quick fix was ready at hand: "Let us bring the ark of the LORD's covenant from Shiloh, so that it may go with us and save us from the hand of our enemies" (4:3).

Nowhere else in Scripture does the ark receive such close and extended attention as it does here, even if, as it would appear, those directly involved in the capture, exile, and return of the ark gained no spiritual benefits as a result. But the author of 1 and 2 Samuel must have hoped that those living after the ark was gone might learn important lessons from the story of the golden box that became a stumbling block to Israel and a terror to her Philistine neighbors.

Scripture says surprisingly little about the ark. Aside from one reference to the ark in heaven (Rev. 11:19), the only other New Testament reference is in the list of sanctuary furnishings in Hebrews 9:4-5, where the author is eager to move on: "We cannot discuss these things in detail now," he writes. He doesn't either, now or later.

Old Testament references to the ark are likewise rare. Outside the Pentateuch and the historical books (the "former" prophets), the ark appears only in Psalm 132:8 and Jeremiah 3:16. The Jeremiah passage is instructive, however, for it warns against relying on the ark as a kind of magical object. In anticipation of a restored Jerusalem, Jeremiah declared: "Men will no longer say, 'The ark of the covenant of the LORD.' It will never enter their minds or be remembered; it will not be missed, nor will another one be made." Similarly, Jeremiah mocked the people's high-sounding rhetoric in honor of the temple (7:4) when their wicked deeds had turned it into a "den of robbers" (vs. 11). Unless there was a reformation, said Jeremiah, the temple would become another Shiloh (vs. 12).

So here we are at Shiloh. From the smoldering ruins of Solomon's temple, the author of 1 and 2 Samuel takes us back to that earlier holy place and gives us a stiff dose of the ark, three chapters plus, to help us understand the difference between holy objects, holy places, and a holy people.

The elders of Israel were following a noble tradition when they called for the ark to lead them into battle. The ark had often led the way at key points in Israel's history—the move from Sinai (Num. 10:33-35), the crossing of the Jordan (Josh. 3, 4), and the march around Jericho (Josh. 6). In one case, Numbers 14:44, Scripture actually links a military defeat to the absence of the ark, describing how the Amalekites repulsed Israel on the borders of Canaan when the people presumptuously went into battle "though neither Moses nor the ark of the LORD's covenant moved from the camp." Given such a record, no wonder the Israelites erupted with cheers when Hophni and Phinehas brought the ark into camp (1 Sam. 4:5).

The Philistines, by contrast, were petrified when they learned the cause of the uproar and in their terror produced an interesting version of Israel's history: " 'A god has come into the camp,' they said. 'We're in trouble! Nothing like this has happened before. Woe to us! Who will deliver us from the hand of these mighty gods? They are the gods who struck the Egyptians with all kinds of plagues in the desert. Be strong, Philistines! Be men, or you will be subject to the Hebrews, as they have been to you. Be men, and fight!' " (vss. 7-9).

Informed Israelites might be forgiven a smile at such a story. First, the Philistines weren't clear as to whether there was one god or many. (Ironically, many of the Israelites weren't sure either!) Second, the event wasn't all that unique, at least as far as Israel was concerned. Against Jericho, for example, the ark had indeed led the way in battle (Josh. 6). But maybe the Philistines meant that nothing like this had happened *to them* before. Third, the Philistines mistakenly had the Israelite "gods" striking the Egyptians with plagues in the wilderness. Fourth, and here any Israelite smiles would likely turn to a wince, the Philistines spoke of themselves as masters over Israel, an uncomfortable echo of Egyptian bondage.

But for all the glitches in the Philistine story, it was fundamentally correct in recognizing that this "god" was indeed unique. For a god to identify himself with an enslaved people, deliver them, and lead them to a new land was unheard of. Furthermore, to remember that act of deliverance as something that took place at a particular point in time was to recognize, however dimly, that this was a god who acted in history, not just through the processes of nature. Israel's God was Creator and Master of nature, not part of nature itself.

So the Philistines knew enough history to be afraid. Israel's God was different from anything they had ever known, and the ark was the symbol of His presence. They were frightened and had reason to be.

So why didn't they just surrender, turn tail, and run? What could mere men do against the gods, especially this God? That's exactly what these very human Philistines intended to find out. They set out to conquer the gods and did! Instead of four thousand casualties, as in the first battle, thirty thousand Israelites fell, while the rest fled to their own tents (4:10). In short, the giddy Israelites lost, while the frightened Philistines won and won big.

Just how big was the Philistine victory? Three passages in this section of 1 Samuel raise the problem of large numbers in the Old Testament. The most "extreme" case is 6:19 ,where the standard Hebrew text and the Septuagint state that God struck down 50,070 men of Beth Shemesh. Both the NIV and the NRSV read seventy, electing to follow a few Hebrew manuscripts. But in 4:2 and 4:10, both dealing with the number of Israelite casualties, no manuscript variants allow an easy way out. According to 4:2, the Philistines struck down four thousand Israelites in the first battle; according to 4:10 they killed thirty thousand in the second.

Are those numbers too large? Some prefer to take the biblical data at face value; others say that hyperbole is involved; still others argue that the multiple meanings for the Hebrew word 'aleph (thousand) lie at the root of the difficulty, since the same Hebrew word can also mean "chieftain" or "clan" (compare Mic. 5:2 and Matt. 2:6 in KJV and NIV). If the problem lies in the interpretation of the Hebrew word *'aleph*, then the Philistines could be said to have killed four chiefs in the first battle and thirty in the second; or, destroyed four squads in the first and thirty in the second.

Regardless of how one might resolve the problem, however, the magnitude of the second Philistine victory in comparison with the first remains constant. The ratio was four to thirty, whether thousands, chieftains, or clans—or simply hyperbole. The point of the story requires a smashing victory for the Philistines, and that is perfectly clear however one interprets the word *'aleph*.

The stunning Philistine victory notwithstanding, the author of 1 Samuel says nothing about the jubilation in the Philistine camp, choosing rather to focus on a sobering catalog of woes for Israel—defeat and total breakup of Israel's army; slaughter of thirty thousand troops; capture of the ark; death of Eli's two sons, Hophni and Phinehas (4:10, 11).

When the Benjamite messenger arrived in Shiloh with the news from the battlefield, the ninety-eight-year-old high priest apparently was able to handle the word about the death of his sons. But when he heard that the ark was lost, he was so stunned that he fell off his chair and died of a broken neck. At about the same time, his grandson was born, hauntingly named Ichabod by his mother, "the glory has departed" (vs. 21).

With Jerusalem's destruction vividly in their minds, the author's audience would immediately recognize the parallels: high priest dead, his sons dead. Even a newborn son was no cause for joy, for the mother died during birth: "She did not respond or pay any attention" (vs. 20). Worst of all, "the glory has departed from Israel, for the ark of God has been captured" (vs. 22).

To the Philistines and Back (5:1–6:21)

The victors carried the ark of Israel's "defeated" God into the temple of Dagon, the Philistine god. Such recognition for a defeated deity may seem puzzling to us. But the Philistines were no monotheists. Even many Israelites were something less than monotheistic at this very time (see 7:3). In any event, the Philistines soon learned that the LORD was no defeated deity. However dormant He may have been when summoned by Israel, He suddenly came alive when the Philistines captured His sacred box. Twice, Dagon fell on his face before the ark, the second time with significant bodily damage (5:3, 4). Terrified, the Philistines played poison ball, tossing the ark from Ashdod to Gath to Ekron, each city attempting to escape the heavy hand of the LORD.

Finally, Ekron called for a national assembly. "Send the ark of the god of Israel away," they pleaded; "let it go back to its own place, or it [He] will kill us and our people" (5:11). So after a seven-month reign of terror among the Philistines, the ark went back home. In the field of Joshua of Beth Shemesh, the Israelites greeted it with great joy (6:14, 18)—short-lived joy, to be sure, for seventy of their number (6:19; 50,070 according to the Septuagint and most Hebrew manuscripts) were struck down for looking into the ark (Hebrew; NIV)—or, according to the Septuagint, simply for failing to rejoice with the others at the ark's return (NRSV). Fear reigned again, and the people of Beth Shemesh asked the citizens of Kiriath Jearim to come take the ark off their hands.

The sojourn of the ark from Israel to the Philistines and back again shows that both Israel and the Philistines thought of the ark in magical terms. In spite of the importance of the covenant for ancient Israel, its ethical dimensions, etched on stone within the ark, were too easily slighted in favor of the "magic" of the ark itself. The sins of Hophni and Phinehas against the covenant are named explicitly in 1 Samuel 2—theft (vss. 12-15); sexual immorality (vs. 22); and dishonoring one's parents (vs. 25). Yet these were the very men who brought the ark into the camp of Israel to ensure success in battle.

The ethical nucleus at the heart of the covenant meant that God's use of the ark's power, whether to hurt or help, could be selective. Uzzah was stricken for steadying the ark, even though his act *appears* to have been well-intentioned (2 Sam. 6:6, 7). By contrast, Hophni and Phinehas could commit myriads of evil deeds and still handle the ark without risk. Their day finally came, of course, but they were struck down by the Philistines, not by the ark. In short, because the ark was only a symbol of God's presence and not a part of God Himself, one could never be certain whether a touch to the ark might be harmless or deadly.

Since the Philistines were much more steeped in magical concepts of the holy than the Israelites, God allowed the ark to take on a more magical appearance in their hands. Israel could be thoroughly wicked and not be at all affected by the presence of the ark. But for seven months, the Philistines experienced nothing but terror from it, though admittedly not the same kind of terror that touched Uzzah or the men of Beth Shemesh. Scripture says nothing about the LORD striking down any of the Philistines for touching or viewing the ark in an inappropriate manner. It seems to have moved from city to city among the Philistines without difficulty.

Excursus: The LORD and the Gods ('Elohim)

In the light of the cross, Revelation 12:7-9 clarifies the struggle between good and evil and the beings arrayed on both sides. There, "Michael and his angels" fight against the "dragon and his angels," and the dragon is explicitly identified as "Satan" (vs. 9). In the Old Testament, however, Satan is rarely mentioned. More typically, the supernatural beings arrayed against Yahweh, Israel's God, are simply described as "gods" ('elohim), a general term that can refer to any supernatural being, including God Himself.

The biblical account of the ark's visit to the Philistines focuses attention on the way the LORD related to non-Israelite peoples and their "gods" ('elohim). In some ways, the LORD's treatment of the Philistines was similar to His treatment of Israel. For a time, He even seems to have been more active among the Philistines than He was in Israel. And during that time, the Philistines treated the LORD and His sacred box with great respect. They put the ark in the temple of their "god" ('elohim) Dagon (5:1-5); they credited (blamed) the LORD for their plagues (vs. 7); perhaps they even prayed to Him ("the outcry of the city went up to heaven," vs. 12); and they grappled seriously with the question of an appropriate guilt offering (6:4, 5).

As far as the LORD was concerned, though His hand was heavy upon them, He did not destroy them, even though they were worshipers of Dagon. The LORD seemed to accept their guilt offering; one may even surmise that He heard their prayers. How did this differ from His treatment of Israel? For one, He made no demands upon the Philistines to keep His covenant. His covenant was with Israel, no one else. But it's also clear that He gave the Philistines no rest until they returned the ark to Israel, perhaps being more persistent with them than He was with His own people. Israel could wander off for years at a time and the ark would remain dormant. Among the Philistines, however, the pressure was insistent until they sent the ark home.

David's role in Israelite-Philistine relations suggests that it was not impossible, maybe even simple, for Philistines to convert to the worship of the LORD. Before becoming king of Judah, David joined himself to Achish, king of Gath (1 Sam. 27) and narrowly escaped being called up to battle against his own people (1 Sam. 29). After David's abortive attempt to bring the ark up to Jerusalem, he took it to the home of Obed-Edom the Gittite, whom most commentators believe to be from the Philistine city of Gath (but see "Obed-edom" in the *Seventh-day Adventist Bible Dictionary* for alternatives). During the three months that Obed-Edom kept the ark, "the LORD blessed him and his entire household" (2 Sam. 6:11). And when David had to flee from Jerusalem at the time of Absalom's revolt, one of the most faithful contingents supporting the exiled king consisted of Ittai the Gittite and the six hundred men who had accompanied David from Gath (2 Sam. 15:18-22). Apparently these were Philistines who had accepted the LORD as their God.

More surprising for the Christian monotheist is the evidence in the Old Testament that the LORD recognized the power of the other "gods" (*'elohim*), even while maintaining a kind of loose control over them. In the first commandment, the LORD did not deny the existence of other *'elohim*, but simply forbid Israel to have any other *'elohim* "before me" (Exod. 20:3; Deut. 5:7). In practical terms, that meant the exclusive worship of the LORD in Israel while leaving the other *'elohim* to the other nations.

The biblical evidence for the commonly accepted idea of national deities is clear, though not plentiful. Some of the more striking passages are noted here.

From Jephthah: The bastard judge Jephthah assumed the concept of national deities in his diplomatic exchange with the Moabites: "Will you not take what your god Chemosh gives you? Likewise, whatever the LORD our God has given us, we will possess" (Judg. 11:24).

From David: The fugitive David, on the run from King Saul, revealed a similar theology in his across-the-valley dialogue with the king. Claiming that his enemies have driven him away from his "share in the LORD's inheritance and have said, 'Go, serve other gods,' " he added a plaintive appeal: "Now do not let my blood fall to the ground far from the presence of the LORD" (1 Sam. 26:19, 20).

From Naaman the Syrian: Perhaps the most picturesque confirmation of the idea of the national deity comes from the Syrian general, Naaman. If he wanted to be healed of his leprosy by Israel's God, he had to go in person to the land of Israel's God. After his healing, he gave a powerful testimony to his conversion: "Now I know that there is no God in all the world except in Israel" (2 Kings 5:15). Even more striking, however, was his request for "as much earth as a pair of mules can carry, for your servant will never again make burnt offerings and sacrifices to any other god but the LORD" (vs. 17). Naaman apparently felt it was possible to worship the LORD only on the LORD's home soil.

Some important nonnarrative passages are also of special interest in connection with the concept of a national "god." One is Deuteronomy 32:8, 9, declaring that while Jacob belonged to the LORD, the boundaries of the nations were set originally by the Most High "according to the number of the sons of God [*'elohim*]" (RSV). However, the standard Hebrew text (followed by the NIV), curiously reads "sons of Israel" in place of "sons of God," suggesting early scribal discomfort with the idea of national deities. The Septuagint, however, has "angels of God," which the 1952 RSV surmised as an original "sons of God" and so rendered the passage. Remarkably, among the Dead Sea Scrolls—a significant cache of manuscripts dating from the second century B.C. to the first century A.D., the first of which were discovered in 1947—a Hebrew manuscript of Deuteronomy 32:8 was found with the reading "sons of God," thus confirming the hunch of the RSV translators.

The implication of such a reading is that all the "gods" (*'elohim*) were under the direction of the Most High but that Israel held a special place as the LORD's own people. That means Dagon and the Philistines could still be part of God's larger plan. While Israel was forbidden to worship the Philistine god, Dagon, Israel's God could work with both Dagon and the Philistines because they were part of the LORD's legitimate domain.

From our perspective, we would be more likely to label Dagon of the Philistines, Rimmon of the Syrians, and Chemosh of the Moabites as part of Satan's domain. Such a sharp distinction between two warring heavenly factions, however, would not be clear until Revelation 12:7-12 identified the cross as the point of transition.

From an Old Testament perspective, another passage, Psalm 82, had already pointed to the "judgment" of the other gods (*'elohim*). There, the true God is said to judge the "gods" for their unjust and wicked behavior. Even though you are "gods," declares the psalm, "you will die like mere men" (vss. 6, 7). The final lines speak a truth with which Christians are more familiar: "Rise up, O God, judge the earth, for all the nations are your inheritance" (vs. 8). Through the revelation of God in Jesus Christ, that rulership of the one true God over every nation, kindred, tongue, and people would become clear for all to see, even if the devil has come down to earth, "filled with fury, because he knows that his time is short" (Rev. 12:12).

Though the truth of God's universal lordship over all peoples and all "gods" (*'elohim*) was not always apparent in the Old Testament, the story of the ark's sojourn among the Philistines is a striking illustration of how the LORD treated the worshipers of another god (*'elohim*) as His own, thus foreshadowing the truth of which Paul spoke: "There is neither Jew nor Greek, slave nor free, male nor female, for you are all one in Christ Jesus" (Gal. 3:28). On the side of the Philistines, one almost senses a longing for the realization of that truth in the poignant scenes of the ark's return: the five Philistine lords following the two milch cows at a safe distance, watching to see if the LORD was leading, wondering if their prayers had been heard and their sacrifice accepted (1 Sam. 6:12); the Israelite harvesters joyfully receiving the ark, offering up the two cows as a thank offering to the LORD (vss. 14, 15); the five Philistine lords returning home, satisfied that the LORD had accepted their gift (vs. 16).

On the Threshold of the Monarchy (7:1-17)

As the events of chapter 7 bring us to the high point of Samuel's ministry, the thoughtful reader may detect a phenomenon that could be called "prophetic overstatement." Close reading of 1 Samuel reveals a contrast between some of the general statements about Samuel's influence and the more precise details given in specific narratives. In 3:20, for example, Samuel is said to be known as a prophet from Dan to Beersheba, that is, from one end of the country to the other. But 7:16, 17 names the specific places on his annual circuit: Bethel, Gilgal, Mizpah, and back home to Ramah, all tightly clustered in Israel's heartland. The implication is that Samuel's specific influence was much more limited than his general reputation. The twenty-year gap between the return of the ark and the religious revival would also suggest a more limited influence. The broad statement would still be true in a general sense, but could be viewed as an "overstatement" in view of a more precise analysis of specific details.

An even more striking example of "prophetic overstatement" is found in 7:13: "So the Philistines were subdued and did not invade Israelite territory again. Throughout Samuel's lifetime, the hand of the LORD was against the Philistines." That contrasts with the detailed descriptions of the Philistine conflicts in 1 Samuel 13 and 14, where the Philistines had even cornered the blacksmith business. On the day of battle, Saul and Jonathan were the only Israelites with sword or spear (1 Sam. 13:22).

The more sweeping statements have a homiletic purpose and can be compared with the dramatic statements from the prophets about the evils of corporate worship. "I hate, I despise your religious feasts," shouted the prophet Amos. "I cannot stand your assemblies" (Amos 5:21). That's a bit strong. But he made his point.

The book of Joshua, with its sweeping statements about the status of the conquest, also exhibits contrasts similar to the ones describing Samuel's influence. Joshua 11:23, for example, declares that "Joshua took the entire land, just as the LORD had directed Moses." Yet in 13:1 the LORD tells Joshua, "You are very old, and there are still very large areas of land to be taken over." The rest of Joshua and much of the book of Judges testify to the sober truth of that latter statement. Still, the first one is a ringing affirmation of God's goodness to His people. It is a "prophetic overstatement," to be sure. But the pages of Scripture frequently testify to such exuberance. Believers are able to look on the bright side of the picture, even when some of the details seem to fall short of the mark. The concept of "prophetic overstatement" becomes crucial in 1 Samuel 7, where the author gives us the last glimpse of Samuel as judge before the thorny question of monarchy faces both him and his people.

Given his eagerness to establish Samuel as the ideal judge, the author's "prophetic overstatement" about the practical benefits of Samuel's leadership against the Philistines is understandable. Though the specific details in the coming narratives might suggest a more sober summary, the author of 1 Samuel has gone to preaching here, and with intensity: "So the Philistines were subdued and did not invade Israelite territory again. Throughout Samuel's lifetime, the hand of the LORD was against the Philistines" (7:13).

The author of 1 Samuel has carefully brought us to this high point of Samuel's life, laying the foundation block by block for what he believed to be God's ideal for His people. By the close of chapter 3, judgment had been announced on the house of Eli. Chapter 4 shows how it happened. Eli, like the collapsed monarchy in the author's day, was old and could no longer see (vs. 15). On hearing the news about loss of the ark, he fell from his chair (throne) and died "an old man and heavy" (vs. 18). His offspring and heirs, Hophni and Phinehas, were also dead, killed by a foreign power because of their great wickedness, because of their failure to respect "the ark of the covenant of the LORD Almighty, who is enthroned between the cherubim" (vs. 4).

The three chapters describing the loss, exile, and return of the ark illustrate the failure of Eli's leadership. More subtly, they also illustrate what happened to Israel when Samuel was not present, for he is never mentioned between 4:1 and 7:3. His return coincides with a remarkable spiritual renewal, a renewal that nowhere mentions the ark that had been returned to Israel some twenty years before.

If Samuel's absence was somehow linked with the two Ebenezer disasters (4:1, 3,10, 11), his presence was instrumental in the Ebenezer victory. The message inscribed on the stone expressed the dramatic turnaround: "Thus far has the LORD helped us" (7:12). Earlier, Samuel had been established as priest (2:35; 3:1) and prophet (3:20). Now, in chapter 7, he is also given the title of judge (NIV = "leader," vs. 6). Eli, too, had judged Israel (NIV = "led," 4:18) but had tarnished the ideal by attempting to pass on his authority to his sons. Though the priestly office was hereditary, judges received their authority from God, not from human lineage. God had judged Eli's attempt to make it otherwise. His sons were killed, and Eli himself died when he fell from his chair (throne). Samuel would yet succumb to the same temptation. But here in chapter 7, he is a judge of the pure type, serving the people under God's appointment.

Under Samuel, the LORD's willingness to again help His people is linked with two striking aspects of the people's response. First, their unqualified repentance; second, their decision to worship the LORD only, with emphasis on the word *only*. Samuel's leadership as judge harks back to the apostasy-oppression-outcry-deliverance cycle that recurs so often in the book of Judges, but with a notable difference, for under Samuel, the people repent. In spite of the many "cycles" in which God intervened on behalf of His people in the book of Judges, only once is there an explicit reference to Israel's repentance, namely, in Judges 10:10-16, where it seems both cavalier and superficial: "We have sinned. Do with us whatever you think best, but please rescue us now" (Judg. 10:15). By contrast, the repentance under Samuel is heartfelt and marked with humility before the LORD (7:4-8).

While the mention of any kind of repentance at all is notable enough, what marks this "returning" to the LORD as truly unique is the use of the qualifier *only*. In the history of God's people from Deuteronomy to the end of 2 Kings, Israel is frequently admonished to serve the LORD *instead of* other gods. But 7:3, 4 is the only time that Israel is called to serve the LORD *only* (Polzin, *Samuel*, 74). Israel responded and "put away their Baals and Ashtoreths, and served the LORD only" (vs. 4).

Polzin argues that the word *only* may be even more significant here: "In 1 Samuel 7 'to serve God *alone*' means not only 'not to serve foreign gods,' it means also 'not to serve kings' " (Polzin, *Samuel*, 78). In short, the author of 1 Samuel could be calling for a "return" to the LORD that is free from both idolatry and monarchy. Samuel is the model of the right kind of leader, the charismatic judge who intercedes with the LORD for His people, who offers sacrifices on their behalf, and who calls them back to the pure service of the LORD only.

Perhaps the strongest evidence for such an interpretation comes from chapter 8 after the people asked for a king. The LORD's response to Samuel equated their request with idolatry: "It is not you they have rejected, but they have rejected me as their king. As they have done from the day I brought them up out of Egypt until this day, forsaking me and serving other gods, so they are doing to you" (vss. 7, 8). In Polzin's words, "Israel's rejection of Samuel the judge, for the proposed service of kings is like its forsaking the LORD for the service of other gods" (Polzin, *Samuel*, 78, 79).

Now if the author of 1 Samuel is portraying the ideal form of leadership in his sketch of Samuel as judge, 1 Samuel 7 allows us to summarize the characteristics of a community living under such a person: (1) a wholehearted "returning" to the service of the LORD, meaning no foreign gods and no king (vss. 3, 4); (2) confession of sin (vs. 6); (3) humility and fear in the presence of the LORD, instead of boastful arrogance (vss. 7, 8); (4) peace with one's neighbors (vss. 12-14). While there is indeed sacrifice, there is no ark and no worship in a formal temple. Thus the author of 1 Samuel dips back to an earlier ideal to help Israel cope with the loss of king and temple. He says, in effect, that God's people can survive quite nicely without the power of a king and without the visible temple. But they must return to the LORD and serve Him only.

The about-face in the Israelite religious experience is vividly illustrated in the return engagement with the Philistines described in chapter 7. Though the ark is not mentioned, other parallels and contrasts are striking. The Israelites were once more in mass assembly, this time at Mizpah, but not in a council of war; Samuel was leading the people in an experience of genuine spiritual renewal. The Philistines heard about Israel's assembly and mounted an attack. Before, when the ark was lost, Israel had been confident and the Philistines afraid. This time, it was the other way around—at least Israel was afraid. But Samuel prayed, the LORD thundered, and Israel won a great victory.

The author's portrayal of God's ideal for His people in 1 Samuel 7 ties in with the prophetic vision for Israel. God's first purpose was to develop a keen sense of right and wrong, a deep appreciation for justice and righteousness. In pursuit of that ideal, it was becoming clear that both sacred rituals and sacred objects, even when originally given by God, could become liabilities. Here in 1 Samuel, all the remarkable signs and wonders connected with the capture and return of the ark apparently did nothing to spark a renewal of true religion. According to Scripture, revival didn't come until twenty years later. Through the covenant tablets that the ark contained, God had intended that the ark be a focal point for the ethical and the personal in His people's relationship to Him and to each other. But the ark had become something magical and mechanical instead. Maybe it would be better to do without the ark. . . .

In a sense, one could say that Jeremiah 3:16 was the necessary preparation for John 3:16, for it spoke of a time when the ark would not be remembered or missed. One day, the followers of Jesus would experience such a time. The principles of the covenant that once were engraved in stone would come again to humanity as a gift of God, but this time embodied in human flesh. "And we beheld his glory, the glory as of the only begotten of the Father, full of grace and truth" (John 1:14, KJV). Jesus shows us a better way. Attempting to put God in a gold box has its problems; 1 Samuel 4 to 7 shows why.

The ideal of 1 Samuel 7 is a marvelous one, however feebly and rarely it may be grasped. Indeed, the author is now ready to open another chapter on Israel's history that illustrates how the compromise of that ideal was a terrible mistake, leading ultimately to the loss of ark, temple, and even homeland.

■ Applying the Word

1 Samuel 4–7

1. *In the Presence of the Sacred.* The stories in 1 Samuel 4 to 7 reveal both a carelessness that makes the sacred appear ordinary and ineffective and a carelessness that makes the sacred quite dangerous. How can my carelessness still make the sacred dangerous today? Have there been times in my life when I have been careless for so long that the sacred simply becomes ordinary? What imparts sacredness to an object or an event? (Summarize your thoughts in a few paragraphs in your Samuel notebook.)

2. *Leaders.* In 1 Samuel, God was concerned not only about idol worship, but the worship of the wrong kind of leaders. List some possible reasons why hereditary leadership was less than ideal for Israel. What parallels in our modern Christian world can you think of? Is the church more at risk from powerful leaders or from the lack of powerful leaders?

3. *God Among the Philistines.* Think good thoughts about the Philistines for a few moments, noting the positive traits revealed in their handling of the ark's capture and return. How can God's way of dealing with them teach me how to work with modern Philistines in my world? What lessons can I learn from the Philistines that would make me more faithful in my worship of the true God?

4. *Overstatement.* Have there been times in my spiritual experience when an "overstatement" has had a positive effect on me by stabilizing, startling, or encouraging me?

5. *Substitutes.* What are the sacred objects in my life? Under what circumstances might I be tempted to use them as a

substitute for a genuine religious experience? What specific steps can I take to avoid giving in to such temptations?

∎ Researching the Word

1. *The Ark.* Using a standard concordance, compile a list of the biblical contexts in which the ark of the covenant is mentioned. Develop your own scheme of organizing the references into categories (e.g., building the sanctuary, leading the people, decision making). Then, using these biblical experiences involving the ark, think through the strengths and weaknesses of linking one's religious experience to a specific sacred object. Write out your thoughts in your notebook. What makes a sacred object helpful, and what makes it dangerous? You may want to include in your study Jeremiah's temple discourse in Jeremiah 7.

2. *Human Repentance, Divine Plan.* On the basis of the book of Judges, study the relationship of human "repentance" to God's saving acts. To what extent is repentance a necessary pre-condition for deliverance? Can you find instances in which God delivered His people apart from their repentance hoping that His grace would trigger repentance? What instances can you find in which He insisted on a change of heart or a change of ways before He would intervene? Compile your list on the basis of the experience of each of the judges who delivered Israel. Summarize your conclusions in your notebook.

∎ Further Study of the Word

1. For general insight, see E. G. White, *Patriarchs and Prophets,* 581-591.

2. For a discussion of 1 Samuel 4 to 7 as an integral part of the author's statement against kingship, see R. Polzin, *Samuel,* 55-79.

3. For a discussion of the problem of large numbers in the Old

Testament, see A. Thompson, *Inspiration*, 214-236.

4. For a discussion of the Lord's relationship to evil, Satan, and the other gods in the Old Testament, see "Whatever Happened to Satan in the Old Testament?" in A. Thompson, *Who's Afraid?*, 43-70.

PART TWO

1 Samuel 8–15

Samuel and Saul:
The LORD Gives;
the LORD Takes Away

CHAPTER THREE

Evil Request, High Hopes

1 Samuel 8–12

Chapter 7 concluded with a glimpse of God's marvelous ideal for Israel: a repentant people, distrusting their own abilities while relying fully on the LORD; peace between Israel and her neighbors; a faithful judge, representing the people before the LORD and taking the LORD's message to the people, reminding them that God is the source of all good. The stone set up by Samuel at Ebenezer said it well: "Thus far has the LORD helped us" (1 Sam. 7:12).

That ideal of chapter 7 doesn't just fade away into the night, it shudders and crashes with the opening words of chapter 8: "When Samuel grew old, he appointed his sons as judges for Israel" (vs. 1). Appointed his sons as judges? Not possible. The authority of the great judges—Deborah and Barak, Gideon, Samson—was not inherited; it came from the LORD. Even priests, for whom authority did pass from father to son, could be cut off by human wickedness right in the face of the LORD's promise of a house that would last "forever." Just ask Eli (1 Sam. 2:27-36). But a judge, attempting to pass his authority on to his sons? Scripture says it happened when Samuel grew old. He appointed his sons as judges—evil sons who became evil judges. The people's wrath was stirred and they came to Samuel with an evil request: Give us a king.

■ Getting Into the Word

1 Samuel 8

Read 1 Samuel 8 to 12 quickly for an overview. Then read it again with an eye on the question of kingship. Make one list of

texts, with brief identifying phrases, that seem to support kingship, and a second list for those that seem to be against it. In a
brief paragraph, answer the question: Was kingship a good idea
or bad? Or, put another way: If kingship was bad, why did God
allow it?

Now focus more closely on chapter 8, guided by the following questions:

1. *God and Samuel.* Outline the interaction between God and
   Samuel in chapter 8. Who appears to be more against kingship? What evidence can you supply for your answer?
2. *Kingship: God's Will?* Read Moses's instruction for appointing a king in Deuteronomy 17:14-20, comparing it with the
   account in 1 Samuel 8, where both God and Samuel describe
   the people's request for a king as a departure from God's
   will. What reasons, if any, does Scripture give for opposing
   kingship? In what ways do these two passage agree or dis-
   agree with each other? Can they be harmonized? If so, how?
3. *Kingship: Help or Hindrance?* Though Samuel's speech in 8:11-
   18 focuses on the shadow side of kingship, Judges 21:25
   envisions a king as the cure for chaos. Reflect on Samuel's
   speech and list the potential benefits from kingship that
   might balance out the negatives. Psalm 72 will help you with
   the list.

■ Exploring the Word

Give Them a King (8:1-22)

Chapter 8 opens up a painful chapter in Israel's history: the people
want a king. Both God and Samuel see it as an evil request, even
though Deuteronomy 17:14-20 assumes that Israel will indeed ask
for and receive a king from the LORD.

Further complicating matters, the undisciplined lifestyle of
Samuel's sons seems to have implicated the prophet himself, making
him partially responsible for the people's request. This subtle criti-

cism of Samuel is a first in the book. Though Samuel's wife is never mentioned, his two sons, Joel and Abijah, do find their niche in Scripture, entering the record as judges at Beersheba, far to the south of Samuel's home in Ramah in central Israel. But Scripture indicates that they were not good judges, contrasting their wickedness with Samuel's integrity. They "did not walk in his [Samuel's] ways" (8:3, 5) but "turned aside after dishonest gain"; they "accepted bribes and perverted justice" (vs. 3).

Their evil practices so exasperated the people that a delegation came to Samuel and asked for a king, openly citing his sons' wicked ways as the reason for the request (vs. 5). Much displeased, Samuel turned to the LORD (vs. 6). Israel had never had a king; the LORD Himself was its leader. Under the judges, if a person was acclaimed leader by popular demand, as in the case of Jephthah, his calling still must be confirmed by a special outpouring of the Spirit (Judg. 11:29). The same was true of most of the major judges: Othniel (3:9, 10), Ehud (3:15), Barak (4:6), Gideon (6:11-16), and Samson (13:3-5). If for Deborah (Judg. 4:4) and the minor judges (Shamgar [3:31], Tola [10:1, 2], Jair [10:3-5], Ibzan [12:8-10], Elon [12:11, 12] and Abdon [12:13-15]), no special mention is made of the LORD's appointment, it was still the case that when a judge was *the* leader of Israel (see Deut. 17:8-13), authority was never inherited.

The principle of divine initiative had not gone unchallenged during the period of the judges. After Gideon's successful battle against Midian, the people were eager to establish his family as a ruling dynasty: "Rule over us," they said, "you, your son and your grandson—because you have saved us out of the hand of Midian" (Judg. 8:22). Gideon himself, however, put a stop to the idea: "I will not rule over you, nor will my son rule over you. The LORD will rule over you" (vs. 23). Though Gideon was scarcely an ideal role model for Israel, having moved dangerously close to idolatry (vss. 24-27) and having taken up polygamy with abandon (vss. 30, 31), one good thing he knew for sure: the LORD alone was Israel's king.

It wasn't as clear to Gideon's seventy sons, however, that they had not inherited their father's authority (Judg. 9:2). Abimelech, the son of one of Gideon's concubines, actually attempted to declare himself king, though both he and his dreams were quickly squelched (vss. 54-56). In any event, when the people came to Samuel to ask for a king, they could not appeal to Israelite tradition for support. Instead, they appealed to the example of the nations around them (1 Sam. 8:5, 20). And that was the rub. Ironically, both Eli and Samuel, by designating their sons to succeed them, may have helped to undermine the Israelite stance against hereditary leadership. The priestly office was indeed passed on from father to son. But because Eli and Samuel were judges as well as priests (4:18; 7:17), they clouded the issue of heredity when they allowed their sons to follow after them. While there is no record that Eli appointed his own sons as judges, Samuel clearly did and with painful results. Now the people wanted to take the next step and have a king. They wanted to be like the nations around them.

That the request for a king displeased both Samuel and the LORD is puzzling in light of Deuteronomy 17:14-20, which assumes that the people would make just such a request. Even their rationale is an echo of Deuteronomy: "When . . . you say, 'Let us set a king over us like all the nations around us' " (Deut. 17:14; compare 1 Sam. 8:5, 19, 20). But when the "displeased" Samuel reported the people's wishes to the LORD, the LORD responded without hesitation: "Grant their request"—though He immediately interpreted it as a rejection, not of Samuel, but of Himself. Indeed, the parallel structure of the LORD's response implies that the people's request was simply another chapter in Israel's long, ongoing tussle with idolatry: "As they have done from the day I brought them up out of Egypt until this day, forsaking me and serving other gods, so they are doing to you" (8:8). In other words, the request for a king was not just a rejection of the LORD; it was tantamount to idolatry (see also 10:19).

Yet the LORD was ready to be gracious—more so than Samuel— and responded positively to the people's request. At the same time, He implied that Samuel had taken the matter too personally: "It is not you they have rejected, but they have rejected me as their king," the LORD told him (8:7). Still, the LORD's very first word to Samuel was an imperative, a command to fulfill the people's desire: "Listen!" "Listen to all that the people are saying to you" (vs. 7). In 8:9 the LORD repeated the command: "Now listen to them." The word for "listen" used here is the same one that heads that most famous of all Jewish verses, the *Shema'* in Deuteronomy 6:4: "Hear, O Israel. . . ." The same word means "obey" and is the very word that Samuel will utter in his famous and fateful line to King Saul: "To obey is better than sacrifice" (15:22).

But Samuel found it hard to "obey" the command to "obey" the people, and he did not respond to the LORD's double imperative. At the end of the dialogue in chapter 8, the LORD commanded him for the third time to "obey" the people: "Listen to them and give them a king" (vs. 22). But all Samuel could do was to send the people home.

The dialogue between Samuel and the people (vss. 10-20) leaves the impression that both prophet and people have departed from the LORD's ideal. If *they* revealed their flawed hearts in asking for a king, Samuel revealed *his* by failing to discipline his sons and by avoiding the LORD's direct command to grant them a king.

Samuel also appears to have only partially fulfilled the LORD's additional commands to "warn" the people *and* "let them know what the king who will reign over them will do" (vs. 9). Probably for stylistic reasons, the NIV and NRSV closely link "all the words of the LORD" with Samuel's description of the king's expected behavior, omitting the Hebrew *and* at the beginning of verse 11. The resulting impression is that the LORD had simply given Samuel the list of negatives regarding kingship as part of the divine warning. Both the KJV and NASB, however, preserve the *and* that prefaces Samuel's interpretation of the king's deeds, suggesting that the description of the king's ways was Samuel's composition at the command of the LORD rather than a direct "revelation" from the LORD Himself. Thus a possible reading of 8:10, 11 is: "Samuel told all the words of the LORD to the people who were asking him for a king. *And* he [Samuel] said, 'This is what the king . . . will do.' "

Literally translated, the introduction to "the king's ways" in 8:9 reads: "Let them know the *mishpat* of the king." The KJV has "shew them the manner [*mishpat*] of the king that shall reign over them." The Hebrew word *mishpat* is usually translated "judgment" or "justice." Along with *chesed* ("kindness") and *tsedek/tsedekah* ("righteousness"), it is one of the three most significant theological words in the Old Testament, one of the three things in which the LORD takes "delight" (Jer. 9:24). It also heads the list of divine expectations in Micah 6:8, where "to act justly" (NIV) is "to do *mishpat*." Rooted directly in the character and actions of God, *mishpat* was to be the key element in the character and actions of the earthly king. Thus, in that great royal psalm, Psalm 72, the opening line declares: "Endow the king with your justice [*mishpat*] O God" (vs. 1).

In 1 Samuel 8 and 10, however, *mishpat* means something closer to "custom," "way," or "regulation" [compare KJV "manner"]. That is especially clear in 10:25 when Saul is formally introduced as king: "Samuel explained to the people the regulations [*mishpat*] of the kingship. He wrote them down on a scroll and deposited it before the LORD." Yet even here *mishpat* seems to retain the element of "justice" that is so dominant in theological settings, for in the absence of any prophetic criticism of kingship, the statement in 10:25 implies that Samuel simply recorded the rights and privileges of both king and people, a commentary detailing the extent of the king's powers but also the limits. In short, 10:25 points to a full and balanced description of kingship, properly written down and preserved.

Just such a *mishpat* of the king is what the LORD had asked Samuel to tell the people in 8:9. But as recorded in Scripture, Samuel's speech in chapter 8 was not a balanced one. Instead, he ticked off all those ways in which the king would diminish their freedoms and tax their wealth. Nothing is said about the good things that the LORD's king should do for the people, the kinds of things listed in Psalm 72, for example: securing just treatment for all, defending the afflicted and needy, and crushing oppressors. Neither does Samuel refer to the contribution of kingship alluded to in Judges 17:6 and 21:25—the order that a king could bring to a society in chaos. Even the negative things Samuel did mention were not extraordinary; indeed, they would have appeared quite reasonable in any other setting. For services rendered, a king would need property, personnel, and income. Everyone knew that. Why would a tithe (8:15, 17) appear so oppressive? It didn't have to be and probably would not have been if Samuel had presented a more even-handed picture of the "*mishpat* of the king."

The people's resistance shows that they perceived Samuel's speech as a thinly veiled attempt to change their minds: "The people refused to listen to Samuel. 'No!' they said. 'We want a king over us' " (vs. 19).

When Samuel told the LORD what the people said, the LORD was again more gracious than Samuel. He did not strike the people down for their wickedness or even attempt to dissuade them, as Samuel had done. "Listen to them," He again told Samuel, "and give them a king" (vs. 22). Samuel couldn't bring himself to obey; he simply sent the people home.

In summary, as chapter 8 introduces the question of kingship, subtle tensions begin to emerge. Samuel and the LORD both agreed that the people's request for a king was evil. But the LORD was gracious, prepared to grant their request and adapt to a less-than-ideal model of leadership for His people. Such graciousness did not come easily for Samuel. Perhaps he was too mortified by the fact that his own sins of omission (failing to discipline his sons) and commission (appointing them as judges) may have laid the groundwork for the people's evil request. It would not be the last time that Samuel's humanity would resist leading the people along the rocky road toward kingship. Yet whatever flaws one might wish to pin on either Israel or Samuel, such flaws did not prevent the LORD from working in and through them. Israel was still God's people; Samuel was still His chosen messenger.

Nevertheless, the tensions in this account remind us that, then as now, when a human decision prompts the LORD to move from Plan A to Plan B, His people can find themselves torn between the original ideal and the divinely sanctioned adaptation. Do we seek to return to the ideal? Or do we wholeheartedly and forever embrace the adaptation? If we are honest with ourselves, we must admit that we, too, often struggle with the same dilemma.

■ Getting Into the Word

1 Samuel 9–11

1. *Saul the Man.* Read through 1 Samuel 9 to 11, writing down the details that reveal Saul's personal characteristics. Prepare a brief character sketch of the man based only on these three chapters. Do you find any indication here of a tendency to depart from the LORD's will?
2. *God's Choice.* List the evidence in chapters 9 and 10 that identifies Saul as the king of God's own choosing.
3. *Is Saul Really King?* Chapter 11 characterizes Saul's early reign in unexpected ways. It hardly sounds like the reign of a king. List and summarize the content of those texts that suggest the tentative nature of Saul's early kingship. Discuss the implications of those texts in a paragraph or two.

■ Exploring the Word

Hesitant King, Forceful Prophet (9:1-27)

Chapter 9 introduces a dramatic change of style and scenery. The confrontation between the people and Samuel is set aside, as are the tensions between Samuel and God. The LORD is ready to give Israel a king even if the prophet isn't. So if Samuel won't go to the king, the LORD will bring the king to Samuel, and that is what happens in the early verses of the chapter. By the end of chapter 9, Saul and Samuel have begun to work together and have set themselves on a course that will prove fateful for them both.

Saul, an outwardly impressive man, enters the scene for the first time in 9:2. Scripture does not explain why the LORD selected a man with such obvious physical advantages to be Israel's first king. When the LORD rejected Saul and turned to David, He made a point of selecting a man who was *not* obviously superior in the physical sense, reminding Samuel that "the LORD does not look at the things man looks at. Man looks at the outward appearance, but the LORD looks at the heart" (16:7). But for Israel's first king, the LORD selected a "man without equal" among his people (9:2).

The picture of Saul that emerges from the narrative, however, is a curious one. He appears gentle and obedient, even insecure. While searching unsuccessfully for his father's asses, he worries that his father might think he is lost along with the asses (vs. 5). He asks counsel from his servant, and it is the servant who points the way to the man of God. "Perhaps he will tell us what way to take," the servant says (vs. 6), a sentence echoing the author's concern for a nation that had lost both temple and king at Nebuchadnezzar's invasion.

Saul readily agrees to visit the seer but worries that they have nothing to give him. His resourceful servant again knows the answer and, indeed, provides the coin (vs. 8), indicating that he will "give it to the man of God so that he will tell us what way to take" (vs. 8). Is this repeated reference to "what way to take" the author's way of revealing Saul's inability to know and act?

Nearing the town, Saul and his servant again ask directions, first from a group of girls (vs. 11), and then once more when they come face to face with Samuel. Not recognizing the man of God, Saul asks Samuel himself how to find the seer (vs. 18). Samuel obliges, identifying himself and hinting of great things ahead for Saul (vss. 19, 20). But Saul recoils from the idea, noting that he is from Benjamin, the smallest tribe in Israel, and that his father's house is the least in Benjamin. "Why me?" he asks (vs. 21).

Good question! The "impressive young man without equal among the Israelites" (vs. 2) had shown no talent for leadership, relying solely on the judgment of others in matters both great and small. Through the end of chapter 10, we hear Saul's voice only once more, an evasive answer to his uncle's query about what Samuel had said. Saul mentioned the asses, but "he did not tell his uncle what Samuel had said about the kingship" (vs. 16). That same shy streak led Saul to hide among the baggage instead of facing the public proclamation of his kingship (vs. 22). And finally, after all the festivities at his public anointing, Saul simply returned quietly to his home in Gibeah (vs. 26). When "troublemakers" (Hebrew = "sons of Belial") made sport of him and insolently refused to bring him gifts, Scripture simply says that "Saul kept silent" (vs. 26). Had he already demonstrated himself to be a man of valor, such a response would more readily be seen as an Old Testament example of turning the other cheek (compare Matt. 5:39). As it is, the reader may be tempted to see Saul's hesitancy as cowardice rather than humility.

Thus, though Israel's first king was a man of dominating physical appearance, the traits that would have marked him as a leader of people seemed woefully lacking. Maybe the "sons of Belial" were right when they asked, "How can this fellow save us?" (10:26).

Yet Saul was the man of God's own choosing. Though Scripture may portray him as hesitant and passive, it leaves no doubt that the LORD's hand was upon him. The day before Saul's arrival, the LORD told Samuel to anoint Saul as "leader over my people Israel; he will deliver my people from the hand of the Philistines" (9:16). When they first met, not only did Samuel drop a hint of Saul's destiny (vs. 20), he repeatedly reinforced it, giving him the place of honor and the choice morsel at the communal meal (vss. 22-24), anointing him in private the next day (10:1), and checking off a sequence of detailed "signs" to convince Saul that the LORD was with him: two men would meet him at Rachel's tomb with the report that the asses were found and that his father was now worried about Saul (vs. 2). Then at the great tree of Tabor, three men carrying goats, bread, and wine would offer him two loaves of bread (vss. 3, 4). Finally, just outside of Gibeah, the Spirit of God would come upon Saul "in power"; a group of prophets carrying musical instruments would approach him; after prophesying with them, Saul would "be changed into a different person" (vss. 5, 6). "Once these signs are fulfilled," said Samuel, "do whatever your hand finds to do, for God is with you" (vs. 7).

But Scripture gives still more proof that God had chosen Saul, stating that "God changed Saul's heart" and that "all these signs were fulfilled that day" (vs. 9). Furthermore, it was the LORD Himself who revealed Saul's hiding place among the baggage (vs. 22). And when Saul finally stood before the people, Samuel declared that Saul was "the man the LORD has chosen" and that there was "no one like him among all the people" (vs. 24). Samuel wrote out the "regulations" of the kingship and deposited the scroll "before the LORD" (vs. 25); and even though Saul returned quietly to his home, with him went "valiant men whose hearts God had touched" (vs. 26).

Thus the author of 1 Samuel has presented Israel's new king as a complex paradox: handsome Saul is also hesitant Saul; he is obedient to specific commands but leaves the uneasy impression that he may not be capable of decisive action. Though Saul is clearly the LORD's choice as well as the people's, the paradox is further complicated by Samuel's seemingly ambivalent attitude toward the new king, an ambivalence revealed in chapter 10 by two striking incidents.

Who Is in Charge: Samuel or Saul? (10:1-27)

The first incident that reveals Samuel's mixed feelings about Saul is one in which Samuel puts Saul in a "double bind" (Polzin, *Samuel*, 107), granting him the freedom of a prophet on the one hand but requiring him to remain subject to Samuel on the other. As described in 10:6-8, Samuel predicted Saul's prophetic experience and the overpowering arrival of the Spirit, which would transform Saul into "a different person." Samuel then gave him a blank check: "Do whatever your hand finds to do, for God is with you" (vs. 7).

But then, like a parent who fears the implications of freedom for an adult child, Samuel took back the blank check. "Go down ahead of me to Gilgal," he told Saul. "But you must wait seven days until I come to you and tell you what you are to do" (vs. 8). Thus Saul was *not* free to do whatever his hand found to do, after all. He was still subject to Samuel, the prophet who anointed him.

The puzzling chronology of the seven-day waiting period becomes a factor in the interpretation of the story at this point. Saul's actual failure to wait for Samuel is reported as coming much later than seven days. As presented in 1 Samuel, Saul's failure is recorded in 13:8 in connection with a battle against the Philistines. Some commentators suggest that the instruction to wait seven days may have been given more than once (see Baldwin, 91). Others use that gap to dismiss the tension between Saul's freedom in 10:7 and the restriction of 10:8, suggesting that verse 7 originally belonged in chapter

13 but was inserted editorially in chapter 10 (see G. Robinson, 60).

The striking placement of the two verses, however, may be crucial to the story, a means of highlighting Samuel's dilemma. From the first, Samuel was convinced that the people's request for a king was wrong; the LORD even agreed with him—only to turn right around and insist that Samuel grant the people's request (8:7, 9, 22). Though Samuel initially avoided the LORD's command by sending the people home without a king, chapter 9 shows the LORD taking matters so firmly in hand that Samuel had no choice but to anoint Saul as king over Israel.

But then Samuel turns into the reluctant parent. No doubt he had pondered the LORD's counsel in Deuteronomy that the king must go to the Levites and write out his own copy of the law, reflecting regularly on its contents (Deut. 17:18-20). But who would keep the king faithful to the law? The LORD had promised Moses that He would raise up "a prophet like you" to guide the people (Deut. 18:18). Was Samuel that prophet? Or was Saul, having prophesied with the prophets, now his own prophet? Both here and after Saul's later rejection, the people posed the question: "Is Saul also among the prophets?" (10:11, 12; 19:24). But in both cases it was a question, not a statement of fact, and that may be revealing, for the Old Testament never credits any other king with combining the prophetic and royal roles. Though David's hymns and prayers and Solomon's wisdom would become part of Scripture, there is no record that these great kings were taken in a charismatic "prophetic frenzy" (10:10; 19:23, NRSV), as Saul was.

In any event, Samuel decided to maintain control. As head of the prophets, he would be responsible for keeping the prophet-king obedient. Thus he put Saul in a double bind, declaring him free—but free to do only what Samuel told him to do.

But the decision to keep Saul in check is not the only puzzle involving Samuel in this passage, for in the Hebrew of 10:8, Samuel's words to Saul are not in the imperative ("Go down. . . ."; "You must wait. . . ." [NIV]) but in the simple future, suggesting that he was predicting rather than commanding: "You shall go down. . . ."; "You shall wait. . . ." (NRSV). Thus, just as

Samuel prophesied Saul's encounters with the messengers, the farmers, and the prophets (10:2-6), such a reading would suggest that he also "prophesied" Saul's trip to Gilgal and Samuel's own arrival seven days later. That would make Saul's panic-driven decision to sacrifice in 13:8, 9 not just a broken command but a failed prophecy, a failure to which Samuel himself contributed by not arriving at the set time. For someone as obedient and as hesitant as Saul, Samuel's unexplained failure to appear as promised must have been a cause of deep agony, and all the more so as he saw his army drifting away. Samuel had told him: "Do whatever your hand finds to do, for God is with you" (10:7). But he also said that he would come in seven days and tell Saul what to do (vs. 8). Was the king free or bound? And how was he to know?

The second incident in which Samuel complicates the paradox of Saul's appointment involves Saul's public anointing in 10:17-25. As the record stands in Scripture, after Samuel summoned the people to Mizpah, he reviewed God's gracious acts on their behalf, delivered a stinging rebuke for their wickedness in requesting a king, and then moved immediately into the ceremony of appointing Saul officially. Imagine the mood of both Saul and the people after they had listened to the bitter conclusion of Samuel's speech: "You have now rejected your God, who saves you out of all your calamities and distresses. And you have said, 'No, set a king over us.' So now present yourselves before the LORD by your tribes and clans" (vs. 19).

Could any king hold his head high after such a scolding? No wonder Saul fled for refuge among the baggage! But the scene is more ominous yet, for in the Old Testament, the selection of someone by the casting of lots is always associated with sinful or shameful deeds. Only two other passages record such a procedure. In one, Achan was identified as the culprit who stole devoted objects from Jericho (Josh. 7:14-21). In the other, Saul's son Jonathan was fingered as the transgressor of the king's oath (1 Sam. 14:38-44). In both of those cases, the death penalty was decreed, though Jonathan was rescued by the people. As for Saul, Polzin puts the matter bluntly: "Saul, as Israel's first king, is singled out as a personification of kingship's sinfulness" (Polzin, *Samuel*, 104).

Saul: Classic Judge, or First King? (11:1-15)

Chapter 10 draws to a close and leads into the story of Nahash the Ammonite with a description of Saul's return home and his silence in the face of sneering "troublemakers." In the continuing narrative of 11:1-11, the idea of kingship is nowhere in sight. When messengers from Jabesh Gilead arrive with their urgent appeal for help against Nahash, they do not go to any kind of royal headquarters but simply make their case to the people. Only after the day's work is done and Saul returns from the fields with his team of oxen does he incidentally pick up the news when he hears the people weeping.

Scripture says that "the Spirit of God came upon [Saul] in power, and he burned with anger" (vs. 6). Shy, hesitant Saul sprang into action. Dicing up his oxen, he sent the pieces throughout Israel with a call to arms. Anyone refusing to join Saul and Samuel against Nahash could expect a similar fate for their oxen, declared Saul. "The terror of the LORD fell on the people, and they turned out as one man" (vs. 7). During the night, Saul led the troops against Nahash and decimated the Ammonite camp.

Both in broad outline and in detail, the story takes us back to the book of Judges. Following the general pattern set in Judges, the Spirit of the LORD comes with power upon an ordinary citizen, using that person to bring a great victory to Israel. The detailed link, however, is with the very last story in Judges, the one pitting the tribe of Benjamin against the rest of Israel over the rape and murder of a Levite's concubine. But in contrast with the other conflict-and-deliverance stories in Judges, this one is an internal struggle, with no judge to deliver the people (Judg. 19-21). Furthermore, both the introduction and the conclusion to the story also declare that there was no king in Israel at that time (Judg. 19:1; 21:25), implying that a land without a king was doomed to anarchy, for "every man did that which was right in his own eyes" (Judg. 21:25, KJV).

Superficially, 1 Samuel 11 seems to provide the royal solution to the kingless chaos of Judges 19 to 21. But some of the detailed parallels are unsettling. First, though Saul dismembered his oxen instead of a human being (11:7; compare Judg. 19:29), his call to arms suggests a certain rashness, a wild swing of the pendulum for the shy and hesitant man who had once wandered about looking for his father's asses.

Second, both Gibeah and Jabesh Gilead, key cities in Saul's rise to power, had badly tarnished their reputations in that earlier account in the book of Judges. Gibeah, Saul's home, was the Benjamite city where the woman had been assaulted (Judg. 19:12-26), while Jabesh Gilead, the city Saul delivered, had rejected its covenant responsibilities by refusing to join with the rest of Israel against Benjamin (Judg. 21:9). As a result, Israel had destroyed the city, dedicating it to destruction (Hebrew = *cherem*) except for the four hundred virgins who were spared to provide wives for the surviving Benjamite males (vss. 10-14). Yet even in this new incident, Jabesh apparently was willing to breach God's covenant again by making a treaty with Nahash (1 Sam. 11:1). Thus Saul the Benjamite was a descendant both of wicked Gibeah and covenant-breaking Jabesh. The bonding with Jabesh Gilead would be evident even after Saul's death, for it was the city that cared for the fallen monarch's remains (31:11-13) and remained loyal to his house for some time (2 Sam. 2:4-7).

One further link with the story of Judges 19 to 21 shadows the account in chapter 11. When Israel came against Gibeah to mete out justice to the rapists and murderers, they demanded: "Now give up the men . . . that we may put them to death" (Judg. 20:13 [Hebrew]). After Saul's deliverance of Jabesh, the people make the same demand with the same words: "Give up the men that we may kill them" (11:12 [Hebrew]), the only other place in the entire Bible in which these words appear.

Who are the culprits in this second instance? The cry for their execution (vs. 12) also turns out to be a tantalizing point in the interpretation of the chapter. Most commentators see the culprits as the "troublemakers" who rejected Saul's kingship (10:27). The common translations of 11:12 point to such an interpretation either by introducing a negative ("Who said that Saul should not reign over us?" [REB; two Hebrew manuscripts; Septuagint; compare Syriac, Targum]) or by adding another question mark ("Who was it that asked, 'Shall Saul reign over us?' " [NIV; so also NRSV]).

The natural reading of the Hebrew, however, is simply, "Who said Saul shall reign over us?" On such a reading, the culprits would be the elders who originally demanded a king (8:4, 5) and anyone else who had supported Saul's kingship. Polzin picks up that natural reading of the Hebrew and argues forcefully that the people were now ready to repent of their evil request for a king. They had seen the LORD use Saul in the classic Israelite pattern of the great judges. If the Spirit can come upon Saul with such power, so the people would have reasoned, we don't need a king like the other nations. Let the LORD be our king and Saul be our judge (Polzin, *Samuel*, 108-114).

Regardless of the identity of the supposed culprits, however, Saul cuts short any talk of executions (11:13). Samuel then calls the people to Gilgal to "reaffirm the kingship." But wait! Had not Saul already been anointed king in private (10:1) and acclaimed in public (10:24)? Why the call to "reaffirm" the kingship? Perhaps the straightforward reading of the Hebrew of 11:12 is correct after all. Maybe the people were ready to reject kingship—indeed, maybe they had already done so. Elsewhere in Scripture the word translated "reaffirm" ("renew," NRSV) "always refers to the renewal or restoration of something actually destroyed, damaged or lost" (Polzin, *Samuel*, 110). Its eight other occurrences include references to Asa's repair of the altar (2 Chron. 15:8), Joash's restoration of the temple (2 Chron. 24:4, 12), and the renewal of "ruined cities" promised by Isaiah (Isa. 61:4).

Thus the story throbs with fascinating questions: If Saul had been a dynamic spiritual leader of firm character, could he have led the people in repentance and spiritual renewal, a return to God's kingless ideal? When the Spirit came upon Saul with power, he rose to the occasion and routed the enemy. Yet even then he called the people to come out after Saul *and Samuel* (1 Sam. 11:7). Was he still reluctant to stand on his own two feet and actually lead Israel?

And why did Samuel insist that the kingship be restored? For reasons not explained in Scripture, he chose not to lead the people back to God's ideal Plan A, even though they seemed ready to follow. He would stay with kingship, God's Plan B. Both Saul and the people obediently followed Samuel to Gilgal. And there they renewed the kingship. One can almost sense the tears of the author, who retells this story after the total collapse of the monarchy. What might have been if the people had been faithful to the call of conscience after God had worked such a mighty miracle in their midst! They had a chance to return to God's Plan A. Or did they?

■ Getting Into the Word

1 Samuel 12

1. *Kingship.* **Read chapter 12 with an eye on the question of kingship. In your notebook, make headings for God, Samuel, and the people. Under the appropriate heading, list the passages that identify who is responsible for the establishment of kingship in Israel. Based on your findings, whom would you conclude is most responsible? Explain your response in a brief paragraph.**
2. *Acceptance and Obedience.* **As you read chapter 12, list in two separate columns the passages that reflect the two different ways that God responded to Israel—first, those that reveal His love and acceptance *in spite of or apart from* the people's obedience; second, those that point to possible rejection *because of* their wickedness. In a summary statement, harmonize or describe the relationship between the two lists.**

■ Exploring the Word

Kingship: Is Repentance Still Possible? (12:1-25)

From the euphoric last line in chapter 11 and its "great celebration" of Saul's appointment as king (vs. 15), we move quickly back into the shadow side of kingship in chapter 12. There, Samuel seeks to convict the people of the "evil thing you did in the eyes of the Lord when you asked for a king" (vs. 17). Was his speech part of the

Gilgal event? If it was, it certainly would have sobered up the celebrants, for Samuel minces no words in his critique of the people and he summons the forces of nature to make his point.

The contrast between the two chapters is so great that most commentators simply think the author of 1 Samuel was drawing on different sources—one in favor of monarchy, the other against.

Even a moderate critic like Ralph Klein declares, "Clearly chaps. 11 and 12 were not written by the same person" (Klein, 113).

But from the perspective of an author writing after the collapse of the monarchy, the chapter is deliberately placed; it is a sober reminder of all the complex factors that led to the failure of kingship in Israel. Although Samuel delivers sharp words against the people, the reader may suspect that Samuel himself bears part of the blame. While defending himself and hearing the people concur that he is innocent of any wrong, he also says that "my sons are here with you" (12:2)—the evil sons who helped trigger the request for a king in the first place (8:2-5). Samuel calls on the LORD and "his anointed" to witness to his innocence (12:5). The people agree. But Samuel's sons are still standing there in the shadows as witnesses to the rest of the story.

Samuel then takes the people through a rehearsal of God's acts of deliverance on their behalf. They have been stubborn; God has been gracious. But when his narrative comes to the people's request for a king, Samuel's memory seems to fail him (perhaps this is an indication that the events in this chapter indeed took place some years after the Gilgal celebration of 11:15). Samuel says it was Nahash's aggression that made the people of Israel want a king like the other nations (12:12). But in 8:2-5, it is the people's exasperation with Samuel's evil sons, not an external threat, that triggers their original request for a king. And according to the events recorded in the previous chapter, it was Samuel himself who insisted on renewing the kingship after Saul had routed Nahash (11:14).

But this was a sermon, not a discussion, and no one was ready to quibble over details. Samuel called for full obedience to the LORD from both people and their king, then summoned special sound effects to underscore his message: "Is it not wheat harvest now? I will call upon the LORD to send thunder and rain. And you will realize what an evil thing you did in the eyes of the LORD when you asked for a king" (12:17).

Thunder and rain at the time of the wheat harvest would be stunning indeed, for in Palestine it never rains in the summer. Never. So when the LORD answered Samuel's request, the people were impressed, standing "in awe of the LORD and of Samuel" (vs. 18). But the thunder and rain were not just a simple confirmation of Samuel's authority or a frightening call to repentance. To those people at that time, it was also a powerful reminder that the LORD, not Baal, the Canaanite fertility god, was in charge of the rain. According to Canaanite mythology, rain fell in winter because that was when Baal was alive. The regular rhythm of wet winters and dry summers was ensured (so thought the followers of Baal) by human fertility orgies at the autumn and spring equinoxes.

But this was summer, when Baal was supposed to be dead. To these people constantly facing the temptation to serve the Canaanite gods, Samuel's point was less than subtle: Baal is dead, but the LORD is alive, and He can bring thunder and rain any time He pleases. If Israel sometimes had trouble remembering that point later in her history, Samuel made sure at least that it was clear for the moment.

Such a thunderous conclusion to Samuel's speech brought the very response demanded by the logic of his presentation: "Pray to the LORD your God for your servants so that we will not die, for we have added to all our other sins the evil of asking for a king" (vs. 19). Repentance! The people were ready to turn away from their evil request for a king and serve the LORD only.

But after bringing them right to the point of repentance, the prophet suddenly cools their ardor: " 'Do not be afraid,' Samuel replied. 'You have done all this evil; yet do not turn away from the Lord, but the serve the LORD with all your heart' " (vs. 20). The people had once demanded with tenacity that they must have a king, and all Samuel's vivid rhetoric could not convince them otherwise (8:19, 20). Couldn't they insist on repentance with equal tenacity? Was kingship all that inevitable? If the LORD Himself would shortly "repent" for having made Saul king over Israel (15:35, KJV), why couldn't the people also repent from their request for a king?

Samuel chose to keep Israel on the road to kingship, assuring the people of God's love and of his own readiness to intercede on their behalf. And it was all very true that the LORD could be with them whether or not they had a king. Indeed, Samuel spoke of an unconditional element in God's love for His people: "For the sake of his great name the LORD will not reject his people, because the LORD was pleased to make you his own" (12:22).

At the same time, however, Samuel reminded the people of the conditional element in their relationship with the LORD: "If you persist in doing evil, both you and your king will be swept away" (vs. 25). "Swept away"—these are the author's last words before turning to the story of Saul's brief reign and his tragic rejection in chapters 13 to 15. Saul would soon be swept away. But the author was more keenly aware of the time when both king and people would be swept away—carried off to captivity in Babylon—because they had persisted in evil.

Once again, Scripture makes it clear that God grants His people freedom to accept or reject His will. Yet all the human actors, even when serving as God's chosen instruments, turn out to be flawed. Israel was God's chosen people, yet often fell short of the mark. The LORD called judges, priests, kings, and prophets to lead them. But they, too, struggled with sin; they, too, had to grapple with rebellion, resistance, and wounded pride. Even in the best of circumstances, they sometimes wavered between God's Plan A and His Plan B, and from our perspective, we may think that they didn't always get it right.

But through it all, the LORD is still master of circumstances and God of His people. None of the human factors even come close to overshadowing the powerful role of the LORD in the troubled history of God's people. As Polzin puts it, the author "never lets us forget that it is God who is directing traffic" (Polzin, *Samuel*, 124).

All one has to do is trace the hand of the LORD as He walked with His people on the tortured road to monarchy: The LORD commanded Samuel to make a king (8:7, 9, 22); the LORD chose Saul and led him to Samuel (9:15-17); the LORD moved Saul to prophesy (10:10); the

Lord publicly chose Saul by lot (10:19-24); the Lord gave Saul victory over Jabesh Gilead (11:6, 13); at Gilgal, Saul was confirmed as king "in the presence of the Lord" (11:15); and the Lord sent thunder and rain at Samuel's request to remind the people that He was master of all (12:18).

Yet that persistent presence of the Lord simply serves as a haunting reminder that resolving the tension between human freedom and divine sovereignty has never been easy. And the paradox appears with painful clarity in Samuel's final words in chapter 12. On the one hand is the glorious promise: "For the sake of his great name the Lord will not reject his people" (vs. 22). On the other is the somber warning: "Yet if you persist in doing evil, both you and your king will be swept away" (vs. 25).

Summary: At the Threshold of Saul's Reign

When the author turns to Saul's actual reign in chapter 13, the first incident would mark the beginning of the end for Saul—as though his reign was a parable illustrating the fate of the monarchy itself and the fate of Israel when led by a king. In summary form, it is helpful to note here how the author, through paradox and pendulum, has brought us to this point.

If the closing scene in chapter 7 reveals the ideal—a people fully committed to the Lord under the leadership of a godly judge (Samuel)—Israel's history frequently fell short of the mark. If a judge was the ideal, then why would the book of Judges end in such chaos and cry out with its last word for a king to restore order (Judg. 21:25)?

Godly Eli fathered evil sons; yet in the midst of their evil, the Lord touched the godly Hannah and Elkanah, and they dedicated their Samuel to His service. Yet for all *his* piety, Samuel, too, faltered, and the wickedness of *his* sons triggered the people's request for a king. Over Samuel's resistance, the Lord selected Saul as their monarch, "an impressive young man without equal among the Israelites" (9:2). The people, judges, priests, and prophets had all fallen short of God's ideal. Would the king too? All Israel knew the answer. And now the author must continue to tell why. He affirmed that God was always there, seeking to bring good out of evil. But what must God do so that His people would seek Him with all their hearts? That was the hard question. And there seemed to be no easy answer.

■ Applying the Word

1 Samuel 8–12

1. *Parents and Their Children.* In the light of the poor example set by Samuel's and Eli's sons, how much responsibility should parents accept for the failures of their children? In what ways should my parents receive both credit and blame for what I am? How does Proverbs 22:6 fit into this situation?

2. *Back to the Ideal?* When God allows His people to move away from the highest ideal of a Plan A to a second-best Plan B, should Plan B then become the standard? Why or why not? Is second best ever acceptable? In my own life, do I still have a vision of God's Plan A for me? What is that plan? Should it still be my goal? What am I doing to realize God's ideal for my life? How does the story of Israel's struggle over kingship provide me with guidance in such matters?

3. *Knowing God's Will.* The LORD seems to have quickly granted Israel's request for a king, even though both Samuel and the LORD saw it as a departure from God's will. At a time when the LORD rarely speaks out loud but allows His people to work through committees, how can I know when it is appropriate to accept a compromise Plan B? What factors should I look for that will indicate if a proposed course is actually God's compromise plan or merely a human solution?

4. *Gentle or Firm?* Does Samuel's speech in chapter 8 suggest that in matters of Christian behavior and actions, hard-line diplomacy may not be as effective as more gentle means of persuasion? How can I know whether to be gentle or firm in

dealing with others? With myself? What Scripture support can I find for each position? Might different circumstances require different means of persuasion?

5. *Faulty Leaders.* If Scripture is explicit in its criticism of prophets, priests, judges, and kings, is it also possible for ordinary believers to recognize when criticism is implicit? In other words, if God's chosen leaders are not always right, when and how can I know if they are wrong? What is my responsibility if I am convinced a leader is in the wrong? To that leader? To the church? To myself? Is that even something I should be concerned about? Why or why not? Does the counsel in Deuteronomy 18:21, 22 apply to a prophet who already holds credentials?

6. *Too Obedient?* Am I in danger of too readily following other people, or is my tendency to resist leadership? Could I lose my ability to stand for the right when the leaders go astray? Does Israel's struggle over kingship suggest any guidelines that can help me understand my responsibilities and tendencies today? If so, what are they?

7. *Too Late to Repent?* Is the possibility of repentance ever gone completely? If so, under what circumstances? If I am willing to repent, will God always accept me? How can I tell if repentance—mine or someone else's—is genuine?

■ Researching the Word:

1. *Judges.* Starting with the word *judge*, use a concordance based on the King James Version to compile a list of passages that can illumine the Hebrew word for *judge*. As in English, the Hebrew verb *to judge* and the Hebrew nouns *judge* and *judgment* all come from the same verbal root. Look for passages that will explain what it means to judge, to be a judge, and to give or maintain judgment. Check to see how modern translations have rendered these words in key passages. Finally, summarize what you think the Old Testament means by *judgment*, comparing it with the traditional concepts of

judge and judgment in our world today.
2. *Seers.* Using a concordance, make a list of the passages in the Old Testament in which the term *seer* occurs. Do any of the passages suggest differences between a "seer" and a "prophet" other than in name? Write out a summary statement of your findings. Check your own results by reading the articles on *seer* and *prophet* in a Bible dictionary.

■ Further Study of the Word

1. For general insight, see E. G. White, *Patriarchs and Prophets,* 603-615.
2. For detailed analysis of the textual variants in 1 Samuel, see commentaries by McCarter and Klein, both of which also tend to explain the tensions between the pro-monarchy and anti-monarchy passages in 1 Samuel by attributing them to different sources and authors.
3. For a literary interpretation of 1 Samuel that retains the integrity and unity of the book, see Polzin's commentary. He sees the tension between pro-monarchy and anti-monarchy passages as being central to the author's purpose.

CHAPTER FOUR

The LORD Was Grieved That He Made Saul King

1 Samuel 13–15

The last words of chapter 12 are a warning from Samuel that had become a grim reality in the author's day: "If you persist in doing evil, both you and your king will be swept away" (vs. 25). In the end, the author wants his story to show how it was that people and king were swept away. Crucial to that story is the downfall of Israel's first king, the king demanded by the people so they could be like the nations around them. Beginning with chapter 13, the focus is on Saul and, for the first time in the story, on the real "evil" in the man God had chosen.

The earlier scenes in 1 Samuel have dropped hints of the character flaws that would grow to tragic proportions: the hesitancy when Saul hid among the baggage; the rash violence in dicing up his oxen as a call to arms. But now the author moves beyond hints, for twice in chapters 13 to 15 God's judgment falls on Saul for specific sins. Almost before his reign begins, it seems, Saul hears from Samuel that it must end. Nor will a son be allowed to follow him. God has chosen someone else.

The lofty standard against which Saul is measured and found wanting may seem troubling because it contrasts so sharply with the experience of his successor. David was an adulterer and murderer—yet he and his sons continued to rule. By contrast, Saul loses the kingship simply for offering a sacrifice in Samuel's absence, and all because the prophet didn't come as promised.

Also troubling, but for different reasons, is the incident that seals Saul's rejection in chapter 15, namely, his failure to obliterate the Amalekites. Though his sin was serious, the issues are clouded by our suppressed horror at God's command to kill women, children, and animals and by the image of Samuel's bloody sword as he "hewed Agag in pieces before the LORD" (15:33, NRSV).

Between these two rejections of Saul, the author gives us a glimpse of noble Jonathan. Couldn't he be king in place of Saul, his father? And then we remember that failure, not success, is the point of the whole story, failure of the people who rejected God as king, failure of all their kings, and finally, the failure of kingship itself. In chapters 13 to 15, we watch the LORD's anointed stumble, stagger, and fall. And we glimpse a brokenhearted God, One who is "grieved that he had made Saul king over Israel" (15:35).

■ Getting Into the Word

1 Samuel 13–15

Read 1 Samuel 13 to 15 through two times quickly; then go back over the same chapters more carefully, and answer the following questions:

1. *The King's Religion.* Based on what you find in 1 Samuel 13 to 15, prepare a two-column list of Saul's activities or attitudes that are directly related to his relationship with God and religion. In the one column, put those items that reveal a positive inclination; in the other, list the incidents that are negative. Any that appear neutral you should put in the positive column, or if you wish, in a separate third column. When you are finished, briefly summarize in two or three paragraphs your impressions of Saul's religious experience.

2. *Important People.* Besides Saul, both Samuel and Jonathan figure prominently in chapters 13 to 15—Samuel in 13 and 15; Jonathan in 14. Read these chapters for the purpose of listening to the stories of these individuals. Then list in your notebook incidents or traits that make you feel good about each of these persons as well as those things that make you uneasy. Write a summary paragraph each about Samuel and Jonathan, comparing their attitudes and behavior with those of Saul.

3. *Chronology*. Since the formal introduction to Saul's reign appears in 13:1 and an overall summary appears in 14:47-52, the question of the chronology of Saul's life is an interesting one. Make note of any items from chapters 13 to 15 that might have a bearing on when these events took place (family, location of headquarters, status of the Philistine threat, etc.). In two or three sentences, summarize your conclusions. Is there sufficient evidence in the Bible to determine whether chapters 13 to 15 are in chronological order and are part of a larger chronological order? What difference does chronology make to the meaning and application of the message?

4. *Foreigners*. Using a concordance and a Bible dictionary, list the important passages from Scripture that describe the relationship between Israel and the Philistines. Do the same for the Amalekites. In a paragraph or two, summarize the differences in Israel's relationship with these two peoples.

■ Exploring the Word

Tardy Prophet, Impatient King (13:1-14)

The lack of official court records may explain why 13:1 is such a puzzle. The verse is missing in the Greek Septuagint, and the Hebrew is hardly correct, reading "Saul was a year old when he began to reign, and he reigned two years over Israel." The Aramaic Targum (a paraphrase of the Old Testament) bravely tries to make some sense of it by rendering it, "Like a one-year-old who has no sins was Saul when he became king." Acts 13:21 gives Saul a reign of forty years, agreeing with one of two passages in Josephus.

At Saul's anointing (1 Sam. 9–11), he was a young man still living with his father. Now he has an adult son, Jonathan, a capable and seasoned warrior. Obviously Scripture is not attempting a complete history of Saul and his reign. Rather, the author has selected key incidents to characterize the man and illustrate his fall.

For those who like to follow a map when they read a biblical story, chapter 13 is a challenge. The biblical manuscripts reveal that the scribes, too, struggled to sort out Gibeah, Geba, and Gilgal. Nevertheless, the general picture is clear: the Philistines were in charge of the area, so much so that they imposed an ancient equivalent of gun control, banning all blacksmiths from Israel. It worked, too, for Saul and Jonathan were the only Israelites with sword or spear (vs. 22). Even farm equipment had to be taken to the Philistines for repair (vss. 19-21).

Jonathan brought matters to a head by attacking the Philistine outpost at Geba. When the Philistines responded by massing for battle, Saul's call to arms turned out to be recruitment in reverse as Israelite warriors looked for any place to hide—"in caves and thickets, among the rocks, and in pits and cisterns" (vs. 6). Some even "crossed the Jordan" (vs. 7), reversing the great theme of Israel's entry into Canaan, for these frightened Israelites were crossing the Jordan in the wrong direction! Thus, instead of two thousand men under his command (vs. 2), Saul's army had dwindled to six hundred (vs. 15), all "quaking with fear" (vs. 7).

The incident that follows not only describes Saul's sin and the judgment against him, but also stirs a certain sympathy for Israel's first king. Though Christian interpreters typically are harsh with Saul (perhaps because of his rejection in favor of David, Jesus' ancestor), Jewish tradition has been more sympathetic, even glowing. Not only is Saul described "as a hero and a saint," but "in all respects his piety was so great that not even David was his equal" (Ginzberg, 4:72).

The biblical account itself, however, avoids both extremes, recording not only Saul's sin and its consequences, but also the features that place him in a more positive light, even at the cost of Samuel's reputation. Note the candor with which the story unfolds, beginning with the description of Saul's dilemma:

> He waited seven days, the time set by Samuel; but Samuel did not come to Gilgal, and Saul's men began to scatter. So he said, "Bring me the burnt offering and the fellowship offerings." And Saul offered up the burnt offering (vss. 8, 9).

Scarcely had he finished the sacrifice when Samuel arrived, confronting him with a question: "What have you done?" (vs. 11). Scripture lets Saul describe his own inner conflict:

> "When I saw that the men were scattering, and that you did not come at the set time, and that the Philistines were assembling at Micmash, I thought, 'Now the Philistines will come down against me at Gilgal, and I have not sought the LORD's favor.' So I felt compelled to offer the burnt offering" (vss. 11, 12).

This was no coward, ready to cut and run. This was no rash military hero, rushing blindly into battle. This was a religious man, seeking the LORD's blessing, distressed because the LORD's messenger had not come as promised.

Samuel's response was immediate and devastating: "You acted foolishly," he said (vs. 13). By breaking God's "command," Saul had forfeited his kingdom; God had already selected a successor. With that, Samuel left. No conversation. No argument—a sharp contrast with the rejection scene in chapter 15. Here, Scripture simply states that Samuel left and that Saul counted the number of soldiers still with him: "about six hundred" (vs. 15).

But now let's explore the nature of Saul's sin: What "command" had he broken? Some argue that it was a *general* command, perhaps a mandate against non-Levites offering sacrifices. Others suggest that Saul may have broken some ritual requirement, even unwittingly. It's even possible that Samuel's command to wait was intended to protect Saul from just that kind of error. But nothing in chapter 13 confirms such suggestions. In fact, the next chapter reports (with apparent approval) that Saul was the protector of proper ritual and also built an altar to the LORD (14:33-35). Elsewhere in Scripture, we know that David's sons served as priests (2 Sam. 8:18, Hebrew, NIV note). And when Solomon offered a thousand sacrifices on the altar at Gibeon (1 Kings 3:4), Scripture implies that the LORD rewarded him for it by promising to give him whatever he might ask (vs. 5).

The more likely interpretation of Saul's sin is that it involved not a general, but a specific, transgression, namely, of Samuel's command to wait:

> "Go down ahead of me to Gilgal. I will surely come down to you to sacrifice burnt offerings and fellowship offerings, but you must wait seven days until I come to you and tell you what you are to do" (10:8).

The apparent time gap between 10:8, where Saul is a young man in his father's house, and 13:8-14, where he is father of an adult son, has prompted the suggestion that the seven-day wait was mandated more than once (e.g., Baldwin, 91). But however one resolves the chronological difficulty, the link between the two passages seems unmistakable. And in that connection, some interpreters suggest that Saul had the perfect alibi: because Samuel didn't come on time, it was Samuel's fault, not Saul's.

Such questioning of God and His messenger is uneasy business, but has biblical precedent. Accepting God's way in the end does not rule out questions en route. Abraham reacted with horror at the thought that the "Judge of all the earth" might not "do right" and he told God so (Gen. 18:23-25). Just as striking is Moses' bold confrontation with God over His threatened judgment against Israel (Exod. 32:9-14). In Moses' case, the LORD "repented" (KJV), or "changed his mind" (NRSV). In short, it pays to question God!

As far as God's judgment on Saul is concerned, since condemnation is the last word here, surely the author wanted us to recognize that Saul was the one at fault. Still, it may be helpful to look at a number of factors (some seemingly contradictory) that could help relieve our uneasiness with the story.

1. Usefulness in God's service is based first on God's call, not on personal goodness or righteousness. Abraham is the premier example of God's gracious call running roughshod over "justice," for God punished both Pharaoh and Abimelech for innocent misdeeds resulting from Abraham's half-truths (Gen. 12:17; 20:2, 17, 18). As for kingship, Jonathan appears morally superior to both Saul and David, yet he never served as king. And David, though much loved as the forgiven sinner, far exceeded Saul in lust and murder. Still, it was David's line that the Lord chose.

2. In times of crisis, God's demands and judgments are often rigorous, even harsh. Saul was Israel's first king, leader of God's people at a crucial point of transition. Impatience and disobedience were critical flaws. Similarly, many of the "troublesome" stories that involve God's judgments against seemingly "minor" sins come at key points when the stability of the community was at risk: the stoning of a man for picking up sticks on Sabbath (Num. 15:32-36); Moses' exclusion from Canaan (Num. 20:9-12); Achan (Josh. 7:24-26); Uzzah (2 Sam. 6:6, 7; 1 Chron. 13:9, 10); and Ananias and Sapphira (Acts 5:1-10).

In two instances, a seemingly plausible alibi (Samuel's tardy arrival and Uzzah's stumbling oxen) is overruled by the larger needs of the community. But the fact that Scripture mentions the alibi makes the stories more difficult for us. Thus we find the death of the one man, Uzzah (2 Sam. 6:7), more troublesome than the death of dozens (or thousands!) at Beth Shemesh who looked into the ark on purpose (1 Sam. 6:19).

3. In an era of authoritarian leadership, God is more likely to expect strict (blind?) obedience than reasonable obedience. In the Old Testament, it was easier to argue with God than with one of His messengers. Nathan, for example, first approved David's plan to build the temple, then reversed himself on advice from God (2 Sam. 7). But in both cases, David was bound to obey. Where prophets and priests are absent, however, as in the wisdom books (Job, Proverbs, Ecclesiastes), one sees the disciplined intellect operating without the benefit of prophetic or priestly guidance. Job, of course, becomes a type of the person who stands alone in a silent universe while still affirming faith and confidence in his Maker and Redeemer.

In the New Testament, shared leadership had become so much the norm that the apostles could even debate among themselves (Acts 15) and Paul could oppose Peter "to his face" (Gal. 2:11).

But Saul had no such freedom. He had to obey the prophet who anointed him. Keeping the letter of the law by waiting seven days was not enough. Failure to wait for the prophet was his downfall and his sin.

4. Chronology. Is it possible that some of Saul's more violent and culpable deeds actually happened before his rejection in 1 Samuel 13? If so, then his rejection might not have been as early in his reign as the present text implies. Evidence from elsewhere in 1 Samuel suggests that its chronology is not always precise. The most telling evidence for such a conclusion appears in connection with David's introduction to King Saul. In 16:18 David the harpist is introduced to Saul as "a brave man and a warrior" and becomes one of Saul's "armor-bearers" (vs. 21). Saul even asks permission from Jesse to let David stay with him (vs. 22). Yet in the story of Goliath, which immediately follows, Saul apparently has never heard of David. "Whose son is that young man?" he asks Abner (17:55). But Abner doesn't know either. Only when David appears with the head of Goliath in tow does Saul ask David directly and learn who his father is. An alternative interpretation of the relationship between 1 Samuel 16 and 17 is suggested in chapter 5 of this volume. But the most obvious impression is that the chronology is somehow not correct.

Are other segments of Saul's story also possibly out of order? The narrative leaves the impression that Saul's rejection in chapter 13 came soon after his selection and anointing in chapters 9 to 11. Yet in chapters 9 to 11 he is a young man, living in his father's house, apparently without wife or family, while the rejection account of chapter 13 (with an uncertain chronology in the first verse) presents Saul as having an adult warrior son, Jonathan. It is also worth noting that in both rejection accounts, Samuel speaks of God's choice of someone else as if it were already an accomplished fact (13:14; 15:28). Yet the public demonstration of that choice isn't recorded until chapter 15. Even then, Samuel needs a nudge and a reprimand from God before he finds the right man. In short, if the key events of Saul's life were known in order, the rejection of chapter 13 might be more understandable. Nevertheless, it must be said that Saul's rejection was no problem for the author, even if Samuel was late for his appointment. This long explanation is mine, not his!

5. Conditional instead of final rejection? Though many commentators note that chapter 13 seems to signal the end of Saul's family dynasty and chapter 15 that of his personal reign, the presence of two rejection accounts is still puzzling. The fact that God continued to work in and through Saul in the battle against the Philistines (chapter 14) may imply that the initial rejection was reversible. Chapter 15 would then be a second chance for Saul, even though Scripture itself does not say so. Scripture does provide other examples of seemingly final judgments that turned out to be conditional, namely, Jonah's prophecy against Nineveh (Jon. 3:4, 10) and Micah's prophecy against Jerusalem (Jer. 26:18, 19; Mic. 3:12).

In sum, if Saul had put things right after Samuel's announced judgment, good things still might have happened for him and his house. After all, in the KJV Old Testament, God "repents" more often than anyone else!

Jonathan Leads the Way (13:15–14:52)

Sandwiched between Saul's two rejections is a remarkable account of a battle against the Philistines in which the hand of God and the sword of Jonathan play prominent roles. Saul is still king and very much part of the picture too. Indeed, he almost seems more worried about staying right with God than he is about fighting the Philistines. But Jonathan is the hero, and God gets the credit.

The story of the battle is bracketed by an introduction describing Israel's dire straits before the battle (13:16-22) and a conclusion that summarizes several positive features of Saul's reign (14:47-52). The battle account itself throbs with the divine presence. In contrast, however, neither the introduction nor the conclusion contains any religious elements.

The full-scale battle was triggered by Jonathan's secret foray into Philistine-held territory. For reasons that remain mysterious, the author makes a point of telling us that Jonathan informed neither his father (14:1) nor anyone else (vs. 3). Earlier, Saul had been in command of two thousand troops and Jonathan, one thousand (13:2). Now their combined forces totaled only six hundred, a figure the author mentions twice (13:15; 14:2).

Ahijah, son of Ahitub, son of Phinehas, son of Eli, "the LORD's priest," was also in camp with an ephod (14:3). Ahijah was the interpreter of

God's will to Saul either through the ephod (vs. 18, Septuagint) or the ark (vs. 18, Hebrew), and probably through Urim and Thummim as well (vs. 41, Septuagint). The author seems eager to show how seriously Saul was now taking his religious commitments.

Jonathan, too, shows himself to be a man of deep religious conviction, but demonstrates it along more practical lines as he confronts the enemy. Accompanied by his young armorbearer, an effective warrior in his own right (vss. 13, 14), Jonathan headed for the Philistine encampment at Micmash. Three times before the battle was joined, Jonathan expressed his conviction that the LORD was in charge (vss. 6, 10, 12). But in contrast with the rash tenacity of his father's religious acts, Jonathan's convictions were marked with a quiet humility that recognized the LORD's freedom to act in His own way. "Perhaps the LORD will act in our behalf," he said, adding that line so familiar to people of faith: "Nothing can hinder the LORD from saving, whether by many or by few" (vs. 6).

Like Gideon, Jonathan expected the LORD to work through signs. But unlike Gideon, he did not go back for a second opinion (Judg. 6:36-40). When the Philistines gave their response, he and his armorbearer clambered up the rocky cliff and went to work, killing twenty warriors (14:14), a rare Old Testament instance of a "reasonable" body count. Their panic intensified by an earthquake (vs. 15), the Philistines were fighting each other by the time Saul and his troops arrived (vs. 20).

The author reminds us repeatedly of God's involvement in the battle, noting that the panic among the Philistines was "sent by God" (vs. 15), though some translations treat *god* here like an adjective (literally, "panic of God"; KJV: "a very great trembling"; NRSV: "a very great panic"). When the Philistines were thoroughly beaten, Scripture says that "the Lord rescued Israel that day" (vs. 23).

Saul's religious life is of special interest in this account. When he discovered that Jonathan was missing from the camp, he called for Ahijah and the ark (Hebrew) or the ephod (Septuagint), seeking divine guidance. But as the tumult in the Philistine camp increased, Saul became impatient. "Withdraw your hand" in 14:19 suggests an interruption of the process of consulting Urim and Thummim, though Scripture does not say so directly.

The other sequence of events that reveals Saul's religious orientation grows out of his oath against anyone who eats "before evening comes, before I have avenged myself on my enemies!" (vs. 24). The troops complied, but then were so famished at the end of the day that they pounced on the spoil, disregarding the prohibition against eating blood (vss. 32, 33). Saul took immediate steps to correct the situation, rolling up a large stone on which the troops could slaughter the animals so that they would "not sin against the LORD by eating meat with blood still in it" (vs. 34). Saul also constructed his "first" altar "to the LORD" at this time (vs. 35), though it is not clear whether the author intended this statement as a compliment or a criticism.

But what about the oath itself? Was Saul justified in imposing such a burden on his troops? If not, was there any acceptable way to reverse it or annul its effects? At the outset, the Hebrew (followed by the NIV) indicates only that the oath was a source of "distress" (vs. 24). The Septuagint (followed by the NRSV) is bluntly critical: "Saul committed a very rash act on that day." Klein's rendition is even more vivid: "Saul committed a great error" (Klein, 130). Jonathan, who unknowingly transgressed the oath when he ate some honeycomb in the forest, was also critical of his father's oath (vs. 29). And when Saul added a further oath, decreeing death for the guilty one in the name of the LORD (vs. 39), the Septuagint records a protest from the troops when the lot came down to a choice between Saul and Jonathan: "Although the troops said it shouldn't be this way, Saul forced them and they cast between him and Jonathan his son" (vs. 42, Klein's translation). Both Klein (131) and McCarter (244) include the missing line from the Septuagint in their translations, though the major modern translations do not (NIV, NASB, RSV, NRSV, NEB, REB, JB).

But however wrong Saul's oath may have been, the narrative is clear that the LORD expected both Saul and the people to honor it. Though God had delivered Israel, He would give no more counsel to Saul until the "sin" (vs. 38), i.e., the broken oath, had been put right. Jonathan recognized the validity of his father's position and was prepared to die. But then the troops finally had their say: "As surely as the LORD lives, not a hair of his head will fall to the ground, for he did this today with God's help" (14:45). And so they "rescued" Jonathan (vs. 45), or "ransomed" him (NRSV). The text does not say whether they simply saved his life, paid money (Exod. 21:30; Num. 3:46-51), or provided an animal substitute (Exod. 13:13, 15; 34:20). Oaths were taken seriously in Old Testament times, even when ill-advised (e.g. Jephthah, Judg. 11:35) or gotten under false pretenses (e.g. Gibeonites, Josh. 9; 2 Sam. 21:1-14). In this instance, as in the case of the defeated Benjamites (Judges 19–21), a detour was found around the requirements of an oath, but in both instances, the avoidance was handled by a third party rather than by the person or persons who made the oath (compare Judg. 21:16-23). In other words, it was not possible simply to call an oath "bad" and then just disregard it. All oaths must be kept, even the "bad" ones.

After the report of Jonathan's rescue, Saul called off the chase, and the Philistines withdrew to their own land. It would appear, then, that God's initial purpose in anointing Saul, namely, to "deliver my people from the hand of the Philistines" (9:16), was in large measure fulfilled, at least for the moment. Even though the dynastic ambitions of Saul's family may have been set aside by Saul's sin in chapter 13, and although Jonathan may have been the key leader in battle in chapter 14, Saul was still king. The chapter concludes with an impressive list of the foes he had defeated (vss. 47, 48), a brief family tree (vss. 49-51), and a final statement about the ongoing "bitter war with the Philistines" and Saul's now-successful recruitment of "mighty" or "brave" men (vs. 52). The success story is glowing enough to suggest that the LORD had indeed forgiven Saul's sin at Gilgal (13:13, 14). But if so, a final rejection is yet to come as a result of Saul's handling of God's command to destroy Amalek.

The Rejection of King Saul (15:1-35)

Without any chronological reference, chapter 15 opens with the words of Samuel to Saul—a command from the LORD to obliterate the Amalekites. But Samuel emphasizes his own authority as well as the LORD's: "I am the one the LORD sent to anoint you king over his people Israel; so listen. . . ." (vs. 1). In the end, this bonding between Samuel and Saul becomes a point of painful and emotional tension.

Except by way of contrast, this chapter does not readily bring to mind Jesus' Sermon on the Mount or His prayer from the cross for the forgiveness of His enemies. In the book of Exodus, Amalek was the first enemy to attack Israel in the wilderness. After Aaron and Hur had supported Moses' hands, ensuring Joshua's victory on the battlefield, the LORD said He would "completely blot out the memory of Amalek from under heaven" (Exod. 17:14). Deuteronomy notes a more sinister evil in Amalek than simply a tribal impulse to defend itself, for when Israel was "weary and worn out, they met you on your journey and cut off all who were lagging behind; they had no fear of God" (Deut. 25:18). Israel was commanded "to blot out the memory of Amalek from under heaven" (vs. 19), a command to which 1 Samuel 15 is clearly linked. Thus, as far as justice in its Old Testament setting was concerned, the Amalekites would be seen as unscrupulous outlaws, sinners against humanity.

But why include "women, children and infants, cattle and sheep, camels and donkeys" in the ban (*cherem*)? Could not the children, at least, have been saved and the animals put to some useful purpose?

Such questions are inevitable in minds accustomed to the individualism of the West. But in cultures where community looms large, individuals can lose their identity within the larger corporate entity. In such cultures, what has become known as "corporate personality" refers to the inclusion of all kindred and possessions within the person of the leader or family head. The clearest biblical example is the story of Achan in Joshua 7. Because he sinned against the "ban" (*cherem*,) Israel's whole army was defeated at Ai (vss. 1-11). The only way to atone for the evil was to destroy Achan and everything that was his (vss. 12-26). And because God was the guarantor of justice, He took a direct hand in enforcing the provisions of the ban, an element of "justice" by no means unique to Israel. For example, according to the Moabite Stone, discovered in 1868, Mesha, king of Moab, took Israelite "men, boys, women, girls, and maid-servants" and "devoted them to destruction for [the god] Ashtar-Chemosh" (Pritchard, 320). In short, Israel's treatment of

Amalek was standard justice.

Saul amassed a huge army, two hundred thousand from Israel and ten thousand from Judah (15:4), though the Hebrew numbers could be interpreted more modestly as two hundred military units from Israel and ten from Judah. The large numbers, however, may have been intended to show Saul's "complete military superiority and his lack of excuse" for failing to carry out the LORD's command (Klein, 149). Before attacking, Saul sent a message to the Kenites to separate themselves from among the Amalekites. They would be spared, for unlike their bandit neighbors, they had shown kindness to the wandering Israelites who had come out of Egypt (vs. 6).

The initial report of the battle in 15:7-9 hints at greedy motives in the people's unwillingness to destroy the "best" of the cattle and flocks, something Saul had difficulty admitting when later confronted by Samuel (vss. 13-15). That reluctance to admit sin was perhaps the greatest contrast between Saul and his successor, David.

Samuel's first clue that Saul had failed came from the LORD Himself. Unfortunately, the violent nature of the ban (vs. 3) and Agag's grisly end at the hand of Samuel (vs. 33) too easily obscure the powerful emotions attributed to both God and Samuel in this chapter. In the NIV, the LORD tells Samuel, "I am grieved that I have made Saul king" (vs. 11). Those same words close the chapter: "The LORD was grieved that he had made Saul king over Israel" (vs. 35). But the tension in the chapter is preserved most vividly by the KJV, which uses the English verb *repent* for both 15:11 and 15:35, as well as in 15:29, where the NIV states that God does not "change his mind." The Hebrew word is the same in all four instances. Thus the KJV twice affirms that God does not repent (vs. 29) yet twice declares that He repented (vss. 11, 35)!

With that tantalizing play on words, Scripture presents the striking paradox that arises when a sovereign God creates free creatures and invites them to obey—indeed, He commands them to obey and threatens them when they don't. And if they persist in disobedience? He repents—even though "he is not a man, that he should repent" (vs. 29, KJV). It is true, of course, that the LORD never needs to repent as a human repents. But the Master of the universe does reserve the right to "change his mind" when human beings change their behavior (compare Jer. 26:3, 13, 19) or even when they intercede on behalf of other human beings (Exod. 32:12-14). In Saul's case, we glimpse the broken heart of God at the failure of one of His children. The NIV translation comes closer to emotional truth when we hear that the LORD was "grieved" over Saul (15:11, 35).

Samuel, too, was emotionally torn over Saul's fate. Both in 15:35 and 16:1, the NIV says that he "mourned" over Saul. In this instance, the Hebrew word focuses simply on deep sorrow, with no overtones of repentance or change of mind. But these verses come at the end of Saul's ordeal. When the LORD first told Samuel of Saul's disobedience, Samuel was more than "troubled" (15:11). The NRSV gives a more straightforward rendition of the Hebrew word: Samuel was "angry"! Angry enough that "he cried out to the LORD all night."

Scripture simply mentions Samuel's night of rage and moves on without comment. Was he angry at God, at Saul, or at himself? Or was he just angry at the world in general as he pondered God's shattered plans and his own? We don't know. But early in the morning, he headed out to look for Saul, finally catching up with him at Gilgal. The conversation that followed is one of the most poignant in all Scripture.

Saul greeted the angry prophet with an exuberant claim of full obedience. Samuel retorted with a question: "What then is this bleating of sheep in my ears? What is this lowing of cattle that I hear?" (vs. 14).

"The soldiers saved some of the best for sacrifice."

"Stop!" cried the prophet. Delivering the message from the LORD, Samuel concluded with a yet more pointed question: "Why did you pounce on the plunder and do evil in the eyes of the LORD?" (vs. 19).

"But I did obey the LORD," Saul protested, mentioning now his own part in bringing back King Agag, though essentially repeating the line about the people's desire to sacrifice the best to the LORD.

Samuel stood firm: "To obey is better than sacrifice," he said. Your rebellion is as bad as divination, your arrogance as bad as idolatry. "Because you have rejected the word of the LORD, he has rejected you as king" (vss. 22, 23).

As the conversation continues, three key Hebrew words heighten the sense of drama and tension. Their nearest English equivalents are: *forgive/bear, listen/obey, turn/repent-relent-restore.*

The first one appears in Saul's alibi. Samuel's announcement of Saul's rejection as king finally had jarred the king into repentance. He confessed his sin against God and Samuel. But he also fell back on an alibi, blaming the people. Literally translated, the alibi reads, "I was afraid of the people, and I listened to their voice" (vs. 24). Years before, God had commanded Samuel to "listen" to the voice of the people and give them a king (8:7, 9, 22). Although the LORD repeated the command three times, Samuel still resisted. Finally, the LORD Himself "listened" to the voice of the people and brought the king to Samuel (9:16). Now the king had "listened" to the voice of the people and with deadly consequences—it had cost him his throne.

Is the author, writing from the ruins of the failed monarchy, trying to tell us something about the dangers of kingship *and* of listening to the voice of the people? From one perspective, kingship was a bad idea from the start, even though God Himself had listened to the voice of the people and made it happen. When Saul listened to their voice, however, it cost him his throne. Was it ever safe to listen to the people?

As Saul moves from alibi to plea, another subtle Hebrew word appears, usually translated as "forgive" (NIV) or "pardon" (KJV, NRSV), a legitimate translation. But note that it is a request for *Samuel* to forgive (15:25). The basic meaning of the word in the sense of "bear" or "carry" would suggest the intriguing possibility that Saul was actually telling Samuel: "Bear my sin." Samuel was the prophet who had anointed him (10:1), had proclaimed him king to the people (vs. 24), had gone with him into battle against Nahash the Ammonite (11:7), and had led out in the confirmation of his kingship at Gilgal (vs. 14). Samuel had given him the blank check: "Do whatever your hand finds to do, for God is with you"—but with restrictions: "You must wait seven days until I come to you and tell you what you are to do" (10:7, 8). When Samuel was late, Saul had sinned, and it was Samuel who told him that his sin had cost him the kingdom (13:14).

"Now I beg you," pleaded Saul, "forgive [bear] my sin and come back [turn] with me, so that I may worship the LORD" (15:25). Reinforcing the suggestion that Saul is making an outright plea for Samuel to bond with him in facing an uncertain future is the use of another key word, the one translated "come back." Though its obvious and first meaning here is spatial, the same word can also be translated as "repent," "relent," or "restore." Is Saul's purpose in asking Samuel to "turn back" more than simple window dressing? Is he asking Samuel to "bear" his sin and join him in a move toward full restoration?

"I will not go back [turn] with you," responded Samuel, reaffirming the LORD's rejection of Saul (vs. 26).

But Saul would not be denied. So when Samuel "turned" (!) to leave, Saul grasped Samuel's robe in desperation. It tore. And Samuel immediately turned the torn garment into a further illustration of rejection. The LORD had "torn the kingdom" from Saul and given it to a "neighbor," a "better" person (vs. 28). And then, lifting a line from Balaam's prophecy (Num. 23:19), Samuel concluded: "The Glory of Israel does not lie or change his mind; for he is not a man, that he should change his mind" (vs. 29).

Still Saul persisted: "I have sinned. But please honor me before the elders of my people and before Israel; come back [turn] with me, so that I may worship the LORD your God" (vs. 30).

Suddenly and without explanation, Samuel caved in: he "went back [turned] with Saul, and Saul worshiped the LORD" (vs. 31). The LORD might not change *His* mind, but Samuel His messenger could change *his*. Was Samuel hoping against hope that the LORD just might change His mind again? In the author's day, the people would surely have heard echoes from the king of Nineveh's speech. A response to Jonah's ironclad threat of destruction, the king's speech reverberates with the same vocabulary as chapter 15: "Who can tell if God will turn [!] and repent [!] and turn away [!] from his fierce anger, that we perish not?" (Jonah 3:9, KJV). Then there was Moses—if the LORD could change His mind on the basis of his powerful intercession, even when the people had not yet repented (Exod. 32:14), maybe He would change it now on the basis of Samuel's intercession *and* Saul's repentance.

Perhaps we now have a clue to Samuel's night of angry shouting to the LORD (15:11). Samuel knew that the LORD had already changed His mind about Saul at least once. Would He change it again? Apparently that was Samuel's hope.

If such a change were to occur, however, the requirements of the ban (*cherem*) would have to be fulfilled first. And so it was that Samuel himself intervened on Saul's behalf and "put Agag to death before the LORD at Gilgal" (vs. 33).

But the story ends there. Samuel went home to Ramah to mourn. Saul went home to Gibeah. "And the LORD was sorry that he had made Saul king over Israel" (vs. 35, NRSV). In the next chapter, He told Samuel that he had mourned long enough. It was time to anoint a new king over Israel. But the readers already know that the fate of King Saul would also be the fate of the house of David. "The Glory of Israel does not lie or change his mind; for he is not a man, that he should change his mind" (vs. 29). Amidst the ruins of Jerusalem, the author and his readers would have plenty of time to ponder that somber truth.

∎ Applying the Word

1 Samuel 13–15

1. *Learning From Saul.* What kind of personal lessons can I draw from the judgments against Saul in these chapters? Do I find these stories a help or a hindrance in my Christian experience? In what ways do they affect my life today?

2. *Learning From Jonathan.* What does Jonathan's relationship to family and work have to say to a godly and efficient person today who happens to be working for someone who is not so godly and not so efficient? Have I ever been in such a situation? If so, how, specifically, could his story be a help to me? Though Saul was king, not priest (or pastor), does Jonathan's experience help me know what to do when my spiritual leaders go astray? In what ways? Summarize your thoughts in a brief paragraph.

3. *Venturing Out.* In church work, could I or should I venture out as Jonathan did without telling those in authority? Why or why not? Would it be appropriate to use this story as an illustration of how an "independent" ministry might trigger

healthy activity on the part of the larger church? Explain your response in a sentence or two.

4. *Rejected and Accepted.* Do I find it encouraging or troubling that the Lord continued to work with Saul even after "judgment" had been declared? What practical effect does it have on my experience to know that God continues to work even with fallen leaders?

5. *Chronology.* Does something such as the puzzling manuscript evidence for the length of Saul's reign (13:1) have any practical effect on my ability to understand the biblical story or appreciate its spiritual lessons? Should it make a difference?

6. *Guidance From God.* Saul had a prophet and a priest to guide him; he also sought counsel through such means as Urim and Thummim and the casting of lots. Should I seek guidance in similar ways? What about Jonathan's signs? In our day, to what extent does "sanctified reason" replace such "supernatural" means of knowing God's will?

7. *Learning From Anger.* How does Samuel's anger (15:11, NRSV) help me know what to do with mine? What aspects of the way Samuel dealt with his anger do I approve of? What aspects do I disapprove of? Why?

■ Researching the Word

1. *The Ban.* Using a concordance, Bible dictionary, and Bible commentaries, study the key contexts that involve the "ban" (*cherem*) or the "devotion" (to destruction) as commanded in 1 Samuel 15:3. According to the *NIV Exhaustive Concordance*, the key Hebrew verb in these verses appears fifty times in the Old Testament and the noun, twenty-nine times. In Bible dictionaries, the relevant articles are typically listed under the heading of *ban* or *devoted.* The major biblical contexts would include Joshua 6 to 8, the events involving Jericho, Ai, and Achan. The ban was used against Israel's neighbors, but also internally within Israel (e.g., Deut. 13:6-18; Judg. 21:10-12). Analyze the ban in terms of potentially

positive ethical implications as well as the more obvious negative ones. Finally, formulate your own position relative to
God's willingness to be "all things to all people" and what
that means for the Christian use of the Bible today. A popular discussion of the "ban" in the context of Judges 19 to 21
is found in Thompson, *Who's Afraid?* in the chapter "The
Worst Story in the Old Testament" (especially pages 124 to
127).

2. *A God Who Repents.* The idea of a God who "repents" (KJV)
stands in a certain tension with the idea of a God who does
not change. Using Young's or Strong's concordances will help
you trace the use of *repent* in the KJV. Comparing the KJV
usage with that in modern versions should be instructive.
Through concordance, Bible dictionary, and Bible commentaries, study both sides of the question, paying particular
attention to Malachi 3:6 in context ("I the LORD do not
change") and to the passages which declare that the LORD
does not repent (Num. 23:19; 1 Sam. 15:29, KJV), as well as
those which describe His "repentance" or change of mind.
Jeremiah 26 and the book of Jonah are important passages.
A fruitful way to conclude your study would be to ask the
question: How is human repentance related to divine repentance? Summarize your conclusions in your notebook.

■ Further Study of the Word

1. For general insight, see E. G. White, *Patriarchs and Prophets*,
   241-251.
2. For a children's version of 1 Samuel 13 to 15, see A. S. Maxwell, *The Bible Story*, 3:174-186.
3. For a literary analysis that closely links the fate of Samuel
   and Saul, see R. Polzin, *Samuel*, 126-151.
4. For the classic discussion of Israelite "corporate" thinking,
   see H. W. Robinson, *Corporate Personality in Ancient Israel.*

PART THREE

1 Samuel 16–31
2 Samuel 1

Saul and David:
Who Is the LORD's Anointed?

CHAPTER FIVE

From Faithful Servant to Hunted Foe—Part I

1 Samuel 16:1–18:9

The early chapters in 1 Samuel (1–7) are dominated by the rise of Samuel, the last of the judges, and the decline of the house of Eli, whose wicked sons delivered the ark into the hands of the Philistines (4–7). This section closes on a high note of renewal and faithfulness, with Samuel as the ideal judge (7:2-17). The people put away their idols "and served the LORD only" (vs. 4).

But with the opening of chapter 8, Samuel has become like Eli, old and afflicted with wicked sons. So the people ask for a king, and in 1 Samuel 8 to 15 we hear the tangled and tragic story of King Saul, a story that concludes with his failure to destroy the Amalekites as the LORD had commanded.

Though originally horrified at the idea of kingship, Samuel now seems to have bonded closely to Saul. Samuel was angry and cried to the LORD all night when he heard that Saul had failed (15:11). But even when Samuel personally stepped in and killed the Amalekite king, thus fulfilling what Saul had failed to do, the LORD still did not repent. The aged prophet went home and mourned, and "the LORD was grieved that he had made Saul king over Israel" (vs. 35).

The next section (chapters 16-23) opens just like the previous one (chapters 8–15), with the picture of a reluctant prophet, resisting the idea of a new anointed king, just as he had earlier resisted the idea of monarchy. But the LORD again intervened, jarring Samuel loose from his attachment to Saul and sending him out to anoint David. That event was virtually Samuel's swan song, for with it, his voice fell silent. Except for the brief reference to his death

(28:3) and his haunting recall at the command of the woman of Endor (vss. 4-25), the prophet will appear only once more in 1 Samuel—faceless and voiceless, a temporary refuge for David (19:18-24).

The focus now shifts. The LORD *had chosen Saul to deliver His people from the Philistines (9:16) but was sorry He had done so (15:11, 35). Now He has chosen David, and Samuel has anointed him king. With two striking statements, almost side by side, the author of 1 Samuel sets the stage for the drama that follows:*

"From that day on the Spirit of the LORD *came upon David in power" (16:13).*

"Now the Spirit of the LORD *had departed from Saul, and an evil spirit from the* LORD *tormented him" (vs. 14).*

The statements are almost side by side. What stands between them? Four words in Hebrew, five in the NIV English: "Samuel then went to Ramah." Samuel is gone. It's now up to David, Saul, and the LORD. *The crucial question is once again: "Who is king in Israel?"*

∎ Getting Into the Word

1 Samuel 16:1–18:9

Read through 1 Samuel chapters 16 to 23 for an overview before returning to a more specific focus on 16:1 to 18:9. Then respond to the following questions:

1. *Spirit Filled.* As you read about the rising fortunes of David and the decline of King Saul in chapters 16 to 23, prepare two lists of passages, one that includes those instances in which the LORD still worked through Saul or blessed his efforts, even though the "Spirit" had left him, the other for all those instances in which David seems to have departed from God's ideal, even though the "Spirit" was with him. In a brief paragraph or two, summarize how you see God's use of flawed vessels (Saul) on the one hand, and on the other, how His indwelling Spirit affects a person's (David's) "freedom" to sin.

2. *Truth*. Set aside a section in your Samuel notebook entitled "Truth." Beginning with the LORD's counsel to Samuel on what to say and what not to say to Saul about David's anointing (16:2, 3), start a list of examples in which God's people have told something less than the truth (i.e., half-truths or lies). Indicate whether or not Scripture records divine approval or disapproval of what was said. Finally, indicate the effect on people and events. Add to this "truth" file as you continue your studies in 1 and 2 Samuel. Two interesting examples of this point occur elsewhere in the Old Testament—the stories of the Hebrew midwives in Egypt (Exod. 1) and of Rahab in Jericho (Josh. 2).

3. *Evil Spirit*. Pay special attention to the "evil spirit from the LORD" in Saul's experience (16:14-23). Does God send evil spirits? What do you think the phrase means?

4. *Goliath*. List the key lines or passages in the story of Goliath that you find particularly inspiring. What effect does the violence in the story have on you? Does it affect your ability to be blessed by what you read?

5. *Who Is He?* On the surface, chapter 17 seems to suggest that Saul did not previously know David, thus standing in a certain tension with 16:18-23. Make a list of the incidents from chapter 17 that could give this impression. Write out as many possibilities as you can think of for resolving or explaining the tension.

■ Exploring the Word

Credentials for a New King (16:1-13)

What right does David have to be king? Chapter 16 begins to answer that question from both divine and human perspectives. Samuel's anointing gave David credentials from the LORD (vss. 1-13). The invitation to join the king's household (vss. 14-23) laid the foundation for a more human legitimacy for David's rise to power, showing that he was not just a rebel out to dethrone the king, but was a loyal servant, subject to the king's authority.

In addition to those obvious structural purposes, chapter 16 also raises tantalizing questions and bristles with fascinating details, beginning with the opening line, the LORD's rebuke of Samuel for his ongoing mourning over the rejected Saul. The rebuke confirms that Samuel had indeed bonded strongly to the man he had anointed as Israel's first king. In spite of the fact that Samuel had twice carried news of the LORD's rejection to Saul (13:14; 15:22-26), hints of Samuel's genuine attachment to Saul are embedded even in the story of Saul's rejection—Samuel's anger and night of crying to the LORD (15:11); his (eventual) willingness to turn back with Saul so that Saul could worship the LORD (vs. 31), even after Samuel had declared that the "Glory of Israel" would not "change his mind" (vs. 29); and finally, the double mention of Samuel's mourning for Saul, once at the end of chapter 15 (vs. 35), and again at the beginning of chapter 16 (vs. 1).

As the reasons for Saul's rejection begin to mount, Samuel's continuing attachment to the fallen monarch leaves a mark on the prophet too. Indeed, the story of David's anointing not only portrays Samuel as reluctant to get on with his mission, but also as lacking in discernment. Without the LORD's blunt intervention, Samuel just might have chosen Eliab, Jesse's firstborn: "Surely the LORD's anointed stands here before the LORD," exclaimed Samuel when he saw Eliab (vs. 6). But the Lord said No. Scripture doesn't say whether the LORD explicitly informed Samuel about the status of each of the other sons. But Samuel's final question, "Are these all the sons you have?" (vs. 11), further suggests that the prophet was in the dark. Though the LORD still used Samuel as His messenger and mouthpiece, the lack of insight reflected in this, Samuel's last recorded conversation, harks back to a similar slowness in his first recorded conversation in chapter 3, that well-known dialogue in the temple that required several attempts before Samuel recognized the LORD's voice, and then, only with Eli's help.

Between those two conversations are other telltale signs that Samuel was very much a human instrument in the LORD's hands.

When the ark disappeared, not only was Samuel powerless to intervene, but he also dropped out of sight for three chapters (4–6) and some twenty years (7:2). When the people asked for a king, Samuel three times resisted God's command to "listen" to the people (8:7, 9, 22). And Samuel was tardy in his appointment with Saul, tempting the new king to offer sacrifices illicitly (13:8), thus forfeiting his kingdom, a judgment that Samuel himself proceeded to announce. No, the prophet Samuel was not perfect. Yet the LORD continued to work through him. Indeed, as the victory over Goliath would show, the LORD could still bless His people even with the rejected Saul holding the office of king (chap. 17). But given the track record of the book's heroes thus far, the reader might well ponder what flaws would emerge in David, the man after God's own heart (13:14). In the author's day, the collapse of David's dynasty was, of course, well known, for the monarchy had disappeared when Babylon destroyed Jerusalem. Would the story of David's rise to power drop any hints as to why?

Samuel balked at the idea of a trip to Bethlehem to anoint Saul's successor. "How can I go?" he asked the LORD. "Saul will hear about it and kill me" (16:2). His concern was understandable, for a journey from Ramah to Bethlehem would take him through Gibeah of Saul (Hertzberg, 137). The LORD suggested that Samuel protect himself with a misleading truth: "Take a heifer with you and say, 'I have come to sacrifice to the LORD'" (16:2).

Such a response in the interest of self-defense is consistent with the Old Testament perspective on truth telling. Although bearing false witness was forbidden in the Decalogue, the primary application of that command was within the judicial process, as the NIV version of the Exodus command makes clear: "You shall not give false testimony against your neighbor" (Exod. 20:16). The judicial context is further clarified in Deuteronomy 19:16-21, where the authorities are directed to punish a false witness by doing to him "as he intended to do to his brother" (vs. 19).

Other settings, however, could call for a more subtle handling of the truth. Here, in 1 Samuel 16, for example, Samuel's lack of full disclosure to an unpredictable Saul is analogous to the midwives' ingenious response to the bloodthirsty Pharaoh (Exod. 1:16-21) or to Hushai's "wise" but misleading counsel to the rebel Absalom (2 Sam. 15:32-37; 16:15–17:23). More tangential is the story of Rahab, illustrating the handling of truth when espionage is involved (Josh. 2). More tangential yet and at a more personal level, the Shunammite woman's less-than-full disclosure to Gehazi allowed her to protect her privacy. She simply did not want to share her heartache with the prophet's servant (2 Kings 4:24-26).

In any event, Samuel arrived unscathed in Bethlehem, though the town elders trembled when they saw him (1 Sam. 16:4), perhaps a reflection of the prophet's reputation as a bearer of bad news.

Allaying their fears, Samuel told the elders to consecrate themselves. He himself consecrated Jesse and his sons, giving them a special invitation to the sacrifice (vs. 5).

Samuel's initial screening involved seven of Jesse's eight sons, though only the three oldest are mentioned by name: Eliab, Abinadab, and Shammah. The LORD cooled Samuel's ardor for the firstborn Eliab, seemingly a worthy successor to Saul. The LORD was not interested in someone who simply looked good from a human perspective. "The LORD looks at the heart," He told Samuel (vs. 7).

Ironically, however, the man of God's choosing turned out to be quite an attractive person after all. David "was ruddy, with a fine appearance and handsome features" (vs. 12). His most notable drawbacks were his extreme youth and the fact that he was the youngest in his father's house instead of the oldest. But no matter. After the anointing, Scripture says that "from that day on the Spirit of the LORD came upon David in power" (vs. 13).

Buffered only by the brief statement that "Samuel then went to Ramah" (vs. 13), the author's unsettling assessment of Saul's situation follows immediately: "Now the Spirit of the LORD had departed from Saul, and an evil spirit from the LORD tormented him" (vs. 14). With Samuel's retirement, the stage is left to the two anointed, spirit-filled men. David is filled with the same Spirit of the LORD that once filled Saul. Saul, by contrast, is now tormented by quite a different spirit, though still "from the LORD."

Excursus: An Evil Spirit From the LORD

The Old Testament manner of attributing evil directly to the LORD becomes more understandable once one recognizes that the Old Testament also keeps Satan almost entirely under wraps. Christians, attuned to the struggle between Christ and Satan for the mastery of human affairs, may be puzzled by an Old Testament world in which the LORD is said to be directly responsible for both good and evil and in which Satan seems to play almost no role at all. Yet that is indeed the state of affairs, for in the entire Old Testament only three contexts explicitly identify "Satan" as a superhuman being opposed to God—1 Chronicles 21:1; Job 1, 2; and Zechariah 3:1—all of which appear in books that were either written or canonized toward the end of the Old Testament period.

Other passages that Christians have interpreted as applying to Satan, including Genesis 3 (the serpent), Leviticus 16 (the scapegoat—Hebrew, *Azazel*), Isaiah 14 ("Lucifer"), and Ezekiel 28 (guardian cherub), are implied rather than explicit and, in fact, have been applied to Satan only in the light of the New Testament. Revelation 12:7-9, for example, is the first passage in Jewish or Christian sources to explicitly identify the serpent as Satan.

Of the Old Testament passages that do mention Satan, the ones most directly helpful for understanding the "evil spirit from the LORD" here in 1 Samuel 16 are the references in Job and 1 Chronicles. In Job, Satan appears in only two scenes in the prologue (1:6-12; 2:1-7) and is entirely subject to the LORD's control. While the author and the reader know about Satan, Job does not. Thus, throughout the book, God, not Satan, is the object of Job's anger (see, for example, 9:13-22; 16:7-17; 19:5-22). Though he makes peace with God in the end (42:1-6), Job never grapples with the reality of Satan, a perspective similar to the one represented in 1 Samuel 16.

The reference to Satan in 1 Chronicles 21:1 is helpful in another way, since the earlier parallel in 2 Samuel 24:1 attributes to the LORD what Chronicles, the last book in the Hebrew Bible, credits to Satan—namely, the instigation of David's census. Thus the two accounts witness to two biblical perspectives on the same event, an earlier one, in which God is responsible for everything, and a later one, in which Satan's role is recognized.

While many scholars simply attribute the "late" appearance of Satan to foreign (Persian) influence, believers who affirm the reality of a personal demonic force in the world can view the LORD's earlier willingness to assume direct responsibility for good and evil in the world as part of His pastoral care for Israel. In polytheistic cultures, the potentially destructive evil demons had to be manipulated and appeased through incantations and magic. Such methods were strictly forbidden in Israel, however, for the LORD was known to be a trustworthy God, not subject to human manipulation. The LORD could harden Pharaoh's heart (Exod. 7:3), release poisonous serpents in the wilderness (Num. 21:6), or send an evil spirit to torment Saul (1 Sam. 16:14), all as part of His plan. He was the sovereign LORD and Master of all circumstances. To be sure, He granted human freedom and expected human beings to assume responsibility for their actions. But the Old Testament typically portrayed Him as ultimately responsible for everything, both good and evil.

In the classic "free-will" understanding of the problem of evil, seen in part in the writings of John Milton and C. S. Lewis, for example, and even more extensively in the writings of Ellen White, the book of Job becomes something of a microcosm of a larger drama. In that larger view, God allows Satan to have access to God's "perfect" world, granting him permission to "test" the good, so that in the end, God's people will be seen to be good for goodness' sake, a vindication not only of God's people but of God Himself.

In the light of the New Testament, Christians can recognize that the history of the human race from the Fall (Gen. 3) to the call of Abraham (Gen. 12) was the period when satanic forces had virtually full rein on earth, even though "Satan" as we know him is not actually mentioned in the Old Testament accounts. Genesis 3:1 simply states that "the serpent was more crafty than any of the wild animals the LORD God had made," a statement that would remain tantalizingly unclear until the revelation of God in Jesus Christ.

A knowledge of Satan's role in the universe can help modern believers grasp the principles of the great conflict between good and evil. If the impact of sin on the world had obscured the "truth" about Satan for a time, the end of the Old Testament period witnessed God's willingness to broaden His people's understanding of the "truth" about the Adversary. Yet that earlier Old Testament perspective is not without its experiential benefits, even for us. A God who is Master of all can be a source of great strength when evil strikes. We, like Job, can turn to our Redeemer for help and healing because He is Lord of all.

Saul's Illness, David's Opportunity (16:14-23)

It could easily be argued that Saul's torments were a result of mental illness, aggravated, no doubt, by feelings of guilt and depression. Recognizing that the evil spirit came from God did not prevent Saul and his staff from realistically treating the evil spirit as an illness for which soothing music was at least a temporary cure (vss. 16, 23). The need for a skilled musician, of course, was the occasion that brought David into the royal household.

When Saul's staff diagnosed the king's problem and suggested a possible treatment, Saul agreed and asked for recommendations. The servant who suggested David knew him not only as a musician, but also as a "brave man and a warrior. He speaks well and is a fine looking man. And the LORD is with him" (vs. 18).

Saul did not hesitate but sent a formal request to Jesse for the services of David, his son. Saul "liked him very much" and even appointed David as one of his armorbearers (vs. 21). The chapter concludes with a further reference to the power of David's music: "Whenever the spirit from God came upon Saul, David would take his harp and play. Then relief would come to Saul; he would feel better, and the evil spirit would leave him" (vs. 23).

The question of David's integrity may trouble the modern reader. How could he serve King Saul in good conscience, knowing that he had been anointed to take Saul's place? Scripture never addresses that question. Had David wished to take the throne by force, of course, the continuing story makes it clear that on two occasions he easily could have killed Saul (24:3-7; 26:7-25). But David steadfastly refused to lay a hand on "the LORD's anointed."

In connection with the matter of David's integrity, it is again pertinent to question the chronological order of the incidents as they now stand in 1 Samuel. The author's logic for placing the two major incidents of chapter 16 at this point in his story is clear: the anointing demonstrates David's divine credentials; the story of his entry into Saul's house begins to legitimize his right to royal power from a more human perspective. Such logic does not require a precise chronology.

For those interested in constructing a chronology, however, both incidents do present puzzling questions. With reference to the anointing, for example, both Samuel's reluctance and his seeming ignorance of the right "candidate" stand in a tension with his firm statements about God's choice of a successor in the two (earlier?) accounts of Saul's rejection. In 13:14 Samuel declares to Saul: "Now your kingdom will not endure; the LORD has sought out a man after his own heart and appointed him leader of his people." In 15:28 Samuel again declares to Saul: "The LORD has torn the kingdom of Israel from you today and has given it to one of your neighbors—to one better than you." How does one correlate such "knowledge" with Samuel's "ignorance" at the anointing?

Similar questions emerge in connection with the story of David's entry into Saul's household. If one assumes that the incidents in 1 Samuel are in chronological order, one would think that the two rejection accounts, replete with the announcement of a successor, would be enough to make Saul forever suspicious and paranoid. Though a more subtle interpretation is possible, as suggested below, a straightforward reading of 1 Samuel would seem to reveal no trace of Saul's jealousy, suspicion, or hatred until 18:8. There, "after David had killed the Philistine" (vs. 6), the women greeted the returning soldiers with their provocative singing: "Saul has slain his thousands, and David his tens of thousands" (vs. 7). That triggered open hostility: "Saul was very angry; this refrain galled him. 'They have credited David with tens of thousands,' he thought, 'but me with only thousands. What more can he get but the kingdom?' And from that time on Saul kept a jealous eye on David" (vss. 8, 9).

Interestingly enough, the author's comments immediately pre-ceding this incident add to the mounting evidence that he was not intending to preserve a precise chronology. If the women's song was a response to the victorious army "after David had killed the Philis-tine" (vs. 6), then how are we to understand that David's killing of Goliath marked the point ("from that day)" when "Saul kept David with him and did not let him return to his father's house" (vs. 2)? And just preceding the account of the women's song, the author records a sweeping summary statement of Saul's overall confidence in David, a statement that implies a lengthier period of full confi-dence on Saul's part: "Whatever Saul sent him to do, David did it so successfully that Saul gave him a high rank in the army. This pleased all the people, and Saul's officers as well" (vs. 5). Given the extended period of confidence that such a statement implies, how was it that Saul "kept a jealous eye on David" (vs. 9), beginning with the army's return after the victory over Goliath?

Adding to the chronological puzzle is the servant's speech when he brought David to Saul's household. Already at that point David was known (though apparently not yet to Saul) as a "brave man and a warrior" (16:18). Even though Saul had appointed David as one of his armorbearers (vs. 21), just prior to David's killing of Goliath, Saul did not recognize David's warrior status, referring to him as "only a boy" (17:33). And after David killed the giant, neither Saul nor Abner *seemed* to know anything about David (vs. 55). The same Saul who had asked permission from Jesse for David's services in 16:19 now poses the question for David: "Whose son are you, young man?" (vs. 58).

Typically, scholars simply have attributed the seemingly impos-sible chronology to the author's use of sources and to clumsy edit-ing. If one adopts a line of reasoning similar to that of Polzin's (*Samuel*, 161-176), however, instead of clumsy editing, one can rec-ognize a skillful portrayal of David's rise and Saul's decline and the increasing tension developing between them. Such inspired artistry does not mean, however, that the author is concerned about pro-ducing a precise chronology. His goal is to demonstrate how gifted people, even those called and anointed by God and filled with His

Spirit, can go horribly wrong. Eli, Samuel, Saul—yes, and David—especially David—are all part of a massive failure. Talent, wisdom, good looks, wealth, and even the Spirit of God cannot prevent the failure of those who depart from God's will. As for David's obvious charm, it may be an unsettling irony to note that "good looks and outstanding physique" (Klein, 166) were also associated with two other men with royal ambitions, namely, Saul (9:2) and Absalom (2 Sam. 14:25, 26), hardly the kind of company to inspire envy or admiration.

Recognizing that the books of 1 and 2 Samuel bring us the story of a failed enterprise makes the introduction to David in 1 Samuel 16 all the more striking. Here is a gifted man, chosen and anointed by God, well-liked and admired, and as Saul's servant noted, "the LORD is with him" (vs. 18). How could such a man possibly fail?

The author of 1 Samuel intends to show us how. But to help us understand the monumental nature of David's fall, he will first tell us about David's rise to popularity, power, and position. If a human perspective tempts us to think that the LORD was too quick to judge and reject Saul for his sins, we may similarly be tempted to think that He was too slow in chastising David for his. But regardless of initial reactions to God's handling of the two men, in the end, believers will find a way of saying with Eli, "He is the LORD; let him do what is good in his eyes" (3:18).

Finally, the stories of Saul and David suggest a thought-provoking practical question: Does the path to belief sometimes seem hard in light of the evil that befalls frail humans? A straightforward answer may not be easy, but in that connection, I have found it helpful to glimpse the LORD's passion and pain when His people are in trouble—His grief over King Saul (15:35), His anguish over a people who respond neither to joyful flute nor mournful dirge (Matt. 11:16, 17), His sorrow as He gazes longingly over the city of His people, crying, "O Jerusalem, Jerusalem, the city that murders the prophets and stones the messengers sent to her! How often have I longed to gather your children, as a hen gathers her brood under her wings; but you would not let me" (Matt. 23:37, NEB).

The Giant—A Story for Believers (17:1-54)

In spite of its violence and gore (or perhaps because of it!), the story of David killing Goliath is an all-time favorite Bible story. Even from a strictly human point of view, the story is a marvelous example of the hopeless underdog coming out on top, the brave little kid beating up on the town bully against all odds.

But for those who believe in God's providence, it is much more than a story. It is a living testimony to a God who acts on behalf of His beleaguered people. Through a sling and a stone in the hand of a courageous shepherd boy, He delivers His people from a dangerous and hostile world. Those elements that have made the story a believer's favorite are worth relishing before we explore its possible role in the larger tapestry of 1 and 2 Samuel.

As I read through the story, having determined not to be distracted by the violence, I found myself drawn to five lines that throbbed with special power for me. Let's take a few moments to share them together as believers:

1. "Who is this uncircumcised Philistine that he should defy the armies of the living God?" (vs. 26). In a world teeming with enemies, God's dispirited and fearful armies long for a glimpse of His power. Behind a mask of uncertainty lurks a smoldering desire to be electrified by someone who believes. God will act to defend His name! Who does this Philistine think he is, anyway?

2. "The LORD who delivered me from the paw of the lion and the paw of the bear will deliver me from the hand of this Philistine" (vs. 37). Small victories are the promise of greater ones to come. Bring on the giants!

3. "You come against me with sword and spear and javelin, but I come against you in the name of the LORD Almighty, the God of the armies of Israel, whom you have defied" (vs. 45). It's not the weapons in our hands, but the banner under which we march.

4. "The whole world will know that there is a God in Israel. All those gathered here will know that it is not by sword or spear that the LORD saves; for the battle is the LORD's, and he will give all of you into our hands" (vss. 46, 47). A world is waiting to know that

our God is alive. But isn't it curious that God's people often are waiting to know the same thing?

5. "So David triumphed over the Philistine with a sling and a stone; without a sword in his hand he struck down the Philistine and killed him" (vs. 50). Little weapons in the hands of little people mean great victories for those who trust in God.

Yes, the story also throbs with violence—too much violence, just as our world throbs with violence—too much violence. But sometimes the Lord uses violence to bring violence to an end.

Does He Know Him, or Doesn't He? (16:14-18:9)

When it comes to the question of relating the story of David and Goliath to the author's larger scheme, the most challenging task is finding the right link with the preceding account in chapter 16, where David is Saul's personal musician and armorbearer, brought to the court by Saul's official request to Jesse, David's father. In short, in chapter 16, Saul knows David very well, while in chapter 17, he seems to be meeting him for the first time all over again. "Still holding the Philistine's head," David stands before the king, at the end of the chapter, and hears Saul ask: "Whose son are you, young man?" (vss. 57, 58).

Most commentators simply attribute the two accounts to different sources, abandoning any serious attempt to find a coherent link between them. Superficially, at least, a major Septuagint manuscript, the *Vaticanus*, would seem to support the "source" explanation, for it has preserved a much shorter version of the Goliath story, omitting those portions that are in tension with chapter 16 (17:12-31, 55-58; 18:1-5).

Yet from within that passage omitted by the Septuagint, 17:12-15 seems to represent a thoughtful attempt to link chapters 16 and 17, referring to Jesse and his eight sons, the three oldest by name, and mentioning David's work with the sheep. Why would an author build such a careful bridge if he didn't mean for the two chapters to be linked together? The author of 1 and 2 Samuel certainly used "sources" in preparing his work. But was he a skilled, Spirit-guided author or merely a clumsy editor? Or, put another way, did he write a book or compile a scrapbook? I follow Polzin (*Samuel*, 161-176) in suggesting an interpretation that sees the tension between chapters 16 and 17 as part of a skilled and deliberate plan by the author, integral to his portrayal of David and Saul.

If we take the events in 1 Samuel as the author has given them, then by the time David defeats Goliath, Saul has both solid accomplishments and acute embarrassments on record. His public anointing was a mixture of both, since his selection and acclaim as king was preceded by Samuel's stinging attack against the whole idea of monarchy. No wonder Saul hid among the baggage (10:17-25)! Scripture then records his successful battle against Nahash the Ammonite (11:1-11), but it was a victory followed by the people's call for reprisals. Only Samuel's intervention saved the day and led to a reaffirmation of kingship (vss. 12-15). Next comes Saul's Gilgal rejection (13:8-14), followed by the Micmash victory over the Philistines, a victory sparked by Jonathan's bravery but marred by Saul's rash oath (14:1-46). Finally, the victory over Amalek was tarnished by the disobedience that led to Saul's final rejection (15:4-26).

By chapter 16, then, Saul has some reasons for confidence but even more reasons to be "tormented" by the evil spirit (vs. 14), regardless of its source. David is there to help the king. But how reliable is the judgment of this king from whom the Spirit of the LORD has departed (vs. 14)? That is certainly the question a thoughtful reader will have in mind as the Goliath story unfolds.

Just as in the Micmash encounter of chapter 14, Saul was again virtually reduced to hand wringing. There, Jonathan sparked the victory; here, in chapter 17, it would be David. And in both cases, the king simply tagged along for the ride. Under such circumstances, how would a tormented king likely respond when his young musician and armorbearer volunteers to battle the giant? Is it not possible that Saul's words to David were of a piece with those of David's older brother Eliab (vs. 28), but dripping with sarcasm and scorn instead of anger? "You are not able to go out against this Philistine and fight him," Saul exclaimed; "you are only a boy, and he has been a fighting man from his youth" (vs. 33).

When David refused Saul's armor (vss. 38, 39), Saul may not have realized that David still intended to battle Goliath. Thus, when he saw David actually heading out to meet the giant, his question to Abner could have been charged with both incredulity and scorn: "As Saul watched David going out to meet the Philistine, he said to Abner, commander of the army, 'Abner, whose son is that young man?' " (vs. 55).

Abner returned a nonanswer: "As surely as you live, O king, I don't know."

But the king was urgent: "Find out whose son this young man is" (vs. 56).

Polzin notes that the author's frequent use of demonstratives in chapter 17 tends to identify people and objects in a derogatory manner. Included in his list of examples are the references to Goliath as "*this* man" (vs. 25), "*this* Philistine" (vss. 26, 32, 33, 37), and "*this* uncircumcised Philistine" (vss 26, 36). The demonstratives in Saul's two questions to Abner (vss. 55, 56) imply a similar derisiveness: "*that* [Hebrew: this] young man" and "*this* young man."

From a human point of view, Saul had reason to be upset. After all, the Philistines were on the run, but to David's credit, not Saul's. And if Saul was indeed seething over David's brash courage, then his reference to David's paternity could be tinged with the same derision that marked his later slur at Jonathan's maternity: "You son of a perverse and rebellious woman!" (20:30).

When Abner brought David before the king, "still holding the Philistine's head" (17:57), Saul's question was curt and pointed: "Whose son are you, young man?" he demanded.

David's straightforward answer, "I am the son of your servant Jesse of Bethlehem" (vs. 58), innocent as it may sound, may have included a barbed note of defiance. As Polzin notes, David's use of *servant* not only echoes Goliath's disdainful use of the term in *servants of Saul* (vs. 8) and *subjects* (vs. 9), but also Samuel's earlier warning that the Israelites themselves would become "servants [NIV: slaves]" of their king (8:17, KJV).

The ongoing narrative also implies that Saul's question to David contained a threat of coercion. Previously, David had divided his time between Saul's court and his father's flock (16:19-21). Now, in view of David's demonstrated military prowess, Saul was demanding that David renounce his natural paternity and become Saul's son, a designation that Saul himself would actually use for David later in the narrative (24:16). Here, David's resistance resulted in firm and coercive action by Saul: "From that day Saul kept David with him and did not let him return to his father's house" (18:2).

In sum, just as Saul had reacted with threats to Jonathan, the leader in the earlier victory over the Philistines (14:39, 44), so he now threatened David, the leader of another victory over the Philistines. That may explain why the author chose this point to say that "Jonathan became one in spirit with David, and he loved him as himself" (18:1). In Polzin's words, "Jonathan, who has had his own run-ins with Saul, is pleased with David's simple yet defiant response. As the people saved his life in chapter 14, so will he save David's in the story to come" (Polzin, *Samuel*, 176).

Jonathan's commitment was by no means a loose admiration from afar. Scripture goes on to say that he made a "covenant" with David, then gave him his robe, tunic, sword, bow, and belt (18:4). The symbolism is powerful, for David, the young king-to-be, now has had his hands on three significant sets of armor and weapons: Saul's (17:38, 39), Goliath's (vs. 54), and Jonathan's (18:4). No wonder the singing of the women drove Saul to exclaim: "What more can he get but the kingdom?" (vs. 8).

■ Applying the Word

1 Samuel 16:1–18:9

1. *Truth.* Have there been incidents in my life in which a half-truth would have kept innocent people from being hurt? What course did I follow? Why? Would I do so again? Have I sometimes used the same kind of reasoning to justify quite selfish purposes? What can safeguard me from using either truth or error in ways that hurt other people?
2. *Evil Master.* Could I conscientiously work for someone who

is under the influence of an "evil spirit from the Lord"? Why or why not? If I suspect that a church leader is falling short of God's ideal because of the influence of an "evil spirit," what is my responsibility? To confront? To cooperate? To bring healing?

3. *God as All in All.* What benefits could I experience if I were to adopt an Old Testament perspective on Satan, ignoring his existence at the level of practical everyday living and simply focusing my attention completely on God? What negatives might result from such a perspective?

4. *Gentle Violence.* Does the story of David and Goliath suggest that I should support violent means in the battle against violence? If so, to what extent? Does knowing Jesus mean a better way that forever rules out violence? Explain your answer in a paragraph.

■ Researching the Word

1. *Samuel.* Study the life experiences of Samuel for the purpose of understanding how closely he patterned his life after God's ideal. Prepare two lists of incidents and passages, one in which Scripture explicitly rebukes or admonishes the prophet (e.g., "How long will you mourn for Saul? . . ." 16:1; "the Lord does not look at the things man looks at. . . ." 16:7), the other for passages or incidents that may appear to be worthy of rebuke or admonition but that are not explicitly so handled in Scripture (e.g., Samuel's poor parenting skills, 8:3; his tardy arrival at Gilgal, 13:8). Based on what you find, write two summaries addressing the following issues: (1) the effect of human flaws on the effectiveness of a prophet and (2) the appropriateness of uninspired believers criticizing prophetic messengers.

2. *Satan.* Using an exhaustive concordance, do a word study of the word *satan* in the Old Testament, looking up all the instances of the Hebrew word (*satan* or *hasatan*, with the article). Summarize the Old Testament use of the term, in-

dicating which of the passages directly or indirectly refer to God's opponent in the traditional Christian sense. Then with the help of commentaries, study the four major Old Testament passages that Christians have interpreted as applying to Satan: Genesis 3 (the serpent); Leviticus 16 (the scapegoat; Hebrew, *Azazel*); Isaiah 14 ("Lucifer"); Ezekiel 28 (guardian cherub). If possible, discover when in the history of interpretation the application to Satan has been made, and correlate this with the evidence suggested by the Old Testament passages. Summarize your conclusions for each passage.

■ Further Study of the Word

1. For general comment on the anointing of David and his battle with Goliath, see Ellen White, *Patriarchs and Prophets*, 637-648.
2. For a popularized treatment of the ninth commandment, see A. Thompson, "When the Truth Is a Lie," in *Lyrics of Love: God's Top Ten*, 79-86; reprint of "Thou shalt not hurt thy neighbor with lies or with the truth," *Signs of the Times*, November 1988, 20-22.
3. For a popularized analysis of the "absence" of Satan in the Old Testament, see A. Thompson, "Whatever Happened to Satan in the Old Testament?" in *Who's Afraid?*, 43-70. In the same book, the "great controversy" theme from an Old Testament perspective is presented in the chapter "Behold It Was Very Good—and Then It All Turned Sour" (25-42).
4. For the most accessible presentation of the Greek *Vaticanus* version of 1 Samuel and its variations from the Hebrew text, see R. Klein, *1 Samuel*, vol. 10 in Word Biblical Commentary.

CHAPTER SIX

From Faithful Servant to Hunted Foe—Part II

1 Samuel 18–23

David was at risk now, supported and encouraged by the king's son, but hated and hunted by the king himself. Saul wanted to kill him. And if he couldn't do it himself, he would get others to do it for him. Yet it never happened. Why? Because the LORD was now with David instead of with Saul. That was the difference and the reason.

But then a paradox. Instead of trusting in the LORD, David, the LORD's anointed, began to tell lies, lies that may have saved his own life, but cost many innocent people theirs. Was this the man to be king over all Israel? That's a question worth pondering in the light of all that happens in chapters 18 to 23.

■ Getting Into the Word

1 Samuel 18–20

Read through chapters 18 to 20 twice to get a feel for the whole section. Then respond to the following questions:

1. *Saul's Hostility.* List all the ways, both direct or indirect, by which Saul attempted to kill David. Then make note of any passages that might suggest David incited Saul's hostility by unwise or foolish acts. In a paragraph or two, summarize your reaction to both men as seen in chapters 18 to 20.
2. *Truth.* Add additional incidents to the "truth" section of your

Samuel notebook. Are any of the lies or half-truths in chapters 18 to 20 justifiable on biblical grounds? Why or why not?

3. *Jonathan*. Pay close attention to the figure of Jonathan in chapters 18 to 20. Write a brief paragraph characterizing him in comparison with David. How are they alike? How are they different? On what, do you think, was their close friendship based?

4. *Chesed*. Using a concordance, do a word study on *chesed* ("kindness," "unfailing kindness," "lovingkindness"), starting with 1 Samuel 20:8, 14, 15 and following up with other Old Testament contexts. Check the meaning of the word in a Bible dictionary. Does the human story in chapter 20 help to illumine the nature of divine *chesed*? How?

5. *Prophecy*. Using a concordance, do a word study on *prophecy* and *prophesy* and other related words. Check the meaning of the key words in a Bible dictionary. Briefly summarize how you would evaluate the biblical evidence for the kind of "charismatic" experience that seems to have seized Saul in 19:18-24. What evidence in Scripture might assist us in making a judgment on the value of "prophesying"?

■ Exploring the Word

Jonathan and David Against the King (18:1–19:24)

Following up the victory over Goliath, chapters 18 and 19 portray Saul as someone who is now intent on destroying David. The two chapters are virtually a catalog of Saul's evil intentions and his numerous attempts on David's life. But all his plots fail. Why? Because the LORD was in control of both men. "The LORD was with David" (18:12, 14, 28), while Saul was haunted by God's (evil) spirit (18:10; 19:9, 23).

As the story unfolds, Saul becomes increasingly angry and frustrated; David grows ever more popular. David "takes hearts by storm, and everyone falls for him" (Hertzberg, 154). Even Saul recognizes what has happened: "Saul was afraid of David, because the LORD was with David but had left Saul" (18:12).

The pattern for David's rise is set early in the chapter. First we learn that Jonathan had made a covenant with David and had given him his own armor (vss. 3, 4). Then the author tells us that because David was so successful in all his endeavors for the king, Saul gave him a high rank in the army (vs. 5). But before reporting Saul's anger at the women's praise of David and the undying jealousy that it sparked (vss. 6-9), the author notes that Saul's promotion of David had "pleased all the people, and Saul's officers as well" (vs. 5). David is well on his way—the king's son, the people, and Saul's officers were all on his side.

Although Saul kept trying to eliminate David through a variety of indirect means, when he himself took spear in hand against David, it was always because of the "evil spirit" from God (vs. 10) or the LORD (19:9). In short, the author was convinced that when Saul was at his irrational worst, the LORD was in control. Could it be that the author wants us to ponder whether the LORD's evil spirit was the cause or the result of Saul's rebellion and disobedience?

In 18:10 the evil spirit "from God" was also part of Saul's prophetic experience. The NRSV states that the spirit "rushed upon Saul, and he raved ["was prophesying," NIV] within his house," a clear example of the author's negative view of certain types of "prophecy." The first record of Saul's prophesying, shortly after his anointing (10:6, 10-13), appears at first glance to value prophecy positively, though the question, "Is Saul also among the prophets?" (10:11, 12), makes the matter less certain, especially when that same question is posed negatively in 19:20-24 in connection with the LORD's use of "prophecy" to sidetrack Saul's murderous attempt on David. Though the NIV preserves "prophecy" or "prophesy" in all three passages, the NRSV renditions suggest a more nonrational experience, with "prophetic frenzy" in the first passage (10:6, 10, 13), "raved" in 18:10, and "prophetic frenzy" (19:20, 23) or simply "frenzy" (vss. 20, 21, 24) in the last context.

After the incident in 19:20-24, no more instances of "prophecy" are recorded in 1 and 2 Samuel, and the only two examples in 1 and 2 Kings hardly encourage confidence: the "frantic prophesying" of the prophets of Baal on Mt. Carmel (1 Kings 18:29; NRSV, "raved") and the "prophesying" of Ahab's four hundred "lying" prophets, who led Ahab to his death at Ramoth Gilead (1 Kings 22:10, 23)! Ahab used the same term in connection with the true prophet Micaiah, but in a voice loaded with scorn: "He never prophesies anything good about me" (22:8, 18). Many other true prophets also appear in the historical books, including Gad and Nathan in the service of David, but none of them are actually said to have "prophesied." And in the entire history of the monarchy, the one and only king who was known to have prophesied was Saul. In short, our author would tell us that prophecy can be a dubious matter, and often simply dangerous. And certainly it was not wise for a king to be among the prophets.

David twice eluded Saul's spear, thrown while Saul was in his "prophetic" frenzy (18:11). As a result, Saul became "afraid" of David, the first of three references to his fear in this chapter. Here he was afraid "because the LORD was with David but had left Saul" (vs. 12); in 18:15, it was because Saul "saw how successful he [David] was"; and in 18:28 it was because Saul "realized that the LORD was with David and that his daughter Michal loved David."

Chapter 18 overflows with such narrative asides about Saul's inner thoughts. In addition to the comments about his being afraid of David (vss. 12, 15, 29), the author also tells us that when the women sang about David's exploits, Saul was "angry" and "galled" (vs. 8). But the most striking way in which the author reveals the inner Saul is to have him talking to himself about his evil plans for David. It happens five times in this one chapter: verses 8, 11, 17, 21, 25. Such insights, however, reveal only Saul, never David; David's thoughts are not for us to know. Even his voice is heard only twice in the chapter—on both occasions, a self-deprecating comment about his unworthiness to marry the king's daughter (vss. 18, 23).

But if our author's pollsters weren't talking to David about his feelings, they certainly were talking to everyone else. In addition to the sweeping statement of approval in 18:5, the chapter includes two other affirmations of David's popularity. According to verse 16, "All Israel and Judah loved David, because he led them in their campaigns"; and the chapter concludes by stating that David had "more success than the rest of Saul's officers, and his name became well known" (vs. 30).

Amidst all this rising tide of general popularity, David's marriage to Michal at the cost of one hundred Philistine foreskins—David made it two hundred for good measure—stands out as particularly noteworthy. Saul first promised his daughter Merab to David, then reneged. (Was it revenge when David later handed over her five sons to the Gibeonites to be "killed and exposed . . . on a hill" before the LORD [2 Sam. 21:8]?) David's marriage to Michal had its moments too. But for now, at least, the author has added the king's daughter to David's impressive group of supporters, a following that already included the king's son (vss. 1, 3, 4), his officers (vs. 5), all the people (vs. 5), and all Israel and Judah (vs. 16). Only the priests remained. But those would soon be on board too. Was there anything that David couldn't have? He was so talented, so gifted, so popular. . . .

Saul's designs on David's life become more intense in chapter 19. He even instructed Jonathan and all the attendants to kill David (vs. 1). But honest and innocent Jonathan pulled no punches, first warning David of the danger and then declaring his intention to discuss David's fate directly with the king. And he was persuasive too—at least temporarily—for Saul took an oath: "As surely as the LORD lives, David will not be put to death" (vs. 6).

Honest and innocent Jonathan told the whole story to David and convinced him to return to the royal court. It seems unreal and almost foolhardy, but "David was with Saul as before" (vs. 7)—until another war with the Philistines brought more fame for David. Then the "evil spirit from the LORD" triggered another spear-throwing incident as David was playing his harp for Saul (vs. 9, 10).

Though David eluded Saul's spear, he was warned by his wife, Saul's daughter Michal, "If you don't run for your life tonight, tomorrow you'll be killed" (vs. 11). With Saul's men already watching the house, Michal defied her father by helping David escape through a window, recalling the Jericho incident when Rahab helped Joshua's spies escape in a similar manner (Josh. 2:15). If the house was part of the city wall (as Rahab's was), David would have escaped outside the city.

As part of the coverup, Michal put an idol (Hebrew *teraphim*) in David's bed, covering it with a garment and putting goat's hair at the head (vs. 13). As the story is told, it is debatable whether this idol-in-the-bed ruse actually bought any additional time for David, though Michal's lie, "He is ill," did (vss. 14-17). She told yet another lie when her father confronted her, declaring that David had threatened to kill her if she didn't help him escape (vs. 17). The unsettling truth is that from this point on in the story, David and his supporters were willing to sacrifice the truth to preserve life. One might build a case for lying in view of Saul's demented condition. But that does not resolve the dilemma: Once a person begins to tell lies, even for good reasons, can such a person really be trusted?

Regardless of the ethics of the story, however, it is now clear that both Saul's son Jonathan and his daughter Michal are more loyal to David than to their father. Though David will one day take the throne, this incident marks his departure from Saul's court, never to return again.

Chapter 19 closes with yet one more escape—David's brief sojourn with Samuel at Ramah. The incident reveals Saul's sorry plight, on the one hand, and the prophet's support for David, on the other, both of which are important to the author's developing story. Concerning Saul's situation, the NRSV rendition reflects the stark realism of the Hebrew text: "He too stripped off his clothes, and he too fell into a frenzy before Samuel. He lay naked all that day and all that night" (vs. 24). The NIV has a more polite version: "He stripped off his robes and also prophesied in Samuel's presence. He lay that way all that day and night." Scripture does not explain the tension between the statement in 15:35, "Samuel did not see Saul again until the day of his death" (NRSV), and the incident in 19:24, in which Saul is "in Samuel's presence." The Hebrew of both passages is clear, though the NIV tries to solve the "problem" by adding an additional verb in the earlier passage: "He did not *go to* see Saul again" (15:35). The facts are that the Bible writers simply were not as worried about chronological precision as we think they should have been.

The critics' mockery of the so-called contradictions in the Bible may have even tempted conservative Christians to fight the battle on the critics' turf instead of letting the Bible speak for itself. As a result, conservative interpreters of Scripture have too often imposed twentieth-century demands on Scripture rather than following the Bible's own logic.

In this instance, the author may have sought to soften the tension between chapters 15 and 19 simply by referring to Samuel's presence in 19 without recording any of his words. But chronology was not our author's worry, in any event. The Spirit had burdened his soul with a deep concern for God's people. In an effort to rouse them from their lethargy, he first tells the story of Saul's failure, then the story of David's rise as the prelude to the story of David's fall—and all of it simply to illustrate what happens when God's people turn away from Him. How tragic to superimpose our views on the Bible, letting *our* worries about chronology hinder us from hearing the *real* message that the Spirit prompted the author to write.

David on the Run (20:1-42)

Like the violent story of David and Goliath in chapter 17, so the moving story of David and Jonathan in chapter 20 has a life of its own, quite apart from the author's use of it in the overall scheme of 1 and 2 Samuel. David and Jonathan finally realized that David was no longer safe in the royal court. In that context, the relationship between them has become a symbol of a friendship that endures.

The story bristles with oaths and strong words affirming the bond between the two men. Of special interest is the use of the word *kindness* (*chesed*) to refer to a binding commitment. In 20:8, David called upon Jonathan to show "kindness" because of the "sacred covenant" (NRSV; Hebrew, "covenant of the LORD") between them. Turning the tables in 20:14, 15, Jonathan asked David for "unfailing kindness" to him and his family. *Chesed* is an important word in the Old Testament, lying at the heart of the well-known verse, Micah 6:8: "What does the LORD require of you? To act justly and to love mercy (*chesed*). . . ." It is also the key word in the repeated refrain of Psalm

136: "His love [*chesed*] endures forever." Translators struggle to find words that express the richness of the Hebrew concept. Generally, "covenant loyalty" is taken as its most basic meaning, one that emerges from the conversations of chapter 20, for in 20:14 Jonathan referred to the "*chesed* of the LORD" and in 20:8, David asks for *chesed* on the basis of the "covenant of the LORD" that existed between them.

As for the role of the story in the author's developing narrative, scholars again are inclined to see a couple of features as indications of sources and rough editing. First, why would David and Jonathan innocently discuss the question as to whether David's life actually was at risk, when Saul had already sought to take David's life so many times? Second, in light of his repeated attempts to kill David, how could Saul possibly wonder why David didn't show up at the feast (vss. 26, 27)?

It is possible, however, to argue for a coherent narrative in which the dominant features of each of the characters are either reflected or further developed (see Polzin, *Samuel*, 187-194). Saul's life, for example, has already been shown to be chaotic because of the "evil spirit" from the LORD. And if we treat the narrative thus far as continuous, then we have evidence that Saul's eyesight or his memory or both could be so bad that he couldn't even recognize his own armorbearer in the battle against Goliath. In short, at this point in his life, we should not expect either clear logic or alert memory from Saul.

But what about Jonathan's seeming ignorance of Saul's plots against David (vss. 2, 9)? Jonathan was not insane, just naive. Always innocent, straightforward, and trusting, he consistently put the best possible construction on people's motives, even those of his demented father. In 19:4, for example, he directly confronted Saul about the plots to kill David, extracting an oath from his father: "As surely as the LORD lives, David will not be put to death" (vs. 6). Jonathan would believe such an oath.

Given an erratic Saul and a naive Jonathan, chapter 20 serves to confirm Saul's evil intentions. But even more, it shows that Jonathan had awakened to reality. By the end of the chapter, he, too, knew that David's life was at risk. After Saul's angry words at the feast and his attempt to spear Jonathan (vss. 30-33), Jonathan left the table in "fierce anger," refusing to eat "because he was grieved at his father's shameful treatment of David" (vs 34). Still true to character, Jonathan was less concerned about himself than he was for his father's treatment of David. But Jonathan now knew what David had discovered long ago: David was not safe in Saul's presence.

As for David's own thinking, Polzin suggests "David cannot be serious here—unless, of course, his entire strategy in having Jonathan lie about his absence [20:5-8] is to provoke Saul to an angry outburst that would remove Jonathan's misconceptions, not his own" (Polzin, *Samuel*, 189). Such a conclusion is hardly explicit in 1 Samuel, for the author has yet to interpret David's inner thinking for us. He has told us all about Saul's motives and plans (18:8, 11, 17, 21, 25). Even the thinking of the general population and the army is part of the story (vss. 5, 16, 30). But David's mind remains closed to us. Jonathan, of course, scarcely needs "interpretation," because he has been so consistently open, honest, and straightforward. Earlier, when he didn't think his father's "starvation" oath was wise, he said so (14:29); and when his father questioned him, he admitted what he had done and declared his readiness to face the consequences: "Here I am, I will die" (vs. 43, NRSV).

Jonathan's past record and David's future course come together, then, in a striking way, for it would appear that David manufactures a lie in self-defense and asks Jonathan to tell it to Saul on David's behalf: David will hide in the field, but Jonathan is to tell Saul that David has gone to a family sacrifice in Bethlehem (20:5, 6). Some interpreters, perhaps reluctant to attribute more lies to David than absolutely necessary, suggest that David really did go to Bethlehem. Yet verses 5 and 24 both imply that David spent the whole time hiding in the field. Furthermore, Scripture nowhere describes such a trip to Bethlehem; it simply was the alibi that Jonathan was to pass on to Saul.

In any event, if it is the first of many lies for David, it is the only one attributed to Jonathan, but a lie that was not his. He simply repeated the one put in his mouth by his covenant-bound friend,

David (vss. 28, 29). Because of Saul's violent reaction, Jonathan finally saw the light or, more accurately, the dark. Did David deliberately plan it that way to awaken his friend? We can only guess.

As the chapter closes, we know that David is capable of telling lies, while Jonathan somehow still seems transparent in spite of his willingness to share in David's plan. What does all that mean for the covenant between them? Could their promises to each other be trusted?

■ Getting Into the Word

1 Samuel 21–23

Read 1 Samuel 21–23 through twice for an overview; then respond to the following questions:

1. *Truth.* Add the appropriate incidents from chapters 21 to 23 to the "truth" section in your Samuel notebook. In Matthew 12:1-8, read Jesus' comments on David's dealings with Ahimelech. To what extent did Jesus approve of David's actions and words? Can you justify David's lies to Ahimelech the priest? Write a brief paragraph explaining why you would approve or disapprove of what David did.
2. *House of Eli.* In a Bible dictionary, read about Abiathar and the house of Eli. Do any of the biblical passages say that the Nob massacre fulfilled the prophecy of doom against the house of Eli?
3. *Counsel.* List the instances in chapter 23 in which David directly seeks counsel from the LORD. In light of the predictions of 23:9-13, which were unfulfilled because David heeded the divine warning, how far can we generalize in saying that God's predictions are all conditional? Is there any connection between the kind of "prophecy" revealed in chapter 23 and the doom declared against the house of Eli? Was the punishment against the house of Eli also conditional?

■ Exploring the Word

Massacre at Nob (21:1–22:23)

Chapters 21 and 22 relate one of the most tragic and costly events in David's rise to power, the death of the priests of Nob. Step by step, the author has shown David gaining support. First, Samuel the prophet anointed David (16:1-13) and later sheltered him (19:18-24); then, at the recommendation of Saul's own staff, David joined the royal court; even Saul "liked him very much," appointing him as one of his armorbearers (16:21). After the victory over Goliath, Saul gave David a "high rank in the army," which "pleased all the people, and Saul's officers as well" (18:5); the women were especially pleased, crediting David with tenfold more success than the king himself (vs. 7).

After reporting that the women's singing had aroused Saul's jealousy (vss. 8, 9), Scripture not only describes Saul's various attempts on David's life (both direct and indirect), but also begins to show how the key people in the realm gave their support to David. Jonathan, the crown prince, admired David in connection with the victory over Goliath (vss. 1, 3, 4), then twice intervened directly with Saul, the first time, successfully (19:4-7); the second time, almost disastrously, putting his own life at risk (20:33). During that second intervention, Saul told Jonathan that his friendship with David would cost Jonathan the throne (vs. 31). Jonathan told the whole story to David, assisting in his escape (vss. 35-42), thus becoming the second member of Saul's own family to do so. Earlier, Michal, Saul's daughter and David's wife, had also helped David escape, deliberately deceiving her father as part of the plan (19:11-17).

Samuel, Jonathan, and Michal had all knowingly contributed to David's cause. Now the priests would come on board, too, but quite unwittingly and at great cost, assisted by more lies from David.

When David arrived at Nob, Ahimelech the priest reacted with fear. "Why are you alone?" he asked (21:1). Scripture does not explain the priest's fear. Perhaps he had a premonition of David's true status with Saul. But David assured Ahimelech that he was simply on a secret mission for the king and that his men would meet him at a designated place (vs. 2), both statements apparently false. Reassured, the priest gave David holy bread and the sword of Goliath (vss. 6-9). David then fled to Achish, the Philistine king of Gath (vs. 10).

Jesus' use of this story to support His disciples' right to eat grain on the Sabbath (Matt. 12:3, 4) raises interesting questions, especially since David's visit led to the devastation of Nob, including the death of eighty-five priests (22:18, 19). Jesus' point was that human need takes precedence over ritual requirement, and He referred specifically (and only) to David's eating of the sacred bread. He said nothing about the "truthfulness" of David's words. Indeed, He took them at face value, referring to David's "companions" (Matt. 12:4), even though the Old Testament record does not confirm the presence of such companions until 22:1, 2, when David's family and four hundred men join him at the cave of Adullam.

If Jesus said nothing about David's lies, neither does the author of 1 Samuel, at least not explicitly. And he proceeds to describe David's next lie, one enacted in the presence of Achish. The fact that the Philistines referred to David as "the king of the land" (21:11) may have unsettled the fugitive. In any event, feigning madness, David managed to escape to Adullam (21:13-22:1).

Were David's lies justified? It may be one thing to lie to the demented Saul, but why tell lies to an innocent priest and to a foreign king? However one answers such questions, it is becoming clear that this king in the making can play fast and loose with the truth. As far as the priests were concerned, the results would prove deadly.

Two incidental references are worth noting in the author's lead-up to the slaughter of the priests. First, David took his parents to the king of Moab and entrusted them to his care (22:3, 4). Through Ruth, David himself was part Moabite (Ruth 4:17), though his Moabite blood did not prevent him from meting out brutal treatment to the Moabites after he had become king (see 2 Sam. 8:2). Second, the prophet Gad appears for the first time (22:5). He continued to serve David throughout his reign and left a written record of his work (1 Chron. 29:29). In terms of the author's overall purpose, both references reveal a further buildup of support for Saul's enemy: another prophet had aligned himself with David, and even the king of Moab was willing to give him a hand.

But now the author opens up perhaps the ugliest chapter in the life of Saul—the slaughter of the priests of Nob. When Saul berated his officers for not telling him about Jonathan's covenant with "the son of Jesse," who—Saul wrongly assumed—was seeking the king's life (22:8), only Doeg the Edomite responded to the king's accusation. From the words of Doeg, who had observed David's visit to Nob, we learn that Ahimelech had also "inquired of the Lord" for David (vs. 10), a point that Ahimelech himself confirmed after he had been summoned to stand before the king. Interestingly enough, the priest who had trembled at David's arrival now stood fearless and confident before King Saul. He simply could not believe that Saul would question David's loyalty: "Who of all your servants is as loyal as David, the king's son-in-law, captain of your bodyguard and highly respected in your household?" (vs. 14). And Ahimelech noted that this wasn't the first time he had inquired of the Lord on David's behalf (vs. 15).

Saul was adamant: Ahimelech and his father's family must die. "Turn and kill the priests of the Lord," Saul commanded his guards (vs. 17). But they refused. Only Doeg the Edomite was up to the task, not only killing the priests, but meting out a full *cherem*, "devoting to destruction" the whole town of Nob: "men and women, its children and infants, and its cattle, donkeys and sheep" (vs. 19). In short, Saul was more "conscientious" in fulfilling the requirements of *cherem* against the priests of the Lord than he had been against the Amelekites. The Lord had commanded that *cherem* be directed against Jericho and Amalek, both enemies of Israel (Josh. 6; 1 Sam. 15). Saul had turned it against the spiritual leaders of his own people, a horrifying symbol of the depths to which he had fallen. The only priest to escape the slaughter was Abiathar, the son of Ahimelech. He fled to David, who promised to protect him: "The man who is seeking your life is seeking mine also" (22:23).

The destruction of the priests of Nob and the flight of Abiathar broke Saul's last formal tie with the Lord. Prophets, family, and now the priests had given their support to David. Even Saul's own guards now felt they could selectively flaunt the orders of their chief. In short, virtually all the people of note within Israel were supporting and protecting David.

The Chase Continues (23:1-29)

Chapter 23 shows that Saul could still muster support among the masses in his struggle against David. The people of Keilah were ready to hand David over to Saul, even though David was the one who had delivered them from the Philistines (vss. 5, 12). The Ziphites, too, offered to cooperate with Saul against David (vss. 19, 20). But these mere human agents couldn't compete with the help available to David. Chapter 23 makes it clear that the LORD Himself was on David's side. Relying for the moment on the LORD instead of on lies, David successfully queried the LORD four times in this chapter. The first two responses helped him defeat the Philistines (vss. 2, 4); the last two helped him escape from Saul (vss. 9-12).

That picture of David's successful communication with the LORD contrasts sharply with Saul's past and future—his failed attempt in 14:37, when Jonathan had unwittingly transgressed his father's oath, and his "successful" but macabre communication through the woman of Endor in chapter 28. In short, Saul could rely only on mere human sources of knowledge, while David was in touch with the LORD.

The various means used by the LORD in chapter 23 to guide and deliver David also shed light on the nature of prophecy and providence. Two of the "predictions" in response to David's inquiries were clearly conditional. When David asked if Saul would seek to capture him in the city of Keilah and if the people of Keilah would hand him over, the divine response was "yes" in both cases (vss. 11, 12). As a result, David and his men left the city, making the predictions irrelevant. Finally, just as the LORD used David to deliver Keilah from the Philistines (vs. 5), so He used the Philistines to deliver David from the hand of Saul, for just as Saul and his men were closing in on David (vs. 26), a messenger arrived with news of a Philistine attack. Saul then broke off his pursuit to fulfill his royal duties, defending Israel against the Philistines. That close call earned a special name for the place, translated in the NIV as "rock of parting" (vs. 28), a symbol of God's providential intervention on David's behalf.

Also in chapter 23, Jonathan appears once more before his untimely death. "Don't be afraid," he told David when they met in the Desert of Ziph. "My father Saul will not lay a hand on you. You will be king over Israel, and I will be second to you. Even my father Saul knows this" (vs. 17). Jonathan was too optimistic about his own future. But his name has gone down in history as the symbol of a friend who is faithful, honest, and true, even unto death. David needed a friend like that, especially after he became king. Too bad Jonathan was gone.

David and Saul—A Summary

In 1 Samuel 16 to 23, the author sketches a vivid picture of a gifted David in conflict with a demented Saul. At the command of the LORD, the prophet Samuel shifts his loyalties, anointing David to be king in Saul's place. At that point, two sentences set the stage for all that follows:

> From that day on the Spirit of the LORD came upon David in power (16:13).
> Now the Spirit of the LORD had departed from Saul, and an evil spirit from the Lord tormented him" (vs 14).

Under the guidance of the Spirit, David enters the royal household, winning everyone's heart, including Saul's (vss. 14-23). The stunning victory over Goliath catapults David into national fame at the same time that it excites the king's envy. By the time chapter 23 closes, Saul has twice flung his spear at David and once at his own son, Jonathan. And he has commanded the destruction of all the LORD's priests.

But Saul's desperation simply works against him. David's popularity with the crowds keeps growing, and step by step, he gains the support of significant people—the prophet Samuel; the king's son, Jonathan; the king's daughter, Michal; and Abiathar the priest, the lone survivor of the massacre at Nob. But most importantly, the LORD is with David. In chapter 23, when David calls, the LORD answers. He even protects David by sending the Philistines to distract King Saul from pursuing the young fugitive.

The final chapters in Saul's demise are yet to come, and David continues to be very much a part of the picture. But in several ways, David has reached a peak in chapter 23. Except for the hostility of Saul, everything seems to be going his way. And that is why we must remind ourselves that we are hearing not the story of a great success, but of a great failure. If we look beyond the external glory, the danger signs are already there. This gifted and brilliant young man begins to reveal a streak of ruthless expediency. He will tell lies, perhaps even justifiably. But lies are still lies, and the results can be deadly. In short, the traces of heart disease are already there in the man after God's own heart.

■ Applying the Word

1 Samuel 18–23

1. *Covenant.* **What covenants have I made that I should honor forever? Do I know someone with whom God is calling me to make or renew such a covenant? What should I do to bring about such a covenant?**
2. *Anger.* **To what extent does overwhelming anger have the same effect on people as an "evil spirit from the LORD"? Are they the same? Under what circumstances am I tempted to erupt in such anger?**
3. *Guidance.* **Does God expect me to ask Him directly for guidance, as David did in chapter 23? Why or why not? Does the Bible provide me with guidance that is at all similar to such direct instruction? When no priest or prophet is around, how do I know the LORD's will for me today?**
4. *When Enemies are Friends.* **Have there been occasions when**

the LORD has sent the Philistines to distract my enemies in the same way that He sent them to distract Saul from pursuing David? How can I know God has been involved, rather than mere happenstance?

■ Researching the Word

1. *Truth.* Starting with the items you have included in the "truth" section of your Samuel notebook, study how "truth telling" in general relates to God's command in the Decalogue against bearing false witness. Use a concordance to check out the key words, especially those translated as "false witness" in the English translations. When you have completed the word-study, return to the two major incidents in 1 Samuel 16 to 23, God's command to Samuel to mislead Saul (16:1-3) and David's false statements to Ahimelech the priest at Nob (21:1-9). How would you evaluate the rightness or wrongness of both incidents? Does the outcome in each instance make a difference in your answer? In what way?
2. *Prophecy.* If you have already done a word study of *prophecy* and *prophesy* in the Old Testament, do the same for the New Testament, following up with articles in a good Bible dictionary. When you compare the role of a prophet in Old and New Testament times, what differences do you see? How does that inform our expectations of prophecy in our day?

■ Further Study of the Word

1. For general comment on the struggle between David and Saul, see E. G. White, *Patriarchs and Prophets*, 649-661.
2. For a survey article on prophets and prophecy in both Testaments, see J. B. Payne, "Prophecy, Prophets," in *New Bible Dictionary*, 975-986.
3. Classic studies of *chesed* ("kindness," "unfailing kindness,"

"loving kindness") in the Old Testament include "The Covenant-Love of God," by N. H. Snaith, in *The Distinctive Ideas of the Old Testament*, 94-130, and *Chesed in the Bible*, by N. Glueck.

CHAPTER SEVEN

When Both Men
Know the Score

1 Samuel 24–2 Samuel 1

High drama and close calls mark the last days of Saul's kingship. Twice the hunted had the hunter in his grasp, once by accident and once by design. But when David confronted him with the evidence, Saul declared David to be in the right and promised to call off the chase. Saul believed his own words and returned home; David kept on the move (24:22; 26:25). Indeed, after the last incident, he was so fearful of Saul's intentions that he escaped to the Philistines, never to see Saul again.

The LORD's hand is seen to be powerful in several incidents in these chapters. On the two occasions when he easily could have killed Saul, David said it was the LORD who had delivered Saul into his hand (24:10; 26:23). Was it a test of David's integrity? The LORD also worked through Abigail to protect David from himself when he was ready to obliterate the house of Nabal. Both Abigail and David testified that the LORD had intervened to restrain him (25:26, 34). And Scripture says that it was the LORD who finally struck the fatal blow to Nabal (vs. 38).

The author also tells us that the LORD protected David by putting Saul and his men "into a deep sleep" when David and Abishai crept into camp and took Saul's spear and water jug (26:12). And when the Amalekites plundered Ziklag, David "found strength in the LORD his God" (30:6) and said that recovering the spoil and the captives was the LORD's doing (vs. 23).

But if the LORD is powerfully present in certain incidents, He is notably absent from others. After his first close call with David, Saul could still talk about the LORD, expressing the wish that the LORD would reward David's integrity (24:19) and asking David to swear "by the LORD" not to destroy Saul's family (vs. 21). After their second encounter, however, while David takes the name of the LORD on his lips ten times, Saul doesn't use it even once (26:16-24). Yet later he still swears "by the LORD" not to harm the woman of Endor (28:10), even though the LORD's refusal to respond by "dreams or Urim or prophets" (vs. 6) was the very reason Saul had sought out the medium in the first place (vs. 7). Finally, the "departed" Samuel, reaffirming Saul's doom, spoke the LORD's name seven times, declaring that the LORD would deliver Saul and the army of Israel into the hands of the Philistines.

However, in the actual descriptions of the final battle, Saul's death, and David's lament (1 Samuel 31 and 2 Samuel 1), the LORD's role in the disaster is never mentioned. Perhaps that is understandable, given the statement back in 16:14 that the Spirit of the LORD had departed from Saul. But is there a connection with the notable absence of any reference to the hand of the LORD in chapters 27 and 29, the chapters describing David's escape to the Philistines and his thoroughly deceptive ways of dealing with Achish his host? Achish, quite unaware of David's deceitfulness, actually affirms David's integrity in the name of the LORD: "As surely as the LORD lives, you have been reliable" (29:6). If only Achish knew! And we are left to ponder what David might have done had he actually gone into battle with the Philistines against Saul: Turn on his gracious host? Fight against his own people?

In what might seem providential, the other Philistine commanders intervened, refusing to allow David to accompany them. But our author says nothing about the hand of the LORD in the matter. Was that intentional? Perhaps. David, the man after God's own heart, was on the rise. But when he decided to follow the inclinations of his own evil heart instead of walking in the ways of the LORD, the implications were unsettling.

And for the first readers of 1 Samuel, those implications would be a painful reminder both of Israel's past and her present, for when the Philistines killed the LORD's anointed in battle, they again controlled the land of Israel, just as they had once before after they had killed the anointed priests, Hophni and Phinehas, and captured the ark. In short, the end of 1 Samuel is a return to the beginning. Ironically, in both instances, the Philistines assembled at Aphek (4:1; 29:1). This time, however, it wasn't the ark that was in exile, but David, the new "anointed one" of the LORD, *an exile in a city provided by Achish, his Philistine master.*

In that earlier hour of darkness, the prophet Samuel had been a figure *of hope. He "cried out to the* LORD *on Israel's behalf, and the* LORD *answered him" (7:9). In the days that followed, "the Philistines were subdued and did not invade Israelite territory again. Throughout Samuel's lifetime, the hand of the* LORD *was against the Philistines" (vs. 13).*

But then the people had asked for a king, and the LORD *granted their request, even declaring that Saul would "deliver my people from the hand of the Philistines" (9:16).*

Now both Samuel and Saul were dead. The Philistines again controlled *the land. What kind of hope was represented by the handsome and talented son of Jesse? The readers of 1 Samuel would be keenly aware of the fact that their condition again mirrored those of 1 Samuel 4 and 31. A foreign power controlled the land. Many, including their king, were in exile. Their temple was gone. So was the ark. As we read the story of David's rise and fall, it will help us understand if we remember what the first readers knew and what they remembered. The downfall of the house of Eli foreshadowed the disaster that struck Saul. And King Saul's demise foreshadowed the failure of David's house and the failure of kingship in Israel. For all the glory that was David's and Solomon's, the end of the monarchy put quite a different light on what had gone before.*

■ Getting Into the Word

1 Samuel 24–26

After reading through 1 Samuel 24 to 2 Samuel 1 for an overview, return to chapters 24 to 26 and read them through once more, paying attention to the following study suggestions:

1. *Persuasive Peers.* List the passages in which peers or associates attempt to convince others to change their minds. Based on what you have seen in 1 Samuel 24 to 26, write a brief paragraph on the effect that associates, both good or bad, can have on our decisions.

2. *Close Calls.* Study David's "close calls" in chapters 24 and 26, listing the similarities and the differences between them. Can you identify a distinct lesson to be learned in each chapter? What is the lesson in each case?

3. *Integrity.* List the passages in which David is shown to be blessed with extraordinary integrity. How does he understand his relationship with the LORD in those instances?

4. *Geography.* By referring to the maps and articles in a Bible dictionary, plot the location of each of the major incidents in chapters 24 to 26. How does geography help you understand the flow of the story?

5. *Normal.* List the passages in these chapters in which Saul seems to be "normal." Does Scripture suggest that he is only occasionally under the influence of an "evil" spirit? Explain your answer.

■ Exploring the Word

Close Calls

Chapter 23 concluded with a close call for David. Just as Saul and his troops were "closing in on David and his men to capture them" (vs. 26), a Philistine raid summoned Saul back to his royal duties. But close calls continue to be a dominant feature in the last cluster of incidents leading up to Saul's death. Twice the LORD delivered Saul into David's hand. Though obviously close calls for Saul, these same incidents were close calls of another kind for David as his men urged him to kill the LORD's anointed. But David remained firm in his convictions and passed the test.

Sandwiched between those two incidents, however, is another close call, one that required the LORD's special intervention to save David from himself. He was powerfully close to taking vengeance with his own hands when the LORD sent the wise and beautiful Abigail to prevent him. David unashamedly gave thanks: "Praise be to the LORD, the God of Israel, who has sent you today to meet me" (25:32).

David will experience yet one more close call before Saul dies, nearly going into battle against his own people and the LORD's anointed. Though the author does not reveal David's intentions, the Philistine commanders intervened, sparing us the agony of having to work through the dilemma with him (29:3-11).

The Cave (24:1-22)

In chapter 24, Saul returned to the chase, learning of David's whereabouts from an unnamed informant. Almost immediately the author brings the incident to a climax. Saul had gone into a cave "to relieve himself" (24:3, NRSV; Hebrew, "to cover his feet"), the very cave in which David and his men were hiding. Citing an otherwise unknown quotation from the LORD ("I will give your enemy into your hands for you to deal with as you wish" [24:4]), David's men urged him to kill Saul. David refused, but did stealthily cut off a portion of Saul's robe. Scripture does not explain how he escaped detection. Perhaps Saul fell asleep.

Why did David's conscience smite him for cutting off a corner of Saul's robe? Possibly because the robe symbolized Saul's royal authority (see Polzin, *Samuel*, 209). Just as tearing the "skirt" of Samuel's robe (15:27, KJV) was interpreted by Samuel as the LORD's tearing the kingdom from Saul, so here, the cutting of the "skirt" (24:4, 5, 11, KJV) of Saul's robe may have suggested to David an inappropriate grasping of royal power. The LORD had promised him the kingdom. But David must wait for the LORD to deliver it to him. He could not seize the kingdom for himself.

The dialogue between Saul and David is laden with emotion on both sides. David called Saul "my father" (vs. 11) and bowed before the king with his face to the ground (vs. 8). The Hebrew verb is the same one used for an act of worship. David presented the piece of Saul's robe as evidence that he was not guilty of "wrongdoing or rebellion" (vs. 11). He appealed to the LORD to judge him innocent by delivering him from Saul's hand (vs. 15).

The biblical account shows that Saul, also, was deeply moved. And nothing in the narrative suggests that his emotions were any-thing but genuine. He addressed David as "my son" and "wept aloud" (vs. 16). He admitted that David was in the right and even declared that he knew David would be king (vs. 20). Finally, he had a request for David: "Swear to me by the LORD that you will not cut off my descendants or wipe out my name from my father's family" (vs. 21).

Scripture says that "David gave his oath to Saul." But after noting that Saul returned home, the author's last word in the chapter is that "David and his men went up to the stronghold" (vs. 22). David did not believe Saul was trustworthy. He was right.

Good Woman, Bad Man (25:1-44)

Chapter 25 opens with a brief notice of the death of Samuel. All Israel assembled, mourned, and buried him at his home in Ramah (vs. 1). Essentially the same note is repeated in 28:3 in the story of the woman of Endor. Samuel was gone, and there was no mediator between the two men he had anointed to be king over Israel. But then, except for the incident in 19:18-24 in which Samuel briefly sheltered David, Scripture records no effort on his part to keep Saul from pursuing David.

With David now in a full-fledged Robin Hood mode, our author tells the story of Nabal and Abigail, a story with a double message: the beautiful Abigail representing the LORD's gracious intervention on David's behalf; the surly Nabal symbolizing the fate of a foolish and demented Saul.

If the initial paragraphs imply that David was taking inappropriate advantage of Nabal by offering Mafia-like protection to the wealthy landowner, the story later corrects the impression. One of Nabal's own workers gave an unflinching testimonial, arguing that David deserved to be rewarded (vss. 14-17). Judged by the provisions eventually provided by Abigail, David's claim seems modest for a crew of six hundred men: two hundred loaves of bread, two skins of wine, five dressed sheep, five bushels of roasted grain (see NIV note), a hundred cakes of raisins, and two hundred cakes of pressed figs (vs. 18). But if the gift was modest, David still accepted it as gladly as he did Abigail's gracious intervention.

In contrast with the previous incident, in which David stoutly maintained his own integrity even in the face of urgent pleading by his own men, here, he is vulnerable. His passions are aroused; he is in danger of burdening his conscience and compromising his future usefulness as king, as Abigail will so ably remind him (vs. 31). David's impulse was to strike out in revenge because Nabal had paid him back "evil for good" (vs. 21). He vowed to obliterate all the males connected with Nabal.

That "natural" impulse contrasts sharply with the ideal articulated by Abigail and then confirmed by David. The story shows that Jesus' ethic in the Sermon on the Mount was not a New Testament novelty. Both David and Abigail recognized what the LORD required. And David was grateful that the LORD had sent Abigail to keep him from sin (vss. 33, 34). Ironically, after David became king, an attractive woman would lead him into sin; here, the LORD sent a beautiful woman to keep him from sin.

If David and Abigail represent God's work through and for human beings, Nabal illustrates all the opposite traits. In subtle ways, the author has portrayed him as a stand-in for Saul. Polzin notes that like Saul in chapter 24, Nabal in chapter 25 becomes an object of mercy: "David chooses not to kill the man who has returned evil for good" (Polzin, *Samuel*, 210, 211). Abigail also establishes the link between Nabal and Saul when she prays: "Now let your enemies and those who seek to do evil to my lord be like Nabal" (25:26, NRSV). Throughout the narrative, Saul is the one seeking to do evil to David. In chapter 24, David calls Saul "my father" (vs. 11), Saul calls him "my son" (vs. 16). Similarly, in 25:8 David presents himself to Nabal as a son. Even Nabal's response to David's request recalls Saul's words: "Who is this David? Who is this son of Jesse?" asks Nabal (25:10), echoing Saul's questions about the "stripling" on the battlefield with Goliath (17:56-58). And Nabal was dangerously close to the truth when he exclaimed, "Many servants are breaking away from their masters these days" (25:10).

Nabal's end came at the LORD's initiative, not David's (vs. 38). So it would be for King Saul too. In the very next chapter, when faced with another opportunity (temptation?) to kill Saul, David spoke an uncanny truth applying to both Nabal and Saul: "The LORD himself will strike him; either his time will come and he will die, or he will go into battle and perish" (26:10).

For minds attuned to Jesus' attitude toward one's enemies, David's reaction to Nabal's death is an uncomfortable one: "Praise be to the LORD, who has upheld my cause against Nabal for treating me with contempt" (25:39). At a more descriptive level, however, Nabal's fate vividly illustrates the Old Testament view of retribution. Boomerang-like, sin comes back on the head of the sinner. David said that the LORD had "brought Nabal's wrongdoing down on his own head" (vs. 39).

The concluding words of chapter 25 are alive with political over-tones. After Nabal's passing, David asked Abigail to become his wife. Though the author does not say so explicitly, David's marriage to the wealthy widow with Calebite ties (vs. 3) would strengthen his power base in Judah. His marriage to Ahinoam of Jezreel in Judah (vs. 43; compare Josh. 15:56) served the same function. Scholars generally agree that this Ahinoam could not have been Saul's wife by the same name (14:50). It would have been unthinkable for David to live with the king's wife while Saul was still alive.

But Saul was playing politics with wives too. He weakened David's claim to royal authority by giving David's wife, Saul's daughter Michal, to another man, Paltiel (25:44). The political implications of Saul's action become clearer when David later demands Michal's return as a precondition for any settlement with the house of Saul. In 2 Samuel 3:13-16, we glimpse the anguish caused by David's request.

Spear and Jug (26:1-25)

The spear-and-jug incident in chapter 26 again brings David to a potentially deadly contact with Saul. A case can be made for identi-fying this incident as an expansion of the one in 23:19. In both in-stances, the Ziphites report David's whereabouts to Saul at Gibeah and promise to deliver him into Saul's hand. Both passages locate David on the hill of Hakilah in the vicinity of Jeshimon (23:19; 26:1, 3). But regardless of how one deals with the chronology, this last recorded contact between Saul and David serves to reveal David's faithful commitment to preserving the life of the LORD's anointed as well as showing the LORD's continued action on David's behalf.

The incident reveals something of a daredevil streak in David. What ordinary mortal would invade the enemy's camp just to take the king's spear and water jug? But that's what David did, taking with him Abishai, one of the notorious sons of Zeruiah (David's sister) who would make life so tumultuous once David became king.

As in the similar incident in the cave of En Gedi (24:1-7), David had to battle a powerful human impulse to kill Saul. Here, the case is made by his companion Abishai. But, as before, David resisted. And the LORD Himself stepped in to protect the daredevil by putting Saul and his men into a "deep sleep" (26:12). When safely across the valley, David rebuked Abner, Saul's bodyguard, but not quite as pointedly as some English translations might suggest, for the *you* in 26:16 is in the plural, thus constituting a rebuke of the entire camp for their failure to guard the LORD's anointed. The NIV gets the plural effect by adding *your men* to the *you*. The author does not explain how Abner and his men could be culpable if the LORD Himself had put them all into a deep sleep.

The dialogue between David and Saul in chapter 26 is not quite so poignant as it is in chapter 24. Saul's emotions were under control even as he admitted his wrongdoing and invited David to return home. His concluding words pronounced a blessing on David: "May you be blessed, my son David; you will do great things and surely triumph" (vs. 25).

David did not accept Saul's invitation to return home. Indeed, he was now so frightened of Saul that he fled to Gath in the land of the Philistines for the express purpose of escaping Saul's net (27:1). According to 27:4, his strategy worked, for Saul gave up the search when he heard that David was in Gath.

But if the dialogue in chapter 26 between David and Saul lacks emotional intensity, it was and is important theologically, for it illustrates once again the concept of a national deity. In the Decalogue, the LORD declared that Israel was to have no other gods before Him (Exod. 20:3; Deut. 5:7). The other "gods" had been assigned to the other nations (Deut. 29:26; 32:8, 9; see excursus in chapter 2: "The LORD and the Gods"). Though it would one day be clear to all Israel that the LORD was God of all gods, here, David notes that to be driven from the LORD's land would be understood as saying, "Go, serve other gods" (26:19). He pleads with Saul not to let his blood "fall to the ground far from the presence of the LORD" (vs. 20). As it turned out, David decided to risk leaving the LORD's land anyway, Saul's invitation to return notwithstanding.

■ Getting Into the Word

1 Samuel 27–2 Samuel 1

Read 1 Samuel 27 to 2 Samuel 1, paying particular attention to the following study suggestions:

1. *David and the Philistines.* **Make a list of all those passages in which David has active contact with the Philistines. In a second column, briefly describe the nature of the contact, and evaluate the quality of his relationship with the Philistines. Finally, write a paragraph evaluating David's behavior towards Achish, noting in particular what judgments the author makes about David's relationship with the Philistines.**
2. *Dead People.* **As you read through chapter 28, the story of the woman of Endor, make a list of those features of the story that do not seem to mesh with your understanding of a person's state after death. Then work back through the story again with your list in hand, noting anything in the narrative that might point to a solution. Summarize your findings in a paragraph or two.**
3. *Providence.* **Read through the chapters for the purpose of identifying those places where the author identifies the LORD's active part in events. Make a list of these passages with brief descriptions; then review the list to see if the author's understanding of "providence" is the same as yours. Describe your conclusions in a paragraph or two.**

4. *Geography*. Using the maps in your Bible or a Bible dictionary, locate the places mentioned in these chapters. Does geography help or hinder you in understanding these stories? How?

5. *Amalekites*. Compare David's handling of the Amalekites in chapter 30 with Saul's handling of the same people in chapter 15. List the similarities and the differences. In a paragraph or two, briefly describe your feelings toward both Saul and David at this point (anger, pity, admiration, indifference, surprise, horror).

■ Exploring the Word

Robin Hood Visits Gath (27:1-12)

David's sojourn among the Philistines is described in chapters 27, 29 and 30. Saul's night visit to the woman of Endor interrupts the narrative but highlights the implications of David's departure at the very time that Saul's rule was coming to an end.

Scripture gives no indication that David's flight to Gath was approved by the LORD. David did not ask; the LORD did not answer or intervene to dissuade him from his decision. The author's candid descriptions of David's double-dealing may reveal why.

David took a crowd with him to Gath: his own two wives along with six hundred men and their families. The size of David's group no doubt strengthened his argument for a separate city in which to live. In any event, Achish, king of Gath, gave him Ziklag to the south, a city that "has belonged to the kings of Judah ever since," the author tells us (27:6).

While in Ziklag, David lived like a robber baron, attacking and plundering settlements at will. He "wisely" left no one alive to tell tales, for he was telling quite a different story to Achish, seeking to convince his Philistine master that he was raiding cities in his own land of Judah. The concluding words of chapter 27 throb with irony: "Achish trusted David and said to himself, 'He has become so odious to his people, the Israelites, that he will be my servant forever' " (vs. 12). A morally sensitive reader might conclude otherwise about who had become odious to whom! But the author does not moralize. He simply describes what David did and concludes with Achish's ironic testimony to a "trustworthy" David.

"Samuel" for the Last Time (28:1-25)

David's position remains ambiguous as the author moves into the story of Saul's visit to the woman of Endor. In the initial lines of chapter 28, a description of the Philistine preparations for war against Israel, Achish makes his point bluntly to David: "You must understand that you and your men will accompany me in the army" (vs. 1).

"You will see for yourself what your servant can do," is David's carefully worded response (vs. 2).

"Bodyguard for life," declares Achish, and David is on a collision course with his own people and the LORD's anointed.

The author sets the stage for the seance at Endor by again referring briefly to the death of Samuel (compare 25:1). He also notes that "Saul had expelled the mediums and spiritists from the land" (28:3). The next few lines vividly depict a lonely, terror-stricken Saul, facing the Philistines at Shunem while his own army assembled at Gilboa: "When Saul saw the Philistine army, he was afraid; terror filled his heart. He inquired of the LORD, but the LORD did not answer him by dreams or Urim or prophets" (28:5, 6). Saul was alone, terribly alone, except for his attendants.

So he asked his attendants to locate a medium for him. His previous efforts to eliminate the mediums apparently were less than thorough, for his men knew where to find one. Taking two men with him, he ventured out into the night (vs. 8). From the later perspective of 1 Chronicles, Saul's visit to the medium was one of his most heinous sins. Summarizing the causes for Saul's rejection, 1 Chronicles 10:13, 14 says that "he was unfaithful to the LORD; he did not keep the word of the LORD and even consulted a medium for guidance, and did not inquire of the LORD." Note the contrast with 1 Samuel 28:6, which says that Saul did, in fact, inquire of the LORD but that the LORD "did not answer him."

After some uneasy initial negotiations in which Saul ironically swore "by the Lord" not to harm the woman (vs. 10), he asked for Samuel. But when the woman saw the old prophet, she let out a full-throated scream, apparently recognizing for the first time that her visitor was, in fact, King Saul (vs. 12).

"Don't be afraid," he said. "What do you see?" (vs. 13).

" *'Elohim,*" was her response, the only time in the Old Testament the word is used to refer to the departed (McCarter, *I Samuel*, 421). The KJV translation ("gods ascending out of the earth") reflects the fact that a plural participle is used as the verb here. *'Elohim*, which can refer to God, gods, angels, or other supernatural beings, is plural in form but can be used in the singular or the plural sense. Here, the initial reference in 28:13 is plural but immediately shifts to the singular in verse 14 as Saul asks about his (or its) appearance.

The story focuses, however, not on Samuel's appearance, but on his message. And it is mostly a repeat, just a bit sharper and more final, for it includes a specific prediction of Saul's death and the defeat of the Israelite army. And through it all, Samuel speaks in the name of the Lord, mentioning His name seven times (vss. 15-19).

Saul fell to the ground, terrorized and without strength (vs. 20). Only after forceful words from the woman and his two companions did he agree to eat the woman's food. The account concludes with a simple, unadorned comment, "That same night they got up and left" (vs. 25).

Excursus: Realm of the Gods, Realm of the Dead

The story of Samuel's appearance at the request of the Endor medium is an amazing one. It is the only passage in the Old Testament that *seems* to bring together the realm of the dead and the realm of the gods. The story is troublesome for both sides of the traditional debate over the nature of the human soul. On the one hand, the fact that the *'elohim* appeared in a form recognizable as Samuel makes the passage difficult to use in support of the immortality of the soul, since the soul is supposed to escape the strictures of the body at death. On the other hand, it is also an uncomfortable passage for those who believe in the holistic concept of soul sleep (conditional immortality).

To put the story in perspective, it is important to grasp the Old Testament understanding of the realm of the dead and the realm of the gods. In spite of the sharp distinction between the human and the superhuman realms in the Old Testament, it was still the case that the superhuman (the *'elohim*) could appear in human form. The other way around, however, was not possible. Humankind could not make the transition to the realm of the *'elohim*—unless, of course, 1 Samuel 28 is seen as an exception. Intertestamental literature, to be sure, taking Genesis 6:1-4 as the point of departure, told tales of the "sons of the *'elohim*" who cohabited with earthly women, with evil results. But even then, the initiative lay with "the sons of the *'elohim.*"

As for 1 Samuel 28, two alternatives are possible: (1) the personification of Samuel by an *'elohim* at the command of the LORD; (2) the return of a dead person from *she'ol* to the world of the living. A survey of the key features of the "realm of the gods" and the "realm of the dead" will suggest that the first alternative is more likely.

A. Supernatural Beings in the Old Testament

1. *'Elohim and other supernatural beings existed in a category apart from humankind.* The Old Testament affirms the existence of a larger world of supernatural beings. While idols were merely metal, sticks, and stones, subject to mockery and scorn by the prophets (Isa. 44:6-20), the *'elohim* (or "sons of the *'elohim*") were very much part of the Old Testament world, supernatural beings under the LORD's supervision. Psalm 82 identifies the two classes of *'elohim*: (1) the singular—the one God in a category by Himself; (2) the plural—good and evil gods subject to God. New Testament cosmology would speak of angels—or principalities and powers—and include Satan among them.

2. *The LORD Himself could appear in visible form.* While the LORD forbade Israel to make likenesses of anything in heaven or on earth, He Himself appeared both visibly and tangibly. In Genesis 18:1, the

LORD was one of three men before Abraham. In Genesis 18:16-33 Abraham argued with the LORD over the fate of Sodom and Gomorrah. And after his night of wrestling, Jacob noted with awe that he had seen God (*'elohim*) face to face, "and yet my life was spared" (Gen. 32:30). On a more cautious note, the LORD refused to show Moses His face, "for no one may see me and live" (Exod. 33:20).

  3. *The angel of the LORD could appear on behalf of the LORD.* Though the LORD Himself sometimes appears to humankind, He also sends "the angel of the LORD" as His stand in, finding Hagar in the desert (Gen. 16:7), confronting Balaam's ass (Num. 22:22-31), and communicating with Elijah (2 Kings 1:3).

  In sum, the LORD was quite capable of sending an *'elohim* in the form of Samuel to serve as His mouthpiece. The fact that "Samuel" spoke in the LORD's name would argue in favor of this interpretation. One scholar has actually said that the narrative in 1 Samuel 28 suggests that Samuel appeared independently of the woman's magical machinations: "Samuel beats the woman to it. He does not allow himself to be conjured up: he appears. He does not come as a dead ghost who is forced to give up his knowledge (as if ghosts have that at their disposal), but he comes as a prophet of the same living God whom Saul has just called as witness to his oath (v. 10)" (Beuken, 8).

B. The Realm of the Dead

  In some ways, the realm of the dead in the Old Testament is a "lively" place, not just one where souls sleep. But if it was in some sense "lively"—just how lively is discussed below—it was still far removed from the Greek idea of the immortal soul. In addition to the normal realm of the dead, however, some kind of spirit world also seems to have been implied by the powerful prohibitions against the practice of magic and necromancy in Israel. Christians would identify such a spirit world with the realm of Satan and his evil angels and would have no difficulty in agreeing with the Old Testament that such a realm is totally off limits to God's people.

  The LORD or His messenger could appear to human beings, and He could respond to Israel's inquiries through "dreams or Urim or prophets" (1 Sam. 28:6). But Mosaic law prohibited contact with "mediums" or "spiritists" (Lev. 19:31; 20:6)—prohibitions well understood by both Saul and the woman of Endor. Saul's known enforcement of them (28:3) was the reason for the woman's fright when she recognized her visitor (vs. 12).

Scholars generally explain this rigorous prohibition against mediums and magic in both theological and practical terms. If the LORD was all-powerful and all-knowing, why would Israel want to manipulate Him? In polytheistic religions, the deities were notoriously unreliable, especially the evil ones, hence the preoccupation with magic and incantation. But Israel's consistent and just God needed no such manipulation.

However one might understand a (demonic) "spirit world" of the Old Testament (a world that was off-limits in any event), the Old Testament still reveals a remarkably clear and consistent picture of the realm of the dead, characterized by the following elements:

1. The Place: She'ol. *She'ol* is the realm of the dead; it is the underworld or the grave. The KJV, according to the summary in Young's *Analytical Concordance*, translates it as "grave" thirty-one times, "hell" thirty-one times, and "pit" three times. The NIV, according to Goodrick and Kohlenberger's *Exhaustive Concordance*, translates it as "grave" fifty-five times, "death" six times, "depth" twice, "depths of the grave" twice, and "realm of the dead" once. The Old Testament knows nothing of a "hot" *she'ol* (or hell) or of any distinctions between good and evil inhabitants. Everyone goes to the same place and in the same condition.

2. The Inhabitants: Dead People, the (Repha'im). The KJV translates *rephaim* as "dead" seven times and as "deceased" once. The NIV translates it "dead" five times, but renders it misleadingly and more freely in three other instances: "departed spirits," "spirits of the dead," and "spirits of the departed." A more descriptive translation is simply "shades," a usage adopted by the NRSV: dead people are merely "shadows" of their former selves.

The NRSV use of "shades" is worth noting: Proverbs 2:18, for example, says of the "loose woman" that "her way leads down to death, and her paths to the shades [*repha'im*]." Note the parallelism of death and shades. Isaiah 14:9, describing the king of Babylon's arrival in the underworld, brings *she'ol* and *repha'im* together: "Sheol beneath is stirred up to meet you when you come; it rouses the shades to greet you."

3. Condition of the Repha'im: Weak. The more sweeping Old Testament passages on the human condition in death declare the dead to be totally separate from all normal earthly activity. One of the clearest examples is Ecclesiastes 9:5, 6: "The dead know nothing," and "their love, their hate and their jealousy have long since vanished; never again will they have a part in anything that happens under the sun." Similarly, Psalm 146:4 (NRSV) states that when the "breath" departs from mortals, "on that very day their plans perish."

But in other passages, we hear something like the pain of tired joints and the rattle of bones among the shades, perhaps a usage that is largely poetic. Job 14:21, 22, for example, though not using the term *repha'im*, describes the condition of a man who has gone to *she'ol*: "If his sons are honored, he does not know it. . . . He feels but the pain of his own body and mourns only for himself." In Isaiah 14, the description of the king of Babylon's arrival in *she'ol* is even more vivid. The fact that the same passage has nature singing for joy and the cedars of Lebanon sighing in relief (vss.7, 8), should allow us to grant the prophet poetic license as he likewise animates *she'ol*, the same *she'ol* that roused the "dead" to greet the king: "It raises from their thrones all who were kings of the nations. All of them will speak and say to you: 'You too have become as weak as we! You have become like us! Your pomp is brought down to Sheol, and the sound of your harps; maggots are the bed beneath you, and worms are your covering' " (vss. 9-11, NRSV).

But such "shades" never escape from *she'ol* to the legitimate world of living people. Thus in 1 Samuel 28, the figure of Samuel was not one of the *repha'im* (shades) but a supernatural being, one of the *'elohim* (gods). Though Saul's attempt to communicate with a *she'ol*-bound Samuel broke all the rules, the LORD used the form of Samuel to send him a message anyway. And even within that message we can glimpse something of the Old Testament view of the realm of the dead, for Samuel says, "Tomorrow you and your sons will be with me" (vs. 19).

In KJV language, one could say that Saul was destined for "hell." But in the Old Testament, so was everyone else, for "hell" was simply *she'ol* or the grave, everyone's destiny regardless of their relationship with God.

Given a basic understanding of the realm of the dead (*she'ol* and *repha'im*) and the realm of the gods (*'elohim*) in the Old Testament, other key words such as *nephesh* ("soul," "life," "person") and *ruach* ("wind," "spirit," "life") can fill out the picture. As for the resurrection hope in the Old Testament, though perfectly clear in Daniel 12:1-2, it is not well developed elsewhere. Yet the idea of the resurrection of the body meshes naturally with the Old Testament understanding of the realm of the dead and becomes very clear in the New Testament. By contrast, the idea of an immortal soul that escapes the body for heaven or hell is entirely foreign to Old Testament thinking.

Fighting on All Fronts (29:1–30:31)

Immediately following the story of Saul's visit to the woman of Endor, the author takes us to the Philistine camp as it prepared to do battle against Israel (29:1). The Philistine commanders reacted with alarm when they saw David and his men march by. Achish frankly admitted that David had been one of Saul's officers but claimed that he had proven his loyalty to Achish.

Such logic, however, simply angered the other Philistine commanders. In the end, Achish had to tell David to go back home, but not before David had crafted another ambiguous masterpiece for Achish: "Why can't I go and fight against the enemies of my lord the king?" (vs. 8) Which enemies, David? Which king?

David and his men returned to a Ziklag in smoking ruins. The Amalekites had raided the city, taking everything worth taking, including the people. Though David's wives were among the captives, it gained him no sympathy. His men talked of stoning him (30:1-6).

Now the LORD reappears as an active player in David's life. David "found strength in the LORD his God" (vs. 6), and when he sought direction through the ephod of Abiathar the priest, the LORD assured him that he should indeed pursue the Amalekites and that he would be successful (vss. 7, 8).

He was, too, recovering not just the people and plunder belonging to Ziklag, but everything the Amalekites had taken from other cities as well. In contrast with Saul's mandate to obliterate the Amalekites in chapter 15, David was not bound by the restrictions of *cherem*. He could help himself to the spoil.

An incident on the return to Ziklag allows the author to put in a good word for David's sense of justice and fairness. When some two hundred of David's men were too exhausted to go on into battle, David left them to guard the "supplies" (vs. 24). After the victory, however, some "evil men and troublemakers" among David's troops didn't want to share the plunder. "Each man may take his wife and children and go," they said, but that was all (vs. 22).

David's response became an enduring statute in Israel, showing that when David was in touch with the LORD and thinking clearly, he had the qualities of an excellent ruler: "The share of the man who stayed with the supplies is to be the same as that of him who went down to the battle. All will share alike" (vs. 24).

Chapter 30 concludes with a touch of politics again, though the author doesn't label it as such. In chapter 25, the politics had to do with wives; here, politics meant sharing plunder with the elders of Judah, David's "friends" (vs. 26). These were the people who shortly would declare David their king (2 Sam. 2:4).

The Cursed Hills of Gilboa (31:1-13)

After telling of David's successful battle against the Amalekites and the distribution of the plunder among his Judean friends, the author takes us back to the Philistine front on Mt. Gilboa to witness Israel's defeat. David, of course, is nowhere in sight.

The sequence of events in 1 Samuel 31 is the same as in the parallel passage of 1 Chronicles 10, though the Chronicler, as usual, adds a concluding moral to explain Saul's rejection. The author of 1 Samuel tells it straight, describing the series of disasters that effectively took Israel back to chapter 4, where the Philistines had killed the anointed priests and captured the ark.

It is a sobering catalog of events: Israel's army fled; the Philistines killed Saul's three sons and wounded Saul; Saul and his armorbearer committed suicide. Seeing their army in flight, the Israelites "abandoned their towns and fled. And the Philistines came and occupied them" (31:7).

When Saul's body was discovered the next day, the Philistine mockery began in earnest. They beheaded him, stripped off his armor, and sent messengers "throughout the land of the Philistines to carry the good news to the houses of their idols and to the people" (vs. 9, NRSV). The NRSV *good news* reflects the word *gospel* in the Septuagint, ironically, the same word for "gospel" used in the story of Jesus.

Saul's armor and head ended up in Philistine temples (compare 1 Chron. 10:10). His headless, naked body was fastened to the wall at Beth Shan, along with the bodies of his sons. The only glimmer of good news for Israel was the bravery of the men of Jabesh who marched all night so they could end the shameful display of bodies on the Beth Shan city wall. They carried the bodies back to Jabesh and burned them. They buried the bones and fasted seven days (31:11-13). The people of Jabesh remembered Saul for his rescue of their city, the event that had catapulted him to national attention and had led to his confirmation as king (11:14, 15). With that poignant glimpse of Jabesh's final homage to their hero, 1 Samuel comes to a close.

David Gets the Word (2 Samuel 1:1-27)

In the opening lines of 2 Samuel, the author brings David on stage to exonerate him from any complicity in the death of Saul and his sons. And at first glance, David's attitude toward the fallen Saul appears to be "right" in every respect.

First, he meted out justice to the Amalekite messenger who brought the news of Saul's death. Hoping to gain special favors from David, the young man had brought him Saul's crown and armband (vs. 10), reporting his own act of "mercy killing" at the dying king's request. His story differs from the account in 1 Samuel 31. It appears he was lying. Most likely, he was a battlefield scavenger who discovered Saul's body before the Philistines did.

But even if the Amalekite was lying, David gave him "credit" for telling the truth. For killing the LORD's anointed (vs. 14), David commanded the young man's execution, repeating the classic Old Testament formula for just retribution: "Your blood be on your own head" (vs. 16).

David then composed a lament for Saul and Jonathan, commanding that it be taught to the men of Judah. Even though the political implications of such a command could be significant in view of the need to build bridges between Judah and the house of Saul, the author does not comment. The lament itself is both poignant and powerful, praising both Saul and Jonathan. Though David's affection for Jonathan is clear, it does not eclipse his positive comments about Saul. Several phrases in David's lament have left an enduring mark in our thinking and vocabulary: "How the mighty have fallen!" (vss. 19, 25, 27), and "Tell it not in Gath" (vs. 20). Most notably, the expression "dry as the hills of Gilboa" comes from David's curse, "O mountains of Gilboa, may you have neither dew nor rain, nor fields that yield offerings of grain" (vs. 21). In all Scripture, Gilboa is mentioned only in connection with the tragedy of Saul's final battle and death.

Was David's lament from the heart? His reputation for doubletalk leaves room for doubt. And the author has let it be known—subtly, to be sure—that David is building a power base that could serve his purposes as king: his wives (25:39-44), his gifts to the elders of Judah (30:26-31), and now a lament celebrating the house of Saul as mandatory learning for the men of Judah.

In the next chapter, 1 Samuel 2, David's politics become overt. But there, the LORD is clearly working with him. By contrast, in chapter 1, except for the references to the killing of Saul, "the LORD's anointed," the LORD's name does not appear, not even in David's lament. Is it possible that the absence of the LORD's name represents the author's subtle critique of this man after God's own heart? In the chapters describing David's questionable relationship with Achish, 1 Samuel 27 and 29, the author also never mentions the LORD. One could argue that when David embarks on an unethical course of action, seemingly leaving the LORD behind, the author cooperates by also dropping out the LORD's name from his description. The LORD will continue to work with David, even in the time of his great sin. But it will also be clear that David often fails to represent the righteousness of the God he professes to serve. Given the record of all Israel's kings, maybe the author is telling us that it is virtually impossible to be a king and stay right with the LORD.

■ Applying the Word

1 Samuel 24–2 Samuel 1

1. *Standing Firm.* What kinds of decisions have I been called upon to make in my life that would have required me to stand for the right regardless of the urging of my companions? How did I face those decisions and with what success?
2. *Help.* If I were to prepare a list of the times when the Lord has sent someone like Abigail to intervene in my life, thus preventing me from sinful actions, what would such a list include? Would it be a short list or a long one?
3. *Respect.* David seemed to be more respectful of his enemy Saul than he was of Nabal. Was that right? Have there been times when I have shown more sympathy to people in authority who did wrong than to ordinary sinners? Or, in our anti-authority age, does it work the other way around? How do the teachings of Jesus suggest that I treat all people with courtesy, regardless of their position?
4. *Trust.* David did not accept Saul's invitation to return home. Apparently, he felt Saul was not reliable. Was David right to distrust Saul? What situations have I faced in which I should have trusted people but didn't or couldn't? What situations have I faced when I did trust and was disappointed? What passages in these chapters help me know when to trust? How can my relationship with the Lord help me make such decisions?

5. *Forbidden Solutions.* Have I ever been tempted, like Saul, to try "forbidden" solutions to my problems? What were the results? How can the story of Saul's visit to the medium keep me from making the same mistake?

6. *Sharing.* Have there been situations in my family and church in which David's principle of sharing (30:24) should have been applied and wasn't? What can I do to make such a principle of equality a reality in my community?

7. *Enemy.* When an "enemy" is struck with misfortune, is it right for me to act more sorrowful than I feel inside? Why or why not?

■ Researching the Word

1. *Words.* Word studies are an excellent way to broaden one's understanding of the biblical perspective on the human condition after death. In this chapter *'elohim* ("God," "gods"), *she'ol* ("grave," "underworld"), *repha'im* ("shades," "dead") have been touched briefly, but are all worth pursuing further. Often, it is fruitful to compare the treatment of the key passages in several translations, especially noting the differences between the classic KJV and the popular modern translations. *Nephesh* ("soul," "life," "person") and *ruach* ("spirit," "wind," "breath") are also helpful for illuminating the biblical view, especially when followed up with the equivalent Greek words in the New Testament: *psyche* ("soul," "life," "person") and *pneuma* ("spirit," "wind," "breath"). For word studies involving the KJV, I have found Young's *Analytical Concordance* easier to use than Strong's *Exhaustive Concordance.* (Strong's is better as a text finder.) For word studies based on the NIV, Goodrick and Kohlenberger's *NIV Exhaustive Concordance* is superb.

2. *Blood and Punishment.* The Old Testament understanding of punishment and retribution can also be approached by means of word study. Using a concordance, scan the entries under *blood* or *head* to locate occurrences of the phrase *your blood*

be upon your own head or its equivalent. Analyze the key passages to ascertain the extent to which sin was viewed as carrying its own built-in reward (the boomerang effect). Such a study can then be the basis for analyzing the passages in Scripture in which divine judgment is directly linked with human sin.

■ Further Study of the Word

1. For general comment and practical applications of the biblical material, see E. G. White, *Patriarchs and Prophets*, 660-696.

2. In recent years, the view that Scripture teaches a consistent understanding of conditional immortality has become increasingly popular, both in scholarly and evangelical church circles. Though sometimes too optimistic in the interpretation of primary sources, the most thorough discussion from an Adventist perspective is L. E. Froom's *The Conditionalist Faith of Our Fathers*.

   The turning point toward conditionalism in scholarly circles may well have been the publication of Oscar Cullmann's 1955 Ingersoll lecture, "Immortality of the Soul or Resurrection of the Dead?" reprinted in *Immortality and Resurrection*, 9-53.

   More recently the discussion has been updated in *Four Views on Hell*, edited by William Crockett. The argument for conditionalism is presented by well-known evangelical theologian Clark Pinnock (135-166). Among the evangelical authors whom Pinnock credits as having persuaded him of the conditionalist view are John R. W. Stott and Edward Fudge. Stott's piece is in *Evangelical Essentials*, co-authored with David Edwards, 313-320. Pinnock says Fudge's book, *The Fire That Consumes*, is the best. Paternoster Press (UK) republished it in 1994.

PART FOUR

2 Samuel 2–12

David:
To the Summit and Back

CHAPTER EIGHT

Taking Charge in Israel

2 Samuel 2–6

Saul was dead. David was an exile in Ziklag, a city given him by the Philistines. How could he become king as the LORD had promised? In chapter 2, we learn that it began to happen in Hebron. There, the elders of Judah anointed David their king. Seven and a half years later, he would rule all Israel (2:11; 5:5).

As described in chapters 2 to 4, winning Saul's supporters was a tedious and bloody affair. It wasn't just a matter of winning. It was war, one that "lasted a long time" (3:1). Battlefield skirmishes, blood feuds, intrigue, treachery, and murder were all part of the story.

As part of a negotiated settlement, David demanded the return of his wife, Saul's daughter Michal. Abner and Ish-Bosheth forcibly removed her from a weeping husband and she became wife number seven for David—at least number seven (3:2-5). But by the time all Israel was ready to anoint David king (5:3), both Abner and Ish-Bosheth had been murdered.

With Saul's family no longer a worry, David set out to consolidate power. He conquered Jerusalem, twice defeated the Philistines, and brought the ark into the city, making Jerusalem the spiritual and political headquarters for the united kingdom.

But all was not well in Jerusalem, even as it moved toward days of glory. Chapter 6 concludes with an angry confrontation between David and Michal over his supposed indecency in dancing before the LORD. David may have been in the right. But the author slipped in that discordant note just before he moved to the heady stuff in chapters 7 to 10. It was an omen of evil things to come.

■ Getting Into the Word

2 Samuel 2–6

For an overview, read quickly through 2 Samuel 2 to 6; then read the section again as necessary in connection with the following study suggestions:

1. *House of Saul.* Set aside a section in your Samuel notebook titled "House of Saul." Based on chapters 2 to 6, make an entry for each of Saul's supporters or family members who had direct or indirect dealings with David. David had sworn a covenant with Jonathan to preserve Jonathan's family (1 Sam. 20:14-16, 42; 23:18); David also had given "his oath to Saul" that he would not "cut off" Saul's descendants or "wipe out [his] name" from his father's family (1 Sam. 24:21, 22). For each name in your "Saul" list, briefly evaluate David's performance relative to his oaths and covenants.
2. *Justice.* As a follow-up to the first question, look more closely at David's handling of "justice" relative to those who killed Saul's family members or supporters—for example, Joab killed Abner (2 Sam. 3); two Benjamites, Baanah and Recab, killed Ish-Bosheth (2 Sam. 4). What was David's reaction? Include, also, David's handling of the Amalekite who claimed he had killed Saul (2 Sam. 1). For a more complete picture of David's treatment of Joab, see his charge to Solomon (1 Kings 2:5, 6) and the description of Solomon's follow-through (vss. 28-35). Write out a paragraph summarizing your evaluation of David's handling of justice.
3. *Truth.* In the "truth" section of your notebook, briefly describe the lies and half-truths that appear in chapters 2 to 6. Evaluate the extent to which each appears to be justified, first in the biblical record and then according to your own sense of "truthfulness."
4. *Geography.* Using the maps in your Bible or in a Bible dictionary, locate the important places in chapters 2 to 6, not-

ing especially how the movement between them affects the
story. Pay special attention to: Hebron, Jabesh Gilead,
Mahanaim, Gibeon, Jerusalem, Valley of Rephaim, Kiriath
Jearim (Baalah of Judah). Check "Arabah" (2 Sam. 2:29) in a
Bible dictionary.

5. *The* LORD. Evaluate how Abner and David relate to the LORD
in this section. In particular, note when they take the name
of the LORD on their lips to confirm a course of action. Write
a brief evaluation of both men, indicating how you see the
consistency of their actions relative to their religious convictions.

6. *Ark*. List "problems" and "joys" that occur to you as you
read chapter 6, the story of the ark's journey to Jerusalem.
Write a brief paragraph summarizing your reactions, noting
in particular if any of the "joys" in the chapter helped solve
the "problems."

■ Exploring the Word

It's Time (2:1-11)

"In the course of time"—the author of 2 Samuel does not tell us
how much time—David asked the LORD whether he should go up to
"one of the towns of Judah" (vs. 1).

"Go up," said the LORD.

"Where?" asked David.

"To Hebron."

Making room for six hundred men with their families, possibly
two thousand people altogether, may have been a challenge for
Hebron. But whether or not there was joy in town, it was the "men
of Judah," not just the people of Hebron, who "anointed" David
king over Judah (vs. 4).

Though the Philistines probably considered David one of their
vassals, they apparently left him alone for some seven years until
they heard that he had been anointed king over the united tribes
(5:17). David had plenty of homework to do in the meantime.

His first recorded act of diplomacy—yes, David could also be a diplomat—was to send messengers to the men of Jabesh Gilead, Saul's most loyal supporters, congratulating them for their "kindness" (*chesed*, "covenant loyalty") in rescuing and burying the body of Saul (compare 1 Sam. 31:11-13). "May the LORD now show you kindness [*chesed*] and faithfulness ['*emeth*]," he said, using two of the most powerful theological words in the Old Testament (2:6). His appeal for their support was thinly veiled: "I too will show you the same favor because you have done this. Now then, be strong and brave, for Saul your master is dead, and the house of Judah has anointed me king over them" (vs. 6, 7).

Scripture records no results from his Jabesh diplomacy, possibly because David failed to support words with deeds. In the rest of Samuel-Kings, the only other mention of Jabesh is in connection with David's belated decision to give the bones of Saul and Jonathan a proper burial in their ancestral tomb (2 Sam. 21:12-14). But it took a three-year famine to prod David into action. In view of his eager diplomatic outreach, the tardy burial is puzzling.

David's attempt at diplomacy, however, certainly wasn't helped by the quirks of geography and the actions of Abner, Saul's commander. Abner had set up Saul's son Ish-Bosheth as king over the rest of Israel (all Israel except Judah), with headquarters at Mahanaim, like Jabesh, on the eastern side of the Jordan, but between Judah and Jabesh. So even if Jabesh had wanted to support David, Abner and Ish-Bosheth literally stood in the way.

Ish-Bosheth appears to have been a mere figurehead, a front for Abner's ambitions, though some scholars suggest that Ish-Bosheth simply was very young rather than incompetent—not forty years old as noted in 2:10. The puzzling chronology at the beginning of Saul's reign (1 Sam. 13:1) shows that the author's chronological information was not always precise. Ish-Bosheth's youth could explain why he accused Abner of sleeping with Rizpah, "my father's concubine" (3:7). Presumably Ish-Bosheth already would have taken Rizpah for himself had he been of age, since a father's concubines customarily belonged to the son (compare Absalom with David's concubines, 16:21, 22).

The two-year reign for Ish-Bosheth (2:10) is another puzzle. In relationship to David's seven years in Hebron as king over Judah (vs. 11; 5:5), two years for Ish-Bosheth would mean a five-year gap, either between Saul's death and the beginning of Ish-Bosheth's reign or between Ish-Bosheth's murder and the beginning of David's reign over all Israel. Neither alternative meshes well with the flow of the narrative.

Excursus: A Shameful Name

A fascinating history lies behind the *Bosheth* in Ish-Bosheth's name, for 1 Chronicles 8:33 and 9:39 list Saul's fourth son as Esh-Baal, not Ish-Bosheth. Similarly, Jonathan's son is Merib-Baal rather than Mephibosheth (1 Chron. 8:34; 9:40; compare 2 Sam. 4:4). The most popular explanation for these variations involves the changing fortunes of the Hebrew word *ba'al*.

Originally *ba'al* was quite an ordinary word meaning simply "lord" or "master," as in Hosea 2:16, but continued association with the Canaanite fertility god by the same name tainted the word. Just as Communists ruined the word *comrade* and as modern homosexuals have co-opted the word *gay*, so the Canaanites took over the word *ba'al* in their world and made it too hot for some to handle. Thus, at some point in the early history of 2 Samuel, devout scribes replaced *ba'al* with *bosheth*, a Hebrew word meaning "shame," reminding readers that the "shameful" word *ba'al* had once been a part of the names of Ish-Bosheth and Mephibosheth.

The Chronicler's lists somehow escaped that fate, as did certain place names, even in 2 Samuel. In one notable instance, 2 Samuel actually retains David's use of *ba'al* to refer to the LORD. After his victory over the Philistines, David said the LORD had "broken out against my enemies before me." And thus the place was called Ba'al Perazim (5:20), correctly interpreted in the NIV footnote as "the lord who breaks out." In other words, Israel's God, the LORD, was the *ba'al* who had broken out to save David.

That process of proper names growing out of ordinary words is also part of the life history of two other words important in the Bible: *Christ* and *Satan*. Originally, *christ*, from the Greek *christos*, which translates the Hebrew *mashiach* ("messiah"), simply meant "anointed one" and could be used for anyone who had been anointed. Every "anointed" priest or king was thus a "christ."

Similarly, *satan* originally meant simply "adversary" or "accuser" and could refer to quite ordinary humans. Hadad the Edomite, for example, was a "satan" (adversary) against Solomon (1 Kings 11:14), as was Rezon, the son of Eliada (vss. 23, 25). That original "adversarial" element is clearly present in the three Old Testament contexts where *satan* is already something more than human and en route to becoming "Satan" with a capital *S* (1 Chron. 21:1; Job 1:6-12; 2:1-7; Zech. 3:1, 2).

Today, Baal, Christ, and Satan are all so specific in their meaning that we could never use them in their original "ordinary" sense without being misunderstood. For similar reasons, devout scribes gave Esh-Baal the new name of Ish-Bosheth, and Merib-Baal the new name of Mephibosheth.

A Family Matter (2:12–3:5)

The struggle between the "house of David" and the "house of Saul" was a family affair with relatives leading out on both sides. Saul's cousin Abner (1 Sam. 14:50) and David's nephew Joab, son of his sister Zeruiah (1 Chron. 2:16), squared off in an encounter that resembled a formal dual. Twelve men from each side tangled with deadly accuracy, each one grabbing his opponent by the head and thrusting him through with a dagger. "They fell down together" (2:16).

In the battle that followed, Joab's men came out on top, losing nineteen men to three hundred and sixty for Benjamin (vss. 30, 31). But the most notable loss was Joab's brother Asahel, a loss significant enough to be counted as a separate casualty. Ignoring Abner's warnings, Asahel had kept up a close pursuit, until Abner thrust him through with his spear (vss. 18-23). At sunset, Joab and Abner agreed to call it quits, and the armies headed home. But Joab would remember Asahel's death.

Chapter 3 opens with a reference to the "long" war between the two houses, noting that "David grew stronger and stronger, while the house of Saul grew weaker and weaker" (vs. 1). The author then inserts a list of six sons born to David in Hebron (vss. 2-5). The list reveals that a different wife gave birth to each one. Only three of the six sons—Amnon, Absalom, and Adonijah—figure in the ongoing history of David's house, each in a way that would bring pain to David and the kingdom.

Abner and Ish-Bosheth (3:6-21)

In 3:6, the author focuses on the house of Saul, stating outright that Abner was "strengthening his own position," obviously at Ish-Bosheth's expense. Accused by Ish-Bosheth of sleeping with Rizpah, Saul's concubine, Abner lashes out, declaring his intention to deliver the kingdom to David, doing for him "what the LORD promised him on oath" (vs. 9). It's not clear whether Ish-Bosheth's accusation was true. But even if it was, he was powerless to intervene, too afraid of Abner even to answer him (vs. 11).

Abner was ready to cast his lot with David rather than continue with the declining house of Saul. He sent messengers to David to "cut a covenant," to translate the Hebrew literally (vs. 12). David was ready, but on one condition: Bring Michal (vs. 13). David sent messengers to Ish-Bosheth with the same demand, and Ish-Bosheth gave the order to take Michal away from her husband Paltiel (vs. 15). Yet it was Abner who ordered the weeping Paltiel to go back home (vs. 16). In short, both Abner and Ish-Bosheth were cooperating to end the rule of Saul's house.

Abner did his homework with the people of Israel. Accompanied by twenty men, he returned to David with a detailed plan of union. It looked good. David feasted Abner and his men and sent them home. Abner said he would "assemble all Israel for my lord the king, so that they may make a compact with you." Scripture says he went away "in peace" (vs. 21).

Joab's Revenge (3:22-39)

No sooner had Abner left than Joab returned from a raid (vs. 22). He was furious when he learned about David's pact with Abner, and he told David so (vss. 24, 25). Was Abner as crooked as Joab said he

was? No way to tell. Most likely, Joab felt threatened by Abner, prob-
ably for good reason. In any event, Joab sent messengers to detain
Abner. Taking him aside "as though to speak with him privately,"
Joab stabbed him, avenging "the blood of his brother Asahel" (3:27).
Scripture does not comment on other possible reasons.

Joab's revenge killing put David in an awkward position. Potentially, he could gain or lose a great deal by Abner's death. If Saul's
supporters thought David was somehow behind Joab's evil deed, the
merger could be off. Yet Abner could be stubborn and strong-minded.
Did David think building the kingdom would simply be a lot less
complicated if Abner were out of the way?

David protested Abner's death, maybe a bit too vigorously. First, he
declared himself and his kingdom innocent, wishing Abner's blood "upon
the head of Joab and upon all his father's house" (vss. 28, 29). Then he
pronounced an enduring curse on Joab: "May Joab's house never be
without someone who has a running sore or leprosy or who leans on a
crutch or who falls by the sword or who lacks food" (vs. 29).

David commanded everyone, including Joab, to tear their clothes
and "put on sackcloth and walk in mourning in front of Abner" (vs.
31). David was highly visible, weeping with everyone else, singing a
lament for Abner and stoutly maintaining a vow not to eat before
the sun went down.

It worked. The author of 2 Samuel says that "on that day all the
people and all Israel knew that the king had no part in the murder of
Abner son of Ner" (vs. 37).

As far as David was concerned, however, two features of the story
are unsettling. First, if it was wrong for Joab to kill Abner, then Joab
deserved to die. Years later, David charged his son and successor,
Solomon, to avenge Joab's murder of Abner: "Do not let his gray
head go down to the grave in peace" (1 Kings 2:6). In 1 Kings, David
declared Abner's killing of Asahel a justifiable wartime act. That made
Joab guilty of murder, shedding blood "in peacetime as if in battle"
(vs. 5). When Solomon carried out David's charge, he confirmed
another aspect of Joab's culpability, namely, that he had acted without David's knowledge (1 Kings 2:32; compare 2 Sam. 3:26).

And that was the rub. Was David so weak that he could not prevent his men from committing violent acts without his knowledge and consent? Or was David being two-faced again, outwardly sorrowful but inwardly pleased that the house of Saul was out of the way? David had not hesitated to execute the Amalekite who claimed responsibility for killing Saul, "the LORD's anointed" (1:15, 16); and he would shortly do the same to the two men who murdered Ish-Bosheth, not because they had touched "the LORD's anointed" but because they had "killed an innocent man in his own house and on his own bed" (4:11). That sounded very much like David's lament over Abner, "Your hands were not bound, your feet were not fettered" (3:34). Yet David left Joab alone, even allowing him to keep his position as army commander.

David's irregular practice of justice in this instance makes the author's conclusion to the story of Abner's murder particularly significant. He lets David condemn himself with his own words: "Today, though I am the anointed king, I am weak, and these sons of Zeruiah are too strong for me. May the LORD repay the evildoer according to his evil deeds" (vs. 39).

That's pretty weak. The opening line of Psalm 72, the classic royal psalm celebrating the ideal king, clearly states the king's first responsibility: "Endow the king with your justice, O God, the royal son with your righteousness." Yet David had to leave justice to someone else because the sons of Zeruiah were too strong for him.

And that brings up the second troubling aspect of this whole incident, namely, the people's blind acceptance of everything the king did. The author records the people's reaction to David's expression of grief for Abner: "All the people took note and were pleased; indeed, everything the king did pleased them" (3:36). Everything? Think again, people. Maybe this was the reason why Israel and her king were in exile and why the temple lay in ruins.

The Last Threat From Saul's House (4:1–5:5)

With Abner gone, the murder of Ish-Bosheth is anticlimactic. The author of 2 Samuel introduces the story with this sobering line: "When Ish-Bosheth son of Saul heard that Abner had died in Hebron, he lost courage, and all Israel became alarmed" (vs. 1). Under those depressing circumstances two of Ish-Bosheth's subjects, "leaders of raiding bands" (vs. 2) took it upon themselves to put Saul's son out of his misery.

But when these two men, Baanah and Recab, arrived in Hebron with the head of Ish-Bosheth, David did not take kindly to their speech that "the LORD has avenged my lord the king against Saul and his offspring" (vs. 8). David commanded their execution. Minus hands and feet, their bodies were hung up by the pool in Hebron. The head of Ish-Bosheth was buried in Abner's tomb (vs. 12).

One other member of Saul's family remained to be reckoned with, Jonathan's son Mephibosheth. While setting the scene for Ish-Bosheth's murder, the author of 2 Samuel had dropped in a few lines identifying Jonathan's lame son and explaining the cause of his lameness (vs. 4), implying that Mephibosheth might also be a potential claimant to Saul's throne. During Absalom's rebellion, Saul's servant Ziba told David explicitly that Mephibosheth was of such a mind, "staying in Jerusalem, because he thinks, 'Today the house of Israel will give me back my grandfather's kingdom' " (16:3).

After David returned to power in Jerusalem, however, Mephibosheth denied Ziba's claim with a show of anguish and passion (19:24-30). But just as the author quotes no disinterested witness to confirm or deny Ish-Bosheth's accusation against Abner, so he quotes no disinterested witness to confirm or deny Ziba's accusation against Mephibosheth. In both cases, we have only the protestations of the accused.

Chapter 5 opens with the report that all the tribes of Israel had come to David in Hebron and asked him to be their king. David made a compact (covenant) with "all the elders of Israel" and "they anointed David king over Israel" (vs. 3). David had now been anointed three times: by the prophet Samuel (1 Sam. 16:13), by the elders of Judah (2 Sam. 2:4), and finally by the elders of all Israel (5:3).

Scripture does not indicate if any one of the anointings would have been sufficient to make David "the LORD's anointed." Saul, of course, was "the LORD's anointed," but 2 Samuel does not use the title for his son Ish-Bosheth. And when David executed the murder-

ers of Ish-Bosheth, his accusation was that they had killed an innocent man, not that they had acted against "the LORD's anointed"
(4:11). For the kings who followed David, the title seems to have
been standard, at least in the psalms. But in the historical and prophetic writings, it is seldom used for the later kings, and the actual
anointing ceremony is reported only sporadically. In the narrative
portions of the Old Testament, the sense of awe in the presence of
"the LORD's anointed" comes mostly from David's speeches about
Saul.

But whether or not it is possible to sort out the anointing proto-
col, it is clear that David is now "the LORD's anointed" and king over
all Israel. It is worth asking, however, if David's great respect for
Saul as "the LORD's anointed," even when Saul was pursuing evil
ends, might not have tempted David to think too highly of his own
position after he had become "the LORD's anointed." While it was
admirable for him to show respect for Saul, when David himself was
"the LORD's anointed," did he expect the same kind of respect, regardless of his behavior? That is the nagging problem for human
authority figures: respect for the office too easily becomes license
for the abuse of authority.

City of David (5:6-25)

The more urgent questions about David's use of authority will
come later. For now he set out to establish his kingdom and did so
with power and skill. A key move was to conquer Jerusalem and
make it his capital, a task that David and his men accomplished with
remarkable ease (5:6, 7). Up to that point, Jerusalem with its Jebusite
population had been something like a "free" Gentile city, aligned
neither with the house of David nor the house of Saul. Thus it was
equally attractive to both sides, common ground that could bond
them together.

A number of leading people in David's reign appear in the narrative for the first time after the capture of Jerusalem, including Nathan
the prophet and Zadok the priest. The sudden appearance of such
people poses the tantalizing question of the "conversion" of native

Jebusites to the worship of the LORD. In the biblical record, the worship of the "true" God at Jerusalem can be traced back to the time of Abraham (Gen. 14:19-24). When paying tithes to Melchizedek, king of Salem (another name for Jerusalem), Abraham identified Melchizedek's "God Most High" as "the LORD, . . . Creator of heaven and earth" (Gen. 14:22). Thus there was precedent for the worship of the LORD in Jerusalem.

But what about the city when David captured it? And how much biblical evidence is there that Israel was willing to accept converts to the worship of the LORD? The legal codes were restrictive, with prohibitions against the Moabites and Ammonites entering the community "even down to the tenth generation" (Deut. 23:3-6) and commands to obliterate the "Hittites, Amorites, Canaanites, Perizzites, Hivites and Jebusites" (Deut. 20:17; compare 7:1, 2). But the historical narratives and some genealogical lists suggest greater openness.

Ruth the Moabitess is the best-known exception, and her vivid statement of conversion to the religion of her mother-in-law Naomi is clear enough: "Your people will be my people and your God my God" (Ruth 1:16). She is in the royal lineage (Ruth 4:16-22) and is listed in Matthew's genealogy of Jesus (Matt. 1:5). Another exception, though not as well known, was Naamah the Ammonite, mother of Rehoboam (1 Kings 14:31), the only one of Solomon's seven hundred wives mentioned by name in Scripture. Rahab, the prostitute from Jericho (Josh. 6:25), would be another notable exception and again one that is listed in Matthew's genealogy of Jesus (Matt. 1:5).

As for Jerusalem and its heritage, the prophet Ezekiel is remarkably blunt: "Your ancestry and birth were in the land of the Canaanites; your father was an Amorite and your mother a Hittite" (Ezek. 16:3). At a stroke, Ezekiel ticks off the first three names in the list of targeted nations in Deuteronomy 20:17: Canaanite, Amorite, and Hittite! These were the people of Jerusalem. And there is no evidence that David obliterated the native population. Apparently many became worshipers of the LORD.

Before moving on from David's capture of Jerusalem to his exploits against his enemies, the author ties together several of David's

Jerusalem activities. First, after noting that David took up residence in the city and began to build it up, the author summarizes: "He became more and more powerful, because the LORD God Almighty was with him" (5:10). Second, he briefly describes the building of David's palace with the help of Hiram, king of Tyre, concluding with another summary statement: "David knew that the LORD had established him as king over Israel and had exalted his kingdom for the sake of his people Israel" (vs. 12). Finally, the author notes that David took "more concubines and wives" in Jerusalem, and "more sons and daughters were born to him" (vs. 13). Their names are listed but, in contrast with the earlier list from Hebron (3:2-5), without the mothers' names. From this second list, Solomon is the only one to play an active part in the kingdom.

David will bring the ark of the covenant to Jerusalem and give it a home there. But before he does, Scripture records two resounding defeats of the Philistines. They finally had gotten wind of David's royal status and were determined to track him down. Scripture indicates that David was in direct communication with the LORD, even receiving detailed instructions on how to attack the Philistines (5:19, 23, 24).

Interestingly enough, after the first battle, when the Philistines "abandoned their idols," David and his men "carried them off" (vs. 21). Just as the Philistines had twice defeated the Israelites, carrying off the sacred ark of the Israelites (1 Sam. 4:1-11), so Israel returned the favor, twice defeating the Philistines and carrying off the idols of the Philistines. And just as David with his six hundred men had lived among the Philistines as loyal subjects of Achish, a Philistine king, so Ittai the Gittite with six hundred Philistine men of Gath now lived among the Israelites, loyal subjects of David, the Israelite king (2 Sam. 15:18).

One final symbolism was probably not intentional, but it is at least interesting to note that the battle that cost Israel the ark also cost her thirty thousand casualties (1 Sam. 4:10). As if to make atonement, when David set out to bring the ark to a place of honor in Jerusalem, he did so with thirty thousand chosen men (6:1). Clearly, this was a day of opportunity, a high day for David and his people.

The Deadly and Blessed Ark (6:1-19)

Bringing the ark to Jerusalem was the last step in David's rise to power and the final preparation for hearing Nathan's covenant oracle and David's prayer of response in 2 Samuel 7. But looming ominously over the journey to Jerusalem is the Uzzah incident. Uzzah died when he reached out and touched the ark, and Scripture portrays God as being directly involved in his death: "The LORD's anger burned against Uzzah," and "God struck him down" (6:7). The joyous procession came to a stunned halt, and David abandoned the project for three months (vs. 11).

The event should be taken seriously, though probably not in the "traditional" way. The element in the story that has tempted religious people to abuse it is the phrase "because the oxen stumbled." Since the mention of that alibi leaves the *impression* that Uzzah was trying to be helpful, but was struck down anyway by a heavy-handed deity, some have interpreted the story to mean that external obedience is more important to God than the internal motives of the heart.

It is not hard to find Old Testament examples pointing in the opposite direction, namely, that God values the motives of the heart more than the external act. One striking incident is the story of Naaman, the healed Syrian leper, who had just confessed the uniqueness of Israel's God: "Now I know that there is no God in all the world except in Israel" (2 Kings 5:15). Yet Naaman knew that his official duties back in Syria would require him to enter the temple of the pagan god Rimmon and bow down there. Explaining his problem to the prophet Elisha, he said: "May the LORD forgive your servant for this." To which Elisha responded: "Go in peace" (vss. 18, 19).

Even with respect to the ark itself, the LORD had shown Himself remarkably restrained when dealing with sinners. Surely the wicked Hophni and Phinehas deserved to be struck down when they handled the sacred ark. But no, they suffered no ill effects; it was the Philistines who did them in (1 Sam. 4:1-11).

As for the Uzzah incident itself, Scripture says almost nothing about any deeper reasons for Uzzah's death, perhaps nothing at all, depending on how one understands the difficult Hebrew of 2 Samuel 6:7. The NIV translates the puzzling phrase in 6:7 as "his irreverent act," while the NRSV chooses to model its translation on the more straightforward rendering of the parallel passage in 1 Chronicles 13:10, a passage that the NIV translates as: "He struck him down because he had put his hand on the ark." If Chronicles has rightly preserved the Hebrew text, then the story says nothing whatsoever about any sinful or perverse motives on Uzzah's part. He simply touched the ark.

Is it possible that Uzzah's motives were indeed pure and that his only sin was in touching a forbidden sacred object? Such an interpretation cannot be ruled out. And in that connection, I would argue that the significance of Uzzah's death was first and foremost for the community. Uzzah's eternal fate may not have been involved at all. Consider the recent history of the ark prior to this move to Jerusalem: Handled by the wicked Hophni and Phinehas, the ark had been a spectacular failure when it came to delivering Israel from the Philistines (1 Sam. 4:1-11). Then it spent seven months among the Philistines, showing them that it was indeed a dangerous box to have around, regardless of how careful and conscientious they were (1 Sam. 5).

But why would the ark be alive among the Philistines but dead in Israel? To be sure, when the Philistines returned it, the ark again had a deadly effect in Israel and in response to obvious sins of arrogance (1 Sam. 6:19, 20). But then the ark went to Kiriath Jearim and was there "a long time, twenty years in all" (1 Sam. 7:2) before the people awoke to their spiritual need and participated in a renewal under Samuel's direction (vss. 2-17). Yet even in that renewal, the ark is never mentioned. It stayed in Kiriath Jearim (called Baalah of Judah in 2 Samuel 6:2), and that's where David had to go when he decided to take the ark to Jerusalem.

Remarkably, between 1 Samuel 7:1 and 2 Samuel 6:1, that is, between the ark's arrival at Kiriath Jearim and David's attempt to bring it to Jerusalem, the only reference to the ark is in 1 Samuel 14:18, a brief comment about its presence with Ahijah in the Israelite camp. Yet in the Septuagint, even that reference is gone, for *ark* has been replaced with *ephod*. In short, as David was bringing the ark to Jerusalem (by unorthodox means, it should be noted), many lingering questions may have been in the minds of the people: Is the ark important in our worship? Is the LORD still present with His sacred box? Given all that had happened to the ark and to Israel, Uzzah's death was a powerful reminder that the LORD was indeed very much alive and an active defender of all that was sacred in Israel.

But if the LORD first got Israel's attention with negative motivation, a display of His power that struck fear to the hearts of the people, He then turned immediately to the positive, a display of His goodness that gave courage and hope. David, with a fair show of anger and fear, had left the ark at the house of Obed-Edom the Gittite, asking the plaintive question: "How can the ark of the LORD ever come to me?" (6:9). We know nothing about Obed-Edom's reaction when the ark arrived. After what had happened to Uzzah, I can't imagine that he was overjoyed. But what can a poor Gittite do when the king brings him a "gift"?

But then the goodness of the LORD took over. He began to bless the house of Obed-Edom and all his possessions (vs. 11). Polzin notes that in the history of Israel that extends from Deuteronomy to the end of 2 Kings, "the house of Obed-edom the Gittite is the only house, be it literal, familial, tribal, or national, the LORD is said to bless" (Polzin, *David*, 65). We don't know what the "blessing" was—except that it was so obvious and so abundant that David heard about it and was inspired to try again (vs. 12). This time, he followed the rules, and the ark made it to Jerusalem without a hitch, becoming a permanent feature there until the Babylonian exile.

The story of Uzzah and the ark is a sobering one. In an age that seldom values sacred objects, it shows us that God's presence in our midst is very real and can be dangerous. It joins the stories of the burning bush and the smoking mountain to remind us that God is active on planet Earth. At the same time, the story tells us that the God who wounds also heals, just as the judgment on Uzzah was followed by the blessing on Obed-Edom.

As important as the story of Uzzah is, however, the startling nature of this divine intervention could distort our view of God's ideal.

On balance, Scripture makes it abundantly clear that the God who was present with the ark would never trade the religion of the heart for a religion of mere externals. In the words of the prophet Micah: "What does the LORD require of you but to do justice, and to love kindness, and to walk humbly with your God?" (Mic. 6:8, NRSV).

Excursus: Who Was Obed-Edom?

An interesting aside to the ark narrative has to do with the identity of Obed-Edom. He was a Gittite—but from which Gath? The best-known one is the Philistine city where David had spent some time. A contingent of six hundred men of Gath under Ittai were some of David's most loyal supporters (2 Sam. 15:18-22). David's influence, possibly combined with the memory of the ark's Philistine sojourn, may have resulted in a number of Philistine converts to the worship of the LORD.

A Gittite could also be an inhabitant from either of two Israelite cities assigned to the Levites: Gath Rimmon in the territory of Dan (Josh. 19:45) or Gath Rimmon in the territory of Manasseh (Josh. 21:25). The name *Obed-Edom* also appears as a Kohathite Levite in 1 Chronicles 26:4-8.

Since Scripture doesn't identify the Gath from which Obed-Edom came, the question comes down to whether David would have been more likely to leave the ark with a Philistine convert or with an Israelite Levite. One almost suspects from the narrative that David was so eager to put some distance between himself and the ark that he just took it to the nearest house and ran, regardless of the nationality of the occupant! From the standpoint of orthodox Israelite religion, a Philistine Gath is the more daring option but also the most popular one among commentators because of David's ties there. Furthermore, David's first attempt to bring the ark to Jerusalem wasn't marked by any special concern for orthodoxy. Taking a different tack, however, some have suggested that given David's mood, he might even have preferred a Philistine home so that any further deadly effects from the ark would affect his enemies rather than his own people!

In short, good arguments can be made for either position. Scripture does not resolve the issue for us. But one thing is sure—whether Israelite or Philistine, Obed-Edom and his family would long cherish the memories of three blessed months when the ark was in their home.

Saul's Daughter (6:20-23)

The Uzzah incident was not the only uneasy moment in the ark's journey to Jerusalem. The author concludes chapter 6 with an unsettling account of Michal's reaction to David's behavior as the ark finally entered Jerusalem. As she watched from a window, she was, in a word, disgusted.

But after mentioning that Michal "despised" David in her heart (vs. 16), the author turns back to the celebration as if to exonerate David. And the enthusiasm in 6:17-19 is contagious: David brought the ark into the tent he had prepared for it, offered sacrifices, blessed the people, and finally gave a present to each person in the crowd: "a loaf of bread, a cake of dates and a cake of raisins" (vs. 19). What a party!

David then went home "to bless his household" only to be confronted by an angry Michal: "How the king of Israel has distinguished himself today, disrobing in the sight of the slave girls of his servants as any vulgar fellow would!" (vs. 20).

David immediately defended himself and with barbed words: "It was before the LORD, who chose me rather than your father or anyone from his house when he appointed me ruler over the LORD's people Israel" (vs. 21). Most commentators agree that David had not danced stark naked before the LORD. According to 6:14, he was wearing a "linen ephod." But the same verse also says that he "danced before the LORD with all his might," and verse 16 refers to his "leaping and dancing." Most likely, the linen ephod couldn't always cope with David's exuberance, sometimes revealing more than David intended and more than Michal appreciated. In David's view, however, the occasion justified his actions.

Instead of recording a response from Michal, the author follows David's defense with one simple sentence: "And Michal daughter of

Saul had no children to the day of her death" (vs. 23).

Poor Michal. Love, not politics, had drawn her to David. Scripture itself tells us that (1 Sam. 18:20). Her father Saul had tried to turn her love into politics, and maybe he succeeded, for Scripture says nothing about David's love for Michal, only that he was "pleased to become the king's son-in-law" (vs. 26). So what does that mean for the passion that drove David to double the required bride price, from one hundred to two hundred Philistine foreskins? Was that the passion of politics or the passion of true love? Scripture never says. But it does say that in spite of all that, Saul still realized "his daughter Michal loved David" (1 Sam. 18:28). She really did. She would even deceive her own father and tell lies to his face in order to protect David (1 Sam. 19:11-17).

But her father, who couldn't keep from playing politics with her, married her to another man while David was on the run—Paltiel son of Laish (1 Sam. 25:44). Did she love Paltiel? Scripture never says. But it does say that Paltiel loved her—well, not exactly, but this is what it does say when David, Abner, and Ish-Bosheth once more began playing politics with Michal: "Ish-Bosheth gave orders and had her taken away from her husband Paltiel son of Laish. Her husband, however, went with her, weeping behind her all the way to Bahurim. Then Abner said to him, 'Go back home!' So he went back" (2 Sam. 3:15, 16).

When David was Michal's first love, she had become his first wife. But now, simply to make her his seventh wife, David tore her away from a man who really cared for her (compare vss. 2-5). David's life was full and exciting—plenty of war, plenty of women. And he could dance "before the LORD with all his might" (vs. 14). Michal stood at the window and watched. No wonder "she despised him in her heart" (vs. 16). No wonder she met David with scornful words when he came home to bless the family (vs. 20). And no wonder David responded with barbed taunts (vss. 21, 22). Poor Michal. The "daughter of Saul had no children to the day of her death" (vs. 23).

A politician would note that Michal's childlessness meant she would never have any offspring who could lay claim to David's throne in the name of the house of Saul. David's house was still getting stronger and stronger. Saul's house was almost gone.

Summary: David on Top

Step by step in 2 Samuel 2 to 6 David approaches his peak. First, the exiled outlaw from Ziklag moves to Hebron and is anointed king of Judah. Then comes the long tussle with the house of Saul: success on the battlefield, the return of Saul's daughter Michal, the violent deaths of Abner and Ish-Bosheth. Finally, David is anointed king of all Israel. A new capital, a double victory over the Philistines, the ark's arrival in Jerusalem as David dances mightily before the LORD— along with everyone else, everyone except Michal, that is.

In 2 Samuel 7, the author will let us hear the lush promises delivered by Nathan the prophet and David's grateful prayer. But the harsh words of conflict between Michal and David remind the readers that all was not well in Jerusalem, even when the city was on the verge of great glory. That would give them plenty to think about now that the glory was gone.

■ Applying the Word

2 Samuel 2–6

1. *Guidance.* **David often had direct communication with the LORD, receiving specific answers to specific questions on what he should do and where he should go. Have I experienced such direct guidance? Should I expect to? If I can't ask a prophet or consult Urim and Thummim, and if the sending of dreams is up to God, not to me, how do I make decisions on how to live day by day? What role does my reason play? Prayer? The Bible? The Holy Spirit? Providence?**

2. *Politics and Piety.* **When David sent a message to the men of Jabesh Gilead, congratulating them for taking care of Saul's body, David was being both gracious and political. Do I separate the two in my life? Can I? How? Should I go ahead with gracious acts even if I know that I am motivated at least partly by "political" concerns? What steps can I take to keep**

"politics" from distorting my Christian experience and my Christian witness?

3. *God's Will.* Abner seems to have known all along that it was the LORD's will to give the kingdom to David. Yet for some time, he still supported the house of Saul. In what ways do I live in two worlds, knowing the will of the Lord, but deliberately choosing to follow my own inclinations? What specific situations in my life can I think of in which the Lord has intervened to jar me loose from a double life?

4. *Temperament.* Am I more like the strong-willed and domineering Abner or the retiring and dominated Ish-Bosheth? Should I attempt to be more like one or the other? Why or why not? How can the Lord help me to bring about changes that have to do with my basic temperament?

5. *Domination.* The lives of both Michal and Ish-Bosheth seemed to have been controlled largely by the decisions of other people. Do I sometimes find myself in such circumstances? How can the Lord help me survive or make changes? How can I know when to endure the efforts of others to control my life and when to resist?

6. *Uzzah and Obed-Edom.* Do I find God's judgment against Uzzah so overwhelming that I overlook the blessing He gave to Obed-Edom? Which aspect of God's dealings make the greater impression on me? In my own life, what specific circumstances have I faced that required me to pay closer attention to God's judgments? In what specific circumstances in my life have God's blessings been more help to me than His judgments? Do I see God as primarily a source of judgment or of blessing?

■ Researching the Word

1. *Jerusalem.* A topic with almost limitless possibilities is the history and development of Jerusalem. Start with a Bible dictionary article on "Jerusalem," noting in particular the discussions of the early history of the city. A standard Bible

atlas will also provide maps or diagrams of the city, showing how it grew and developed through the years.

2. *Obed-Edom and Gath.* This chapter gave a brief overview on the question of Obed-Edom's identity. To explore the matter further, read the entries for "Obed-Edom" and "Gath" in a Bible dictionary. Include Gath Rimmon in your study as well. Locate each Gath on a map, noting the relationship of each to the route of the ark (Kiriath Jearim to Jerusalem) on the occasion when Obed-Edom was its temporary custodian. Then turn to a concordance and check out all the instances of "Gath" and "Gittite" as the basis for formulating your own view on the national identity of Obed-Edom. Finally, list the significant factors leading to your conclusion.

■ Further Study of the Word

1. For general comment on the biblical narrative, see E. G. White, *Patriarchs and Prophets*, 697-711.
2. If the story of Uzzah suggests that the Old Testament God is harsh and legalistic, a good antidote is J. Dybdahl's *Old Testament Grace*, a book exploring the graciousness of God in the Old Testament.

CHAPTER NINE

From Heaven to Hell

2 Samuel 7–12

In 2 Samuel 7 to 12 David hits the apex of his glory, then plummets into the abyss. His climax comes in chapter 7, where he offers to build a house for the LORD. The prophet Nathan says Yes, only to hear the LORD say No. Nathan's oracle and David's prayer combine to make the chapter a rich resource for studying covenant theology. The LORD said He didn't need a house, but would establish David's house—forever. David was profoundly grateful.

The readers of 2 Samuel would know, of course, that David's son had built a house for the LORD, a house now leveled by Babylon. They would also know that David's successor was no longer on the throne but was in exile in Babylon. What did the LORD mean when He said that He would establish David's throne and house forever (7:13, 16)?

Chapters 8 to 10 follow with a catalog of military victories, the story of David's kindness to Mephibosheth, and an account of a battle against the Ammonites. Adultery and murder come in chapter 11, God's judgment in chapter 12: "You are the man" (12:7), and "The sword will never depart from your house" (vs. 10). David has gone from heaven to hell. The rest of 2 Samuel will reveal the cost of enjoying the pleasures of sin for a season.

■ Getting Into the Word

2 Samuel 7–12

Read 2 Samuel 7 to 12 quickly for an overview, then work through it again as needed in light of the study suggestions below:

1. *The* LORD. Make a list of all the passages in chapters 7 to 12 in which the LORD or God is mentioned. Then analyze the narratives where He is present and those where He is absent. Write a brief summary statement describing what you think may be the significance of what you have found.

2. *Truth.* Ponder carefully all the narratives and characters in chapters 7 to 12 for the purpose of updating the "truth" section of your notebook. Write out your comments as appropriate.

3. *An Exile's Perspective.* Try to read chapter 7 through the eyes of someone living during the exile, i.e., after Jerusalem, its temple, and its king are no more. Make a list of those things in Nathan's oracle and David's prayer that would be particularly meaningful or troublesome in exilic circumstances. In a brief paragraph, summarize how you think you would have reacted to the reading of the oracle and the prayer if you were living in the time immediately following Jerusalem's destruction.

4. *Forever.* Make a list of all the "forevers" in chapter 7, noting in each instance the application to which it is made. Then, make note of any elements in the oracle or prayer that could be described as conditional.

5. *Defeated Enemies.* List (with references) the nations and peoples that David defeated militarily. Using the maps in your Bible or a Bible dictionary, locate them on a map, and sketch (or describe) the inclusive borders of David's kingdom.

6. *Mephibosheth.* In connection with the story of Mephibosheth in chapter 9:

    a. *Geography.* Mephibosheth's home in Lo Debar was probably just south of the Sea of Galilee. Using the maps in your Bible or in a Bible dictionary note how that location would relate to Jabesh and Mahanaim, key centers of support for the house of Saul, and to Jerusalem.

    b. *Chronology.* Work out a chronology of Mephibosheth's life, taking 4:4 into account along with the story in 2 Samuel

21:1-14. For the story in 2 Samuel 21, consider the possibility that it may have happened before the events in chapter 9.

   c. *House of Saul.* Update the "House of Saul" section in your notebook. Your comments on Mephibosheth may be have to be preliminary, since he and David interact later in 2 Samuel as well.

■ Exploring the Word

A House for David, a House for the LORD *(7:1-29)*

David is now settled into his own palace, and the LORD has given him "rest from all his enemies around him" (vs. 1). Chapter 5 had described David's building activities in Jerusalem, including the construction of his own palace with the help of workmen sent by Hiram king of Tyre (5:9-12). For the most part, however, chapters 1 to 5 describe the downfall of David's enemies—the Philistines and his opponents from the house of Saul. More enemies will come in chapters 8 and 10 and one more skirmish with the house of Saul in chapter 9, the story of Mephibosheth. But in the author's scheme of things, now is the time to talk about God's plans for David and David's plans for God.

   Nathan's oracle and David's prayer, found here in 2 Samuel 7 and in similar form in 1 Chronicles 17, are the foundation on which Jewish and Christian Messianic hopes are built. Today, an interpreter faces the challenge of attempting to hear these passages from at least five different perspectives, listed here in the chronological order in which each one became viable:

   1. *Monarchy (1000 B.C.):* Glory days. The perspective of David and Solomon and their contemporaries when hopes for the Davidic monarchy were strong and vibrant.

   2. *Exile (after 586 B.C.): Temple and city destroyed, people and king in Babylon.* The perspective of the author of 1 and 2 Samuel and his audience, living with the immediate shock of losing everything near and dear.

   3. *Post-exilic (400 B.C.): Modest temple, no king in sight.* The per-

spective of the Chronicler and his audience, grim appearances but with hopes still alive.

4. *Christian (A.D. 100): Universal community, spiritual kingdom, eternal king.* The perspective of those who accepted Jesus as the promised son of David, thereby dramatically transforming the literal meaning of the promises to David.

5. *Post-Christian Jewish (modern): Return to land and city, maybe a temple, maybe a messiah.* The perspective of certain strands of modern Judaism, refracted in different ways by the various segments of Judaism.

Our primary focus here will be on the second perspective, that of the author of 1 and 2 Samuel, with careful attention to the first, the perspective of those who lived in the days of David and Solomon; appropriate attention will also be given to the third and the fourth, the Chronicler and the Christian.

Given the remarkable story of David's rise to power, trying to experience Nathan's oracle and David's prayer as the author of 1 and 2 Samuel did is something like rereading the campaign promises of an incumbent candidate who has just lost the election or like reading love letters from a once-happy marriage now ended in divorce. From a more biblical perspective, it is like trying to sort out Job's angry words from the lofty speeches of his friends, knowing that from God's final perspective, Job had said what was right and his friends had spoken folly (Job 42:7-9).

From a more recent perspective, it is something like trying to understand the two worlds of Baruch Goldstein, the Brooklyn-born doctor who gunned down forty-eight Palestinians in a Moslem mosque in Hebron in February 1994, but who, some twenty-four years earlier as a grade-school youngster in 1970, had written: "Who will give something to bring about a situation such as this—that all human beings will live in peace, will not murder and will not covet the land of one's neighbor?" (*Newsweek*, 21 March 1994).

It isn't easy to imagine ourselves in the setting of the exile, and then, from that perspective, to "hear" Nathan's glowing words to David and David's grateful response. But by God's grace, His Spirit can help us hear, and in ways that are meaningful for our day too.

An Overview of Chapter 7

David contrasts his fine palace with the LORD's modest tent and says he wants to build a house for the LORD. The prophet Nathan says Yes; the LORD says No—and explains why: He doesn't need a house, never has. But He will establish David's house. David's son will build a house for the LORD's name, not for the LORD Himself. If the son strays, the LORD will punish him but will not withdraw His love. David's house will last forever.

In response, David says nothing about a house for the LORD but expresses awe and gratitude for the promise of an enduring house and asks the LORD to bless it.

Nathan's Oracle (7:1-17)

Nathan's response to David's suggestion is the clearest example in Scripture of a true prophet speaking in the LORD's name, then reversing the message because of a direct word from the LORD. It is possible, however, that this experience is more the rule than the exception. Prophets generally receive their credentials through a vision or some other kind of glorious manifestation of God's presence (theophany). Thus authorized, they then speak in the LORD's name, but not necessarily on the basis of visionary experiences. They interpret the times to God's people on the basis of their own best judgment and His revelations. The LORD promises to empower them (Exod. 4:1-8), to stand by them (Jer. 1:19), to purify them (Isa. 6:7), and to help them speak (Exod. 4:12; Jer. 1:9). Like Isaiah to King Hezekiah, a prophet may counsel resistance to a foreign invader (Isa. 37:6, 7). Or, like Jeremiah to King Zedekiah, a prophet may counsel surrender (Jer. 38:17, 18). And also like Jeremiah, a prophet may give a message from the LORD—then add "many similar words" to it (Jer. 36:32).

In 2 Samuel 7, nothing suggests that David questioned the prophet's authority because Nathan got it "wrong" and then corrected it on the basis of more specific instruction from the LORD. Indeed, the LORD's pastoral concern for people—kings included—

might suggest that Nathan's original affirmation of David's good intentions was just the "right" message. Having already been affirmed by the prophet, David was more prepared to receive the "correction" when it came.

In Nathan's oracle to David from the LORD, the first section (7:5-7) gives the LORD's rationale for *not* wanting David to build Him a house: He never needed one before and doesn't need one now. A tent was quite adequate. Was our author hoping that his exilic audience would recognize that the LORD could easily do without a temple? The temple was gone. Perhaps it should stay gone.

Nathan's oracle says nothing about bloodshed disqualifying David from building a temple. That argument, which David credits directly to the LORD, is recorded by the Chronicler in David's instructions on temple building to his son Solomon (1 Chron. 22:8).

The next section (7:8-11a) describes the specific benefits the LORD intended to give David and his house. In David's day those promises were believable and already mostly in hand: the people would have a home of their own and not be disturbed; the wicked would oppress them no more; God would give them "rest" from all their enemies. The exile, of course, would have thrown all such promises into chaos. But without flinching, the author of 2 Samuel reproduces them for his readers to ponder.

Finally, Nathan confirms the enduring nature of David's house (vss. 11b-16). Here, also, is his only mention of a house for the LORD, though not for the LORD Himself, only for His name. And that house would be built by David's son. David's own house, kingdom, and throne would all endure forever. Forever, forever, forever—three times Nathan repeats it (vss. 13, 16). That sounded good in David's day. But how would it sound during the exile, when house, kingdom, and throne—along with the temple, the house for the LORD's name—were all gone?

David's Prayer (7:18-29)

In David's prayer, the first line would be both painful and ironic for an exilic audience. David says: "Who am I, O Sovereign LORD, and what is my family, that you have brought me this far?" (vs. 18).

How far? All the way to exile? But David was just responding to the LORD's promise: "I took you from the pasture and from following the flock to be ruler over my people Israel" (vs. 8).

David concluded his prayer with a request for the LORD's blessing on his house. Such a blessing is never recorded explicitly in Scripture. As noted earlier, in the entire Old Testament, the only house of any kind directly blessed by the LORD was the house of Obed-Edom (Polzin, *David*, 65).

The succeeding chapters might suggest that David's house was more cursed than blessed. But that wouldn't be the first time an enduring house had been preserved as a continuing example of the LORD's curse. Consider, for example, the LORD's words to Eli: "I promised that your house and your father's house would minister before me forever" (1 Sam. 2:30). How could the LORD punish such a house? Not by obliteration, but by ongoing pain and suffering. Speaking to Eli, the LORD had said: "Every one of you that I do not cut off from my altar will be spared only to blind your eyes with tears and to grieve your heart" (vs. 33). That was the fate the LORD described in His message to Samuel: "I told him that I would judge his family forever" (1 Sam. 3:13).

David's curse on Joab similarly points to punishment that lasts "forever": "May Joab's house never be without someone who has a running sore or leprosy or leans on a crutch or who falls by the sword or who lacks food" (2 Sam. 3:29).

That fits David's case too. As Polzin says, "It is not accidental that the very next 'forever' to follow the eight forevers of 2 Samuel 7 is God's promise of perpetual punishment for the house of David" (*David*, 81). The reference is 2 Samuel 12:10: "Now, therefore, the sword will never depart from your house, because you despised me and took the wife of Uriah the Hittite to be your own." Polzin again: "A sword cannot remain over a house forever unless that house endure forever" (*David*, 81).

Such a somber view of the promises to David is only one perspective, of course. When the Chronicler retells the same history, he produces a much more hopeful view of the future, but in the process, also omits or sharply abbreviates much of the damning evidence documenting the chaos that struck David's house and which contributed to the decline of the monarchy. The Chronicler no doubt helped keep alive the "eternal" promises made to the house of David, thus preparing the way for their ultimate transformation by Jesus' message and ministry, a transformation that envisioned a community with no king but Jesus, where all humankind are brothers and sisters, and all are one in Him.

Revolutionary? Yet the author of 1 and 2 Samuel glimpsed the ideal from afar. Perhaps because he was so close to the disaster of the monarchy, too preoccupied with its evil results, he was not able to articulate the new vision himself. Thus, instead of transforming the promises of an eternal Davidic kingdom, he saw them as promises of never-ending pain, a sword that refused to depart. Christians, too, can profit from such a message. It's a warning worth remembering when we are tempted to arrogance over the LORD's blessings to His people.

Man of War (8:1-18)

Chapter 8 appears to be a summary or a sample of David's military exploits, probably not in any chronological order (Anderson, 130). The list could include victories from throughout his reign. From the standpoint of the author's purpose, the chapter illustrates a couple of points in Nathan's oracle, namely, that wicked people would no longer "oppress" the people of Israel and that God had given David "rest" from all his enemies (7:10, 11). A parallel to 2 Samuel 8 is found in 1 Chronicles 18, with numerous minor changes, additions, and deletions. The most notable deletion is the description of David's brutal execution of two-thirds of the Moabites (2 Sam. 8:2). The Chronicler was intent on giving a "good news" version of David's reign, though he apparently had no qualms about violence in general, since he, too, reported that David hamstrung Hadadezer's chariot horses (2 Sam. 8:4; 1 Chron. 18:4).

The Chronicler augments 2 Samuel 8 when he says that Solomon used the bronze David collected for the "bronze sea and the pillars and the vessels of bronze" (1 Chron. 18:8, NRSV). And he differs

with 2 Samuel 8:4, which has 1,700 horsemen captured from
Hadadezer (NRSV); 1 Chronicles 18:4 has 1,000 chariots and 7,000
horsemen. The Chronicler also gives Abishai, not David, credit for
killing 18,000 Edomites (2 Sam. 8:13; 1 Chron. 18:12). Finally,
2 Samuel 8:18 states that David's sons were "priests" (NRSV);
1 Chronicles 18:17 says they were "chief officials in the service of
the king" (NRSV).

As for the bloodshed implied and explicit in 2 Samuel 8, let's be
realistic. While wishing that David had behaved himself like an English country gentleman, given the violence of his age, we can hardly
expect it. What is remarkable here, however, is that he was seemingly more brutal than usual with the Moabites. After all, David himself was part Moabite through Ruth (Ruth 4:17; Matt. 1:5) and had
entrusted his own parents to the Moabite king for a time while he
was on the run from Saul (1 Sam. 22:3, 4). Yet if ruthless with the
Moabites, David was even more so with the Edomites at one point.
According to 1 Kings 11:15, 16, David and his army stayed in Edom
for six months until they had killed every Edomite male. Such a
foray is particularly jarring in view of the contrasting treatment
Deuteronomy mandates for the Moabites and the Ammonites, on
the one hand, and the Edomites, on the other: "No Ammonite or
Moabite or any of his descendants may enter the assembly of the
LORD, even down to the tenth generation" (Deut. 23:3). But, "Do
not abhor an Edomite, for he is your brother" (vs. 7).

In contrast with the Chronicler's "good news" version, the author
of 1 and 2 Samuel does not hesitate to include the uglier side of
David's history. That fits his overall purpose of showing that all the
kings, David and Solomon included, were thoroughly human, and
their participation in the flawed institution of the monarchy just made
matters worse. But whether or not he included the brutal details
about the Moabites here and the Edomites in 1 Kings 11 for the
purpose of subtly revealing the shadow side of David's experience is
debatable. And certainly his conclusion of the account in 2 Samuel 8
rings with affirmation: "David reigned over all Israel, doing what
was just [*mishpat*] and right [*tsedekah*] for all his people" (vs. 15). If,
as suggested earlier, David fell short of executing justice in connec-

tion with Joab's murder of Abner, here the author of 2 Samuel does not hesitate to affirm David's overall royal performance as "just" and "right," using the very words that are repeated twice in the description of the ideal king in Psalm 72: "Endow the king with your justice [*mishpat*], O God, the royal son with your righteousness [*tsedekah*]. He will judge your people in righteousness [*tsedekah*], your afflicted ones with justice [*mishpat*]" (Ps. 72:1, 2).

Since the parallel account in 1 Chronicles 18:14 includes the same words, both the Chronicler and the author of 2 Samuel were likely citing the views of a previous writer who had left his summary opinion on record in the royal archives. Still, the author of 2 Samuel had no qualms about including that glowing account of David's reign.

In connection with David's administrative skill, it is noteworthy that his list of chief officials at the end of chapter 8 includes three pairs: two military commanders (Joab and Benaiah), two priests (Zadok and Ahimelech), and two from the "state department" (Jehoshaphat and Seraiah). As Anderson puts it, "If this dual structure is intentional, its purpose may have been to lessen the accumulation of power in one pair of hands!" (Anderson, 136).

Mephibosheth (9:1-13)

In my teaching experience, I often have been distressed by my students' lack of chronological and geographical perspective when it comes to well-known Bible stories. They often have only a hazy idea of where the characters fit into the flow of history.

The story of Jonathan's son Mephibosheth is one of those "islands" that seems to float without roots in history—it's simply a touching story of a little boy, crippled when his nurse dropped him in her haste to take him to safety and later treated with great kindness by King David.

But it's much more than just a nice story. It has to do with promises and integrity. And when we take the whole of 1 and 2 Samuel into account, not just chronology and geography are of interest, but also the author's placement of the story in his scheme of things.

To catch the significance of what the story of Mephibosheth means

here, we need to review what has happened between David and
Jonathan and the house of Saul. And I must declare my own bias, for
as I have worked with 1 and 2 Samuel, I have been much attracted
by the figure of Jonathan. Of all the major characters in the story, he
seems to me to come closest to being "good." When he first appears
in 1 Samuel 14, he is a young, unassuming warrior who slips out of
camp to see if the LORD can use him against the Philistines. "Perhaps the LORD will act in our behalf," he says to his armorbearer.
"Nothing can hinder the LORD from saving, whether by many or by
few" (vs. 6). The LORD used Jonathan's simple faith to deliver all
Israel.

When he unwittingly transgressed his father's foolish oath,
Jonathan was ready to admit his deeds and pay the price. He didn't
defend himself; the people did (vs. 45).

When he next appears, immediately following David's victory over
Goliath, instead of seeing David as a rival, Jonathan embraced him
as a friend, even giving David his robe, tunic, sword, bow and belt
(1 Sam. 18:4). When Saul ordered his men to kill David, Jonathan
warned David and then confronted Saul, extracting an oath from his
father: "As surely as the LORD lives, David will not be put to death"
(1 Sam. 19:6).

But Saul still pursued David, attempting to spear him to the wall
(vs. 10). Michal helped David escape (vss. 11-17) and Samuel sheltered him for a time (vss. 18-24). Still on the run, David finally exclaimed to Jonathan in desperation: "What have I done? What is my
crime? How have I wronged your father, that he is trying to take my
life?" (1 Sam. 20:1).

"Whatever you want me to do, I'll do for you," Jonathan told him
(vs. 4). So David had Jonathan tell a lie for him. David told a fistful
of lies—so many, in fact, that the only one Scripture credits to
Jonathan was actually David's lie too—and Jonathan told it for his
friend David (vss. 5-8, 28, 29). Saul responded with a spear thrust at
Jonathan. Scripture says Jonathan was angry—but also "grieved."
Why? Because of "his father's shameful treatment of David" (vs. 34).

That same chapter describes the binding covenant between David
and Jonathan, and it is Jonathan who takes the initiative. It's his voice

we hear affirming love and commitment for David, not the other way around. The only explicit reference to mutuality comes just before Jonathan's final speech, when David "bowed down before Jonathan three times, with his face to the ground. Then they kissed each other and wept together" (vs. 41). The Hebrew of the next phrase is problematic. Literally, it reads: "until David magnified." The NIV translation "but David wept the most" (similarly NRSV) is suggested by the Latin Vulgate. Not that David resisted the covenant with Jonathan; it's just that Jonathan's commitment to David was so overwhelming and dominant.

The two men met just once more before Jonathan died in battle. While David was hiding in the Desert of Ziph, Scripture says that Jonathan went to him and "helped him find strength in God" (1 Sam. 23:16). The two of them "made a covenant before the LORD." Then Jonathan went home (vss. 18).

The essence of that covenant between David and Jonathan was that David would never cut off his kindness (*chesed*, "covenant loyalty") from Jonathan's family (1 Sam. 20:15). "The LORD is witness between you and me, and between your descendants and my descendants forever," Jonathan said (vs. 42). Later, during a brief moment of truth, Saul similarly asked David: "Now swear to me by the LORD that you will not cut off my descendants or wipe out my name from my father's family" (1 Sam. 24:21). Scripture is clear: "David gave his oath to Saul" (vs. 22).

David's powerful emotional reaction to the loss of Saul and Jonathan is recorded in 2 Samuel 1. Nothing in the chapter suggests that his emotion was anything less than genuine. And part of his lament testifies to his affection for Jonathan: "I grieve for you, Jonathan my brother; you were very dear to me. Your love for me was wonderful, more wonderful than that of women" (vs. 26).

But now, only after many years do we finally hear David's question in 2 Samuel 9: "Is there anyone still left of the house of Saul to whom I can show kindness for Jonathan's sake?" (vs. 1; compare verse 3).

The trail started with Saul's servant Ziba, apparently a man of some means, since he had fifteen sons and twenty servants (vs. 10). Ziba told David about Mephibosheth, who had managed to put some

distance between himself and David by living in Transjordan at Lo
Debar near the southern tip of the Sea of Galilee. He was staying
with Makir, son of Ammiel, a man who would later show hospitality
to David during Absalom's revolt (17:27-29).

Maybe twenty years had passed since Jonathan's death.
Mephibosheth was five when he lost his father (4:4) and now had a
young son of his own named Mica (9:12). Mephibosheth appeared
before David with a great show of respect and fear. David told him
not to be afraid, for he intended to show him kindness (*chesed*) for
the sake of his father Jonathan. Mephibosheth would receive back
all the property of Saul his grandfather and would eat at the king's
table in Jerusalem (vs. 7).

On the face of it, David sounds generous. And given what usually
happens to the descendants of a deposed king, Mephibosheth could
be grateful that he was still alive. Indeed, David may have been al-
luding to sole-survivor status when he asked, "Is there *anyone still*
left . . . ?" Twice he asked the question and each time used the word
still. What could he mean?

First, the readers of 2 Samuel would be quite aware of the demise
of Saul's house. Abner and Ish-Bosheth had both been murdered.
And even though David made a point of claiming innocence in both,
his failure to punish Joab implied a weakness that David himself
admitted (3:39). A more cynical person might suspect that David
really wanted the house of Saul out of the way. Furthermore, his
angry words to Michal after he had brought the ark to Jerusalem
reveal lingering hostility to the house of Saul (6:21, 22).

Second, another piece in the puzzle may be the death of the seven
members of Saul's house, described in 2 Samuel 21:1-14, an event
most scholars see as being chronologically prior to the events described in 2 Samuel 9. Even Polzin, who vigorously defends the
author's *literary* decision to locate the narrative of the slaying late in
the book, still admits to a "strong case" for it happening before the
events of 2 Samuel 9 (*David*, 98). If the slaying preceded
Mephibosheth's visit to David, then both his fear in David's presence and David's twice-repeated, "Is there anyone *still* left?" become
understandable.

A case can also be made for seeing David's treatment of Mephibosheth as being both generous and controlling. Polzin notes the ironic twist at the end of 2 Kings, where David's "son" Jehoiachin "ate regularly at the king's table" (2 Kings 25:29)—but, of course, as an exile and as the king's captive in Babylon (*David*, 102, 103)! Similarly, Mephibosheth was under David's control, since David could take away Mephibosheth's property at a stroke (2 Sam. 16:4) and give half of it back again (19:29), though it appears Mephibosheth may have rejected that last offer.

In short, the author of 1 and 2 Samuel would never deny the many good things that David did for his people. But he was also sketching a picture of a man who always gets what he wants—a dangerous tendency that put both king and people at risk.

Technically, David fulfilled his oath to Jonathan and Saul not to obliterate their names from history. And according to the genealogies included by the Chronicler, Mephibosheth's son Mica had a long list of descendants (1 Chron. 8:34-39; 9:40-44). So David kept his promise all right—just rather tardily. In the words of Polzin, "David showed *chesed* to Saul's house only after he allowed the Gibeonites' sword to descend upon most of its occupants" (*David*, 100). And even when he did show *chesed*, he kept a watchful eye on the last member of the house of Saul.

Mephibosheth's story appears in 2 Samuel but nowhere else in Scripture. The fact that the Chronicler's "good news" version of David's life does not include it also suggests that in spite its moments of beauty and pathos, the story foreshadows flaws in David's character that will soon plunge him and his kingdom toward chaos.

■ Getting Into the Word

2 Samuel 10–12

1. *Review.* **Return to the first suggestion in the "Getting Into the Word" section that opens this chapter and look at the references to God in chapters 10 to 12. Write a brief statement on what God's presence or absence means, especially**

in chapters 11 and 12.
2. *Geography.* Using the maps in your Bible or in a Bible dictionary, locate places and peoples mentioned in chapters 10 to 12. In particular, note where the allies came from who came to the aid of the Ammonites.
3. *The Innocent.* From chapter 11, list the innocent people affected by David's passion for Bathsheba. In your notebook, briefly comment on how God's forgiveness for David affected them.
4. *Punishment and Grace.* From chapter 12, list the indications that David's sin had to be "appropriately" punished. Then list the indications that God showed mercy or kindness to David, *not* treating him as his deeds deserved. Comment on what these two lists suggest to you as to the meaning of sin, punishment, and grace.

■ Exploring the Word

Last Battle Before the Storm (10:1-19)

Chapter 10 describes a battle between David and the Ammonites that was triggered by the humiliating treatment meted out to David's men by Hanun, the new king of the Ammonites. Misreading David's cordiality as cunning, the Ammonites seized David's men and left each one with half a beard and half a garment (vs. 4).

Though David's reaction was initially restrained, he began laying plans to even the score. Soon the Ammonites realized they were in for trouble and lined up a number of allies. But led by Joab, David and his men overpowered the Ammonites.

One remarkable passage in this account throws a positive light on Joab. Always the clever strategist, here, he reveals a simple faith in the LORD: "Be strong and let us fight bravely for our people and the cities of our God," he told his men. "The LORD will do what is good in his sight" (vs. 12).

Joab's expression of faith in the LORD didn't make him any less clever. By human standards, he was a gifted commander and set up an effective scheme that led to victory. But for us, perhaps the most encouraging word to emerge from this violent battle is that Joab was a believer. If there was hope for David's crusty general, then there is hope for the most stubborn of our friends and/or enemies. Indeed, there is hope for us too.

The chapter concludes with the report that David defeated the Arameans, the Ammonite allies. They "made peace with the Israelites and became subject to them." Furthermore, they "were afraid to help the Ammonites anymore" (vs. 19).

The Ammonites themselves, however, remained unsubdued. That was unfinished business for David and his men. They would go to war again in chapters 11 and 12—at least, David's men would. David would stay home and get into trouble.

Back in chapter 5, David and the LORD were in active dialogue before he went to battle against the Philistines. Even the summary of his military victories in chapter 8 includes references to David's commitment to the LORD and the LORD's blessing on David: he dedicated his plunder to the LORD (vs. 11), and "the LORD gave David victory wherever he went" (vs. 14). But with that reference in 8:14, the author lets the LORD disappear from David's life until that fateful statement at the end of chapter 11: "But the thing David had done displeased the LORD" (vs. 27). The LORD nowhere appears in chapter 9, the story of Mephibosheth's arrival under David's custody; in the account of the Ammonite battle in chapter 10, the only reference to the LORD is the remarkable testimony from Joab in verse 12. And in the fateful chapter 11, the author seems to avoid referring to the LORD, even where it would have been natural to do so. In verse 1, David sends out "his servants and all Israel" (Hebrew); in verse 11 Uriah refers to "the ark and Israel and Judah," and instead of swearing by the life of the LORD, he swears by David, literally, "by your life and by the life of your soul [*nephesh*]." All those would be prime places for the LORD to appear. He doesn't. Thus, when He *does* appear at the end of chapter 11, it's like a thunderclap from what David had pretended was a cloudless sky: "But the thing David had done displeased the LORD" (vs. 27).

The king who had mounted almost to the gates of heaven would descend into hell. And he wouldn't go alone. For us, it is important to realize that his fall didn't happen all of a sudden. A man with the intense passions of a David must stay close to the LORD. When he fell, he was at least a day's journey away. Earlier, before leaving Ziklag for Judah, he had asked the LORD, "Shall I go up?" And the LORD responded, "Go up" (2:1). David didn't ask that question before he went up to his roof that evening. How different the history of the world might have been if he had!

Falling From the Roof (11:1-27)

All interpreters recognize that chapter 11 marks the turning point of David's fortunes. As Polzin puts it, "at the center of the story of David we find something much more akin to the bursting of a bubble than to the relaxed deflation of a balloon. The tragic turn of events that follows chapters 11-12 is but a consequent reverberation of the explosive events of these earlier chapters" (*David*, 119).

If the author of 1 and 2 Samuel has allowed David to rise to glory with only subtle hints of his darker side, he now lays aside subtlety in favor of bold disclosure. The fact that the Chronicler ignores virtually all the potentially damning events accompanying David's rise to power could confirm the suspicions that those events were indeed potentially damning, though arguing from the Chronicler's silence may not be justified, since the Chronicler doesn't even re-port David's most blatant sins, his adultery with Bathsheba and the murder of Uriah. In fact, the Chronicler never once mentions Bathsheba, and Uriah appears only in his list of David's thirty war-riors (1 Chron. 11:41).

As far as the shape of 1 and 2 Samuel is concerned, however, David's story presents the reader with a choice, laid out by Polzin as follows: "Whether David originally served God but now seriously fails him, or whether readers only now find out the kind of calculating and self-serving person David has always been, is perhaps one of those gaps in the story that must remain unresolved" (*David*, 119).

But even if David's earlier history remains ambiguous, chapters 11 and 12 are dreadfully clear. In chapter 11 *we* suddenly see David.

In chapter 12, *David* suddenly sees himself.

From a superficial point of view, chapter 11 is simply the continuation of the unfinished business from chapter 10, the war against the Ammonites. Since Palestinian winters were generally too soggy for "elective" warfare, spring marked the return of hostilities. Hence the opening words of chapter 11: "In the spring, at the time when kings go off to war, David sent Joab out with the king's men and the whole Israelite army. They destroyed the Ammonites and besieged Rabbah. But David remained in Jerusalem" (vs. 1).

It was not wrong for David to stay in Jerusalem. But his innocence ends at the close of the first verse. And what follows leaves little to the imagination.

From his rooftop advantage, David sees a woman bathing. She is beautiful. He wants her. He sends someone to inquire about her. He doesn't ask *if* she is available; the ongoing narrative makes it clear that he is asking when, not if or whether. Scripture reveals no hesitation on David's part when he learned she was married. With report in hand, "David sent messengers to get her. She came to him, and he slept with her" (vs. 4). Then she returned home.

In the course of time, she sent David a message: "I am pregnant" (vs. 5), the only direct quote from Bathsheba in all of 2 Samuel. David got serious about coverup. Responding to the king's request, Joab sent Uriah home from the front. After asking him about Joab and the war, David said, "Go down to your house and wash your feet" (vs. 8). "Wash your feet" may simply refer to normal refreshment, but could be a euphemism for sexual intercourse (compare vs. 11); David's comment to Ahimelech that "women have been kept from us" (1 Sam. 21:5) implies that soldiers on active duty were to maintain sexual abstinence. Both Uriah's behavior and his words seem to confirm such a view. Yet his loyalty to his fellow soldiers was even more tenacious; he wouldn't go home at all, choosing rather to sleep "at the entrance to the palace with all his master's servants" (11:9).

The next morning, David learned what had happened and again urged Uriah to go home. Uriah was adamant: "The ark and Israel and Judah are staying in tents, and my master Joab and my lord's

men are camped in the open fields. How could I go to my house to
eat and drink and lie with my wife? As surely as you live, I will not do
such a thing!" (vs. 11).

So David kept Uriah the next night too. "At David's invitation, he
ate and drank with him, and David made him drunk" (vs. 13). Uriah
still wouldn't budge. He stayed at the palace all night. As Peter
Ackroyd comments: "Uriah drunk is more pious than David sober!"
(Anderson, 152, citing Ackroyd).

So David wrote a letter to Joab. It was Uriah's death warrant,
delivered by Uriah himself. The fiendish nature of David's sin is
becoming clearer: Joab becomes party to the crime, the army is placed
at risk, and as 11:17 notes, other valiant men fell in the same action
that killed Uriah.

When the messenger brought Joab's report, David further damned
himself by a flippant response: "Say this to Joab: 'Don't let this upset
you; the sword devours one as well as another. Press the attack against
the city and destroy it.' Say this to encourage Joab" (vs. 25).

The chapter concludes with stark simplicity: "When Uriah's wife
heard that her husband was dead, she mourned for him. After the
time of mourning was over, David had her brought to his house, and
she became his wife and bore him a son. But the thing David had
done displeased the LORD" (vss. 26, 27).

The Hebrew of the last sentence contains a striking irony. Literally translated, it reads: "But the thing that David had done was *evil*
in the *sight* of the LORD" (vs. 27, NASB), using exactly the same
words David had sent back to Joab: "Do not let this thing be *evil* in
your *sight*" (vs. 25, NASB margin). It's almost an echo of the Lord's
words to Samuel at David's anointing: "The LORD does not see as
mortals see; they look on the outward appearance, but the LORD
looks on the heart" (1 Sam. 16:7, NRSV).

Three times in his lament for Saul and Jonathan, David had cried,
"How the mighty have fallen!" (2 Sam. 1:19, 25, 27). Now it is true
once more. And the very first line in his lament, "Your glory, O Israel, lies slain on your heights" (1:19), is also true once again, though
a slight paraphrase makes the point more explicit: "Your glory, O
Israel, lies slain on your rooftop."

Waking Up (12:1-31)

Chapters 11 and 12 give some indication of the passage of time involved in David's crimes. A couple of months would have passed before David received the pregnancy report (11:5). After Uriah's death, a time of mourning passed, probably seven days (compare Gen. 50:10; 1 Sam. 31:13). Then Bathsheba was his. Apparently, it wasn't until the child was born that the LORD stepped in to awaken David.

Chapter 12 opens with the simple statement that "the LORD sent Nathan to David" (vs. 1). And Nathan launched right into his story of the rich man who stole the poor man's only sheep to feed to a traveler. David angrily interrupted, exclaiming that the rich man must restore fourfold, "because he did such a thing and had no pity" (vs. 6).

Nathan immediately thrust home the dagger of truth: "You are the man!" he said (vs. 7), then ticked off a quick sketch of all that the LORD had done for David. "And if all this had been too little," the LORD had said, "I would have given you even more" (vs. 8).

In back-to-back oracles, Nathan declared David's twofold punishment, matching sentence with crime. First, because of murder, "the sword will never depart from your house" (vs. 10). Second, because of adultery, "before your very eyes I will take your wives and give them to one who is close to you, and he will lie with your wives in broad daylight. You did it in secret, but I will do this thing in broad daylight before all Israel" (vss. 11, 12).

As the narrative unfolds, the first punishment is realized when the sword falls first on the child born to Uriah's wife, then on three of David's own sons: Amnon, Absalom, and Adonijah—a close approximation to David's impulsive response that the rich man must repay fourfold, though the Talmud interpretation includes Absalom's sister Tamar (13:1) instead of Adonijah (Yoma 22).

The second punishment, the public shaming of David's wives, is fulfilled by the defiant act of his son Absalom: "He lay with his father's concubines in the sight of all Israel" (16:22).

David's confession was simple and immediate: "I have sinned against the LORD" (12:13).

Nathan's assurance of forgiveness was just as immediate: "The LORD has taken away your sin. You are not going to die" (vs. 13). But Nathan also said that because of the contempt David had shown the LORD, the child born as a result of David's sin would die.

Two important points are worth noting here. First, David's sin did not destroy the LORD's *chesed*. The covenant was still intact. Second, preservation of the covenant did not negate the boomerang effect of sin. The LORD might be described as the one responsible for David's punishment, but in a curious sort of way, our modern perspective confirms the ancient dictum of the blood returning upon one's own head. David's example destroyed his influence with his children. In spite of the LORD's forgiveness, again and again and yet again, David reaped the "natural" results of his sin.

Having recognized, however, that the Old Testament confirms an almost automatic relationship between sin and its deadly natural results, we must also note that the Old Testament narratives defy our attempts at tidy categories when it comes to matching up "good" and "obedient" people with the blessings of the LORD. The paradox cannot be resolved. Almost in the same breath, for example, Deuteronomy lays out both tantalizing alternatives. On the one hand, Israel's status with God has nothing to do with her size or goodness but is solely an act of His mercy and love (Deut. 7:7, 8). On the other hand, however, He will "keep his covenant of love" with Israel *if* the people keep His commands (vs. 12). The LORD will preserve His freedom to save apart from any human merit—but also His responsibility to reward sin. And so we struggle to understand His ways with a seemingly well-intentioned Saul, a very good Jonathan, and a clever, self-serving David. Polzin may not be far from the truth when he declares, "The merits or demerits of someone delivered by God are, more often than not, irrelevant to the deliverance itself" (*David*, 91). Jesus was touching on the same phenomenon when He said that our Father in heaven "causes his sun to rise on the evil and the good, and sends rain on the righteous and the unrighteous" (Matt. 5:45).

As for David, his popular appeal to believers of all ages is not without explanation. In spite of the incredible damage caused by his undisciplined passions, David's quick and honest repentance after his sin with Bathsheba is a classic example for all to follow. And in spite of his frequent self-serving lies, wholesome honesty and openness often crop up in the story of his life. When Abigail kept him from bloodguilt, for example, he unashamedly admitted how close he had come to the abyss and praised the LORD for sending her to intervene (1 Sam. 25:32-34). And when his own men were on the verge of blows with each other after the successful recovery of the people and plunder belonging to Ziklag, David quickly and forthrightly laid down a key principle: Those who go into battle will share with those who stay with the supplies, in short, "All will share alike" (1 Sam. 30:24).

After Nathan had left the palace, the child fell ill. David immediately began to fast and pray with an intensity that alarmed his own staff. But he steadfastly resisted their efforts to make him eat. When he surmised, however, that the child was dead, he resumed normal activities. His staff was puzzled by his reaction, as we might be too. Why not a show of grief *after* the child died, as well? David simply explained that he had accepted the finality of the LORD's judgment. Life must now go on (2 Sam. 12:22, 23).

A sign of the LORD's goodness was given to David and his wife. She bore a son, and they named him Solomon. But the LORD Himself had a better idea and another name, reported by the author of 2 Samuel in striking fashion: "Because the LORD loved him, he sent word through Nathan the prophet to name him Jedidiah" (vs. 25).

David has fallen. The LORD has awakened him and even blessed him. Now Joab brings David back to the real world with an urgent summons to come finish the siege of Rabbah; "otherwise I will take the city, and it will be named after me," he reports saucily (vs. 28).

David goes to battle, overwhelms the enemy, and takes much plunder. He puts the Ammonites to forced labor and returns to Jerusalem. It is a great victory. But now David must try to pick up the pieces of his life and his shattered honor. That will get harder and harder, as the remaining chapters of 2 Samuel will show.

From Heaven to Hell: A Summary

While settled in his palace in chapter 7, David hears from the prophet Nathan a panoramic and glorious vision for both David and his people. David's response is marked with awe and gratitude. Chapter 8 follows with a summary of David's military victories, indicating at least partial fulfillment of the LORD's promises through Nathan. The chapter concludes by listing the members of David's administrative team.

Then the LORD disappears from David's life. In chapter 9 he belatedly fulfills his covenant obligations to Jonathan by taking Mephibosheth into his care. Chapters 10 to 12 describe a military campaign against the Ammonites, one that is interrupted by a guided tour of David's palace. He shows us his roof, his bedroom, his dining room, the entrance to the palace where Uriah the Hittite slept with David's servants, the writing room where David wrote the letter to Joab, and finally his bedroom again.

But David isn't giving us a tour of his palace. He is showing us himself. He has fallen from heaven to hell, committing adultery and murder. He has displeased the LORD.

Confronted by Nathan the prophet, David confesses his sin. The LORD forgives and blesses. But David still must pay the price for his sin. And the readers of 2 Samuel will know part of the reason why Jerusalem is in ruins and her king in exile.

■ Applying the Word

2 Samuel 7–12

1. *Forever.* In some ways, the promises to David that involved his throne and his house were not really "forever." What kinds of things can I expect from the Lord that *are* "forever"? Is Jesus' spiritual kingdom more secure in my life than David's material kingdom was for him and his family? What reasons can I list for my answers?

2. *Abused Blessings.* What specific promises and blessings from

the Lord can I recall that I later disregarded and misused to my own hurt and the hurt of others? Given my track record, is it safe for the Lord to bless me? Why or why not?

3. *Gratitude or Arrogance?* Am I able to recognize when gratitude for the Lord's blessings begins to turn to a dangerous arrogance? How?

4. *God's Presence.* How important is it to me to recognize the Lord's presence in my life even when I am doing quite ordinary things? How can remembering His abiding presence in my ordinary affairs of life keep me from dangerous moral crises?

5. *Generosity.* Though David appears to have treated Mephibosheth generously, his behavior can also be interpreted as a self-serving act designed to protect his own dynasty. To what extent do I see my own "kindness" to others as generous, but the kindnesses of others as "selfish"? Would it be better for me to be more probing of my own motives and less so of others'? How can I do so?

6. *Promises.* How conscientious am I in keeping promises? Is late better than never? Am I too conscientious, attempting to keep promises that have become impossible? Or is my tendency to forget promises that I should have remembered?

7. *Guidance.* How would it help protect me from sin if I were more open and explicit in asking for God's guidance? If I see myself slipping toward sin, would it be a helpful wake-up call to ask the Lord, "Shall I go up?" Or could that be just another way to delude myself into getting what I want? Give reasons for your answers.

8. *Forgiveness.* After a sin that hurts other people, am I able to accept the Lord's forgiveness as David did? Or do I tend to think that God has cast me off forever? Why do I feel the way I do?

9. *Grace.* Have I received a special token of God's grace—a Jedidiah—after I have seriously sinned against the Lord and other people? If so, how have I reacted to God's grace? What effect has it had on how I viewed my sin?

■ Researching the Word

1. *Forever.* Study the biblical usage of the word(s) translated as "forever" in our English Bibles. Using a concordance, develop a list of contexts in which *forever* clearly does not mean "endless" time and a list of contexts in which it does. The words are particularly significant for understanding prophecy and the nature of God's punishments and blessings. Write out your conclusions with supporting references.

2. *Comparisons: Samuel and Chronicles.* For an interesting comparison of the differences in the sources used by the author of 2 Samuel and the Chronicler, 2 Samuel 8:1-18 and 1 Chronicles 18:1-17 is a project of manageable size. Compare the two accounts verse by verse, noting each difference as it comes. Write a brief summary, describing the implications of your study.

■ Further Study of the Word

1. For general comment on the biblical narrative, see E. G. White, *Patriarchs and Prophets*, 717-726.

2. For a provocative analysis of the use of the term *forever* in 2 Samuel, relating to both promises and punishments, see R. Polzin, *David*, 54-87.

3. For a popularized presentation of Messianic prophecy from its Old Testament roots through to its developed Christian form, see A. Thompson, "The Best Story in the Old Testament: the Messiah," in *Who's Afraid?*, 130-157.

4. For a survey article comparing God's original plan for Israel with its ultimate expression in Christianity, see "The Role of Israel in Old Testament Prophecy," in F. D. Nichol, ed., *Seventh-day Adventist Bible Commentary* 4:25-38.

5. For a more technical literary analysis of the story of David's house from 2 Samuel 9 and following (sometimes called the "Succession Narrative"), see D. Gunn, *The Story of King David: Genre and Interpretation.*

PART FIVE

2 Samuel 13–24

David:
Wounded King in Decline

CHAPTER TEN

Rape and Revenge, Revolt and Return—Part I

2 Samuel 13–17

David had sinned. The LORD had forgiven. But the costly aftermath of his sin continued on and on. That aftermath is the story of chapters 13 to 20.

In this part of David's story, human weakness and intrigue stain virtually everything and everyone. Only the fringe players really win our affection—the loyal Philistine exile, Ittai the Gittite (15:18-22); the generous Barzillai (17:27-29; 19:31-39). Otherwise, it's only bad news. David's son Amnon rapes David's daughter Tamar; David's son Absalom murders his brother Amnon, then stealthily schemes to take the kingdom and kill his father.

David flees from Jerusalem, going into "exile" and crossing the Jordan in the wrong direction. The strong-willed Joab continues to kill in war and murder in peace, often flying in the face of the king's wishes and acting without his knowledge. But aside from an occasional whimpered protest, David does little to intervene.

By the end of chapter 20, David is again king in Jerusalem, but barely, it seems. The manner of his return heightens the tension between the tribe of Judah and the northern tribes (Israel), a tension that would finally sunder the kingdom in two in the days of Rehoboam, David's grandson. In the final episode of chapter 20, Joab negotiates for the head of the Benjamite rebel Sheba, then returns "to the king in Jerusalem" (vs. 22).

And where do we hear about the LORD in all this? Mostly from the lips of rebels, liars, and foreigners. Except for his oath in the name of the LORD (on demand) to the wise woman of Tekoa (14:11), David's awareness of the LORD's presence is largely focused on three incidents during his escape from Jerusalem. Only once does he talk directly to the LORD, a desperate prayer for the confounding of Bathsheba's grandfather, "O LORD, turn Ahithophel's counsel into foolishness" (15:31). And that does seem to represent a turning point in his fortunes, however small.

Only twice does he talk about the LORD, in both instances revealing a battle with depression. As he sends Zadok back to Jerusalem with the ark, he says: "Take the ark of God back into the city. If I find favor in the LORD's eyes, he will bring me back and let me see it and his dwelling place again. But if he says, 'I am not pleased with you,' then I am ready; let him do to me whatever seems good to him" (15:25, 26).

His second conversation about the LORD comes when the Benjamite, Shimei, curses David, and the king has to put the damper on Abishai to keep him from decapitating Shimei (16:9): "Leave him alone; let him curse, for the LORD has told him to. It may be that the LORD will see my distress and repay me with good for the cursing I am receiving today" (vss. 11, 12).

Finally, only once does the author explicitly interpret the LORD's will for us: "The LORD had determined to frustrate the good advice of Ahithophel in order to bring disaster on Absalom" (17:14).

As we try to imagine how the first readers of 2 Samuel would have heard the story unfold—unravel might be a better term—we can imagine them keenly aware of the fate of David's city, his throne, and the temple built by his son. And we can imagine them pondering the meaning of the two "promises" the LORD had made to David, one positive, the other negative: "My love [chesed] will never be taken away. . . . Your house and your kingdom will endure forever ['ad 'olam] before me" (7:15, 16) and "The sword will never ['ad 'olam] depart from your house" (12:10).

In one sense, at least as far as 2 Samuel is concerned, the narrative of David's rise and fall concludes with chapter 20. Chapters 21 to 24 serve as a kind of interlude before the story of the "succession" continues in the first two chapters of 1 Kings. There, Solomon settles a number of old scores from 1 and 2 Samuel, once more unleashing the sword in the house of David as he establishes his own claim to power.

For plotting to take the throne, Solomon executes his older brother Adonijah (1 Kings 2:25). He also executes David's nephew Joab (vss. 28-35) and demotes Abiathar the priest for their part in the same plot. The author of 2 Samuel sees the demotion of Abiathar as fulfilling the LORD's curse against the house of Eli (1 Sam. 2:27-36; 1 Kings 2:26, 27).

Before his death, David had charged Solomon to bring Joab's blood down on his own head because the infamous "son of Zeruiah" had killed both Abner and Amasa "in peacetime as if in battle" (1 Kings 2:5, 6). Though Adonijah's plot provided the occasion for the execution, Solomon also justified it on the basis of David's charge (vss. 28-35). Similarly, David had charged Solomon concerning Shimei, the cursing Benjamite: "Bring his gray head down to the grave in blood" (vs. 9). Solomon summoned Shimei, telling him to move to Jerusalem and stay there. "The day you leave," Solomon said, "your blood will be on your own head" (1 Kings 2:36, 37). Shimei agreed and kept his word for three years. But when he went to Gath in search of two runaway slaves, Solomon got wind of it and summoned him again. But before executing him, he said to Shimei: "You know in your heart all the wrong you did to my father David. Now the LORD will repay you for your wrongdoing" (vs. 44).

Following that account of Shimei's death at the end of 1 Kings 2, the author states: "The kingdom was now firmly established in Solomon's hands" (vs.46).

But all that ruthless bloodshed was simply the fallout from David's sin and weakness, as described in 2 Samuel. As is clear in His promise to David, the LORD's ideal was something quite different: "I will provide a place for my people Israel and will plant them so that they can have a home of their own and no longer be disturbed. Wicked people will not oppress them anymore, as they did at the beginning and have done ever since the time I appointed leaders over my people Israel. I will also give you rest from all your enemies" (2 Sam. 7:10, 11).

That was God's ideal. What if David had stayed in touch with the LORD, maintaining a firm grip on himself and on Joab? But maybe that wasn't possible with a king in the land. David had grabbed for power. Solomon would too. So would every king in Israel and Judah—until the LORD brought it all to an end.

The story told in 2 Samuel 13 to 20 is not a pretty one. Small wonder that not a single line of it appears in the Chronicler's "good news" version of David's life. And the continuation in 1 Kings 1 and 2 with its ruthless stories about Solomon's rise to power receives the same "silent" treatment at the hand of the Chronicler. This part of David's story is not a source of joy or good news.

One day, a Son of David would bring a true message of joy and good news to the streets of Jerusalem, though it would cost Him His life. His *message would be a radically different one, a message that just might have touched a responsive chord in our author's soul: "My kingdom is not of this world. If it were, my servants would fight to prevent my arrest" (John 18:36). In that kingdom, the King would call His supporters "friends," not servants (John 15:15). And His friends would serve each other as equals, for there would be only one Master, one Teacher (Matt. 23:8-10), a Teacher who would say to His followers: "The greatest among you will be your servant" (vs. 11). That King would teach by example, too, washing their dusty feet—much to their consternation and surprise—and saying, "So if I, your Lord and Teacher, have washed your feet, you also ought to wash one another's feet. For I have set you an example that you also should do as I have done to you" (John 13:14, 15, NRSV).*

That was not the kingdom of David or Solomon. Glimpses of such a realm shine through Nathan's promise to David. But human flesh is weak, even when the spirit is willing. And when the spirit isn't willing, all hell breaks loose. Or, in Nathan's words to David, "The sword will never depart."

In chapters 13 to 20 we read about the sword that won't quit.

■ Getting Into the Word

2 Samuel 13–17 (13–20)

Since 2 Samuel 13 to 20 are so closely linked together, the chapters in this volume that deal with this material (chapters 10 and 11) are also closely linked. You may want to read 2 Samuel 13 to 20 through quickly for an overview, then focus more specifically on particular questions, themes, or persons as suggested below, either for the whole block or separately for chapters 13 to 17 (chapter 10) and chapters 18 to 20 (chapter 11). You might want to experiment, either tracing each point all the way through or taking a cluster of items and working chapter by chapter.

1. *Discipline.* List the occasions when members of David's family, court, or kingdom deserved to be disciplined or punished. Note what action David took or (in your opinion) failed to take and what you think he should have done or left un-

done. Summarize the consequences.

2. *Characters.* Take notes on the people appearing in each chapter, identifying their strengths and weaknesses. Pay special attention to David, Absalom, Joab, and Abishai. Add 1 Kings 1 and 2 to your reading for David and Joab.

3. *The LORD.* Make a list of all the passages that mention the LORD or God in these chapters, noting the person who is speaking (either one of the characters or the author's own comment). Look for patterns, and summarize your conclusions.

4. *Places.* Note how key place names figure in the story, especially Hebron, Gilgal, and Mahanaim. Expand your knowledge of these place names by checking for other references in a concordance or Bible dictionary.

5. *Truth.* In the "truth" section of your notebook, record and evaluate the incidents in which people appear to be telling untruths or acting in ways that are not completely truthful.

6. *House of Saul.* Update your notebook. Evaluate David's role in dealing with Saul's people.

7. *Exile and Return.* Outline the key events and encounters in David's flight from Jerusalem (15:13–16:14) and in his return (19:9–20:3). Compare the two lists, looking especially for patterns in David's actions and thoughts.

8. *Exilic Perspective.* Read the story from the perspective of someone living in exile with Jerusalem, the temple, and the monarchy all gone. Make a list of the things in this passage that would likely be most helpful, most thought-provoking, and most troubling to such a person.

■ Exploring the Word

Rape (13:1-22)

At first, Amnon's rape of Tamar might appear to be simply a story of lust. But given the internal strife in David's house, it may also have been driven by power politics. According to 2 Samuel 3:2, 3,

David's three oldest sons were Amnon (by Ahinoam), Kileab (by Abigail), and Absalom (by Maacah). Since Abigail's son Kileab seems to have disappeared without a comment or trace, the handsome crowd pleaser Absalom was next in line behind Amnon. It is not impossible that Amnon was partly motivated by a desire to humiliate Absalom, putting him in his place by raping Absalom's sister (see Anderson, 172).

Though a political element is part of the story, from the author's perspective, Tamar's rape is linked, first of all, with Nathan's announced punishment of David's sin. A major part of the speech that follows his famous line "You are the man!" focuses on the women in David's life—past, present, and future. Through Nathan, the LORD declared in 12:8 that He had given David his master's *nashim*, the Hebrew generic word for "wives" or "women." While some scholars try to argue from 12:8 that David's wife Ahinoam was Saul's wife by the same name, there is no hint elsewhere in Scripture that David had any relations with Saul's wife Ahinoam or his concubine Rizpah. What is clear, however, is David's relationship with Saul's other women, i.e., his daughters. Saul had reneged on his offer to give his daughter Merab to David as his wife (1 Sam. 18:17) but did give him his daughter Michal (vss. 20-28). Though Saul at one point also gave her to another man (1 Sam. 25:44), David bargained with Abner to get Michal back (2 Sam. 3:13). The LORD had indeed given Saul's "women" into David's hands.

But in spite of David's many women—he was, after all, the "rich" man in Nathan's parable, the one who stole the poor man's only lamb—David still had a problem with women. He stole another man's wife, committing adultery and murder. Therefore, promised Nathan, David would suffer the public humiliation of *his* women in the future (12:11). The rape of David's daughter Tamar was already a partial fulfillment.

Scripture vividly describes the circumstances surrounding the rape. Amnon "loved" the virgin Tamar, but didn't know how he could get her. Virgin daughters of the king were likely well protected! David's nephew Jonadab, son of Shimeah (apparently a variant spelling of Shammah of 1 Sam. 16:9 and 17:13), a "shrewd" man and a friend of

Amnon's (2 Sam. 13:3), suggested a strategy that worked—ask the king to allow Tamar to care for her "sick" brother. Having sent everyone else out, Amnon grabbed Tamar when she brought him the food she had prepared. "Come to bed with me, my sister," he said (vs. 11).

She protested. He overpowered her.

Then, hating her more than he had loved her (vs. 15), he told her to leave. Again she protested. But Amnon called his personal servant and had him throw her out, bolting the door after her. Tearing her robe and putting ashes on her head, Tamar left, weeping loudly as she went.

Her brother Absalom took her under his care. She lived in his house, "a desolate woman" (vs. 20).

The story raises several issues about sexual mores and morality. First is the matter of incest. Pentateuchal laws explicitly forbid a man to have sexual relations with his sister, either the daughter of his mother or of his father (Lev. 18:9, 11; 20:17; Deut. 27:22). Apparently such laws were not in effect in Jerusalem at the time, or at least were not applied to royalty, for Tamar speaks with conviction when she says the king would give her to Amnon in marriage if he would but ask (2 Sam. 13:13). In an earlier era, Abraham also was apparently free to marry his half sister and did not hesitate to say so (Gen. 20:12). McCarter, however, argues that Amnon's crime was indeed incest, noting the author's repeated use of sibling vocabulary (*brother* and *sister* six times each in 13:1-14) and Tamar's strong language in her protest (McCarter, *II Samuel*, 323, 324, 328).

But whether or not Amnon's act was incest, it certainly was rape. The narrative is clear that he had no right to force himself on Tamar. Indeed, Tamar implied that it was inappropriate for her, a virgin, to sleep with him even *with* her consent. Although in the Old Testament world the rape of an unbetrothed virgin was generally seen as a less "serious" crime than adultery (sexual relations with a betrothed virgin or with another man's wife), it was still a grave matter. Virginity was highly valued and expected in a bride. Robinson notes that it is "still a pre-condition of marriage for women in most Asian countries" (G. Robinson, 220).

Deuteronomy 22:13-21 mandated the stoning of a bride who was not a virgin at marriage. In the words of the law code, "She has done a disgraceful thing [*nebalah*] in Israel by being promiscuous while still in her father's house" (vs. 21). Tamar used that exact vocabulary when she appealed to Amnon: "Don't do this wicked thing [*nebalah*]" (2 Sam. 13:12). The torn robe, the ashes, and the loud weeping were all part of her public testimony that she had been violated and would confirm her innocence if a pregnancy were to follow.

Tamar's "desolate" status in her brother's house suggests that she was no longer marriageable. And her plea after the rape, "Sending me away would be a greater wrong than what you have already done to me" (vs. 16), points to the law that required a man to marry a virgin he had raped (Exod. 22:16; Deut. 22:28, 29). In Exodus, the erstwhile virgin's father could nullify the requirement, though the offending man still had to pay the "bride price." The law in Deuteronomy includes no such provisional element. Indeed, it forbids the man to divorce his rape victim "as long as he lives" (Deut. 22:29).

All that made no difference to Amnon. He cast Tamar out of his house, brazenly adding insult to injury.

The royal reaction? The NIV simply states that David was "furious" (2 Sam. 13:21). Both the NRSV and the REB, however, include an additional comment, confirmed both by the Septuagint and the Dead Sea Scrolls: "When King David heard of all these things, he became very angry, but he would not punish his son Amnon, because he loved him, for he was his firstborn" (vs. 21, NRSV).

In short, David had once again shown himself incapable of acting. Amnon's emotions led him to commit sin; David's prevented him from punishing it; Absalom's would lead to blood vengeance, revolt, and contemplated murder of his father. Nathan had spoken truth: "The sword will never depart from your house" (12:10).

The damning nature of the story is further heightened by its frequent echoes of the ghastly story of the dismembered concubine at the end of the book of Judges. Polzin ticks off a long list of similarities (*David*, 136-138). Both stories, for example, involve the sexual abuse of a woman who is treated callously by her male companion:

"Get up; let's go," said the woman's husband in Judges 19:28. "Get up and get out!" said Amnon (2 Sam. 13:15). Both stories describe the crime with the same vivid vocabulary: "Do not do this vile thing [*nebalah*]," protested the old Ephraimite (Judges 19:23, NRSV), exactly the words spoken by Tamar to Amnon (2 Sam. 13:12). And her exclamation "Such a thing is not done in Israel" (vs. 12, NRSV) echoes the expression of horror at the crime in Judges: "Has such a thing ever happened since the day that the Israelites came up from the land of Egypt until this day?" (Judg. 19:30, NRSV).

But perhaps most striking from the standpoint of the author's purpose is the way he uses the last picture in Judges, namely, the violence and the collapse of justice among the tribes, as a pattern for the violence and the collapse of justice in the royal family at the end of David's reign. Just as the woman's protectors failed her in Judges, so Tamar's protectors failed her here. Absalom counseled his sister to be quiet (2 Sam. 13:20); he himself "never said a word to Amnon, either good or bad" (vs. 22). And King David just got angry; that's all (vs. 21). The last word in Judges was that the absence of a king meant no safety or justice: "All the people did what was right in their own eyes" (Judg. 21:25, NRSV). Now it was clear that kingship was no improvement.

Revenge (13:23-39)

Absalom waited two years before striking. His plot fell together neatly: the feast, the invitation, the polite royal refusal, the substitution of Amnon and the king's sons for the person of the king.

Absalom hid his emotions well, for there is no evidence that either Amnon or David suspected foul play—unless it is implied in David's question to Absalom: "Why should he go with you?" (vs. 26). The author simply says that "Absalom urged him" (vs. 27). David then agreed. The fact that Absalom had men who willingly responded to his orders to kill Amnon may suggest that he was already well on his way toward building a power base.

When Absalom's men struck, the rest of the king's sons fled. The rumor reached David that all the king's sons had been killed. Amnon's friend Jonadab was apparently not at Absalom's feast, for he was available to interpret the rumor to David even before the king's sons arrived on their mules (vs. 35). Jonadab seems to have been some kind of double agent, serving both Absalom and Amnon, unless Amnon's rape had driven him into Absalom's camp exclusively. In any event, he reassured David that Absalom had killed only Amnon. Clearly, Jonadab had "insider" information on Absalom's thinking.

With the royal household in an uproar, Absalom fled to the king of Geshur for refuge among his mother's people (3:3; 13:37). The author tantalizes us with a partial picture of David's emotions: "King David mourned for his son every day" (vs. 37). We don't know if the tears were for the son who was dead or for the son who had fled.

The final verse in chapter 13 shows that David finally had come to grips with the death of Amnon, his firstborn. But it is not so clear what his emotions were toward Absalom. Most English translations suggest that David was longing for Absalom. If so, then why did Joab resort to deceit to bring Absalom home from his three-year exile? Even when Absalom did return, he could not see the king's face for another two years. Later, during Absalom's revolt, David leaves no doubt—his emotions are so strong that they dictate his entire governmental policy. "Be gentle with the young man Absalom for my sake," he tells his troops as they go out to battle the very son who is seeking to destroy his father David (18:5). And according to Joab, David's final grief over Absalom almost cost him the kingdom (19:5-7).

Here, however, David's emotions are more ambiguous. Anderson translates the unusual Hebrew of 13:39 as follows: "So the king's anger ceased to be actively directed against Absalom for he had become reconciled to the fact that Amnon was dead" (Anderson, 182). Such a translation prepares the way for the events of chapter 14 and Absalom's return to power and influence.

The Rebel Returns (14:1-33)

Joab, the man who will kill Absalom in the end, is clearly in Absalom's camp as chapter 14 opens. He convinces a "wise woman" from Tekoa to tell David a parable. Though his overall objective is clear, Joab's story of the two feuding brothers is much more complex than Nathan's rich man/poor man tale. In 14:1 the Hebrew preposition *'al* presents an ambiguity that crops up again and again in the narrative: Was David "for" or "against" Absalom? *'Al* can mean either. NIV and REB have David longing "for" Absalom; Anderson has him "against" (Anderson, 182); NRSV and McCarter (*II Samuel*, 335) try to get the best of both: "The king's mind was on [*'al*] Absalom" (vs. 1, NRSV).

In any event, believing that he must convince David to bring Absalom home, Joab develops an elaborate ruse. The "wise" woman portrays herself as a widow whose two sons got into a fight, one killing the other. The clan wants to avenge the killing by taking the life of her remaining son. She pleads with the king to intervene so that they will not "quench" her "one remaining ember" (vs. 7, NRSV).

Given David's inability to bring Amnon to justice for the rape of Tamar, the complexities of the parable match the tangle the king is in. Clearly, Joab's purpose is to bring Absalom home. But the parable itself weaves together three concerns that stand in a certain tension with each other—blood vengeance, blood guilt, and the law of succession.

Blood vengeance was a primitive form of tribal justice in which the *go'el*, the kinsman avenger ("redeemer"), would pursue and take the life of a murderer (Num. 35:6-28). Blood guilt was incurred by the unlawful shedding of innocent blood, a sin that required atonement even if the culprit were unknown (Deut. 21:1-9).

Measured against standards of traditional justice, Absalom was guilty. First, he could not be a *go'el* avenging Amnon's rape of Tamar, since the *go'el* functioned only against enemies of the clan, never within the clan; second, Absalom had incurred blood guilt, since murder for rape did not qualify within the limits of the eye-for-an-eye law (Deut. 19:21).

Although the woman's story did not fully mesh with traditional law, especially with reference to the *go'el*, it did imply that some were demanding judgment against Absalom in order to clear the land of innocent blood. Bringing him to justice, of course, would complicate the question of royal succession, though hardly jeopardize it, as the parable suggested. After all, David did have other sons besides Absalom.

Yet the woman pressed David on that point of succession, arguing that it should take precedent over the legal demands incurred by blood guilt. Had David known what she was asking, he would have recognized it as an audacious request to exempt the royal family from normal justice. In the end, it simply may have been Joab's way of demanding that David formalize what was already happening in actual practice.

Before David could realize that he was on the verge of involving himself in a pronouncement, the woman pushed him a step further. Still disguised, she asked David to guarantee the safety of her remaining son (symbolizing Absalom). Initially, David simply wanted to send the woman home without a decision: "Go home, and I will issue an order in your behalf" (2 Sam. 14:8).

That wasn't good enough. "Let the blame rest on me," she suggested (vs. 9).

So David moved closer to a decision: "If anyone says anything to you, bring him to me, and he will not bother you again" (vs. 10).

Almost good enough—but still not ironclad: "Then let the king invoke the LORD his God," she said, "to prevent the avenger of blood from adding to the destruction, so that my son will not be destroyed" (vs. 11).

At that, David capitulated: " 'As surely as the LORD lives,' he said, 'not one hair of your son's head will fall' " (vs. 11).

Now she could point the finger: The king must bring back Absalom, his banished son. The king agreed—but bluntly asked the woman if Joab was behind it all. She admitted that he was, after which Joab suddenly appeared to thank David for the decision, interpreting it as David's personal favor to him (vs. 22).

But the overall impression is that once again, Joab is a threat to David and his house. Polzin suggests that this "son of Zeruiah" may have wanted David to see a reference to himself in the woman's parable when she spoke of "the man who is trying to cut off both me and my son from the inheritance God gave us" (vs. 16; *David*, 142).

The author, however, will tell us in 17:14 that it was the LORD's will to bring disaster on Absalom. From such a perspective, anyone aiding and abetting David's rebel son would be party to a crime against the LORD. Here, that would mean indicting Joab first, then David, for supporting him. David simply cannot stand up to Joab. Time and again, he capitulates, to his own harm and the harm of the country. In this instance, he lays the foundation for Absalom's destructive revolt.

Given the dubious motives driving first Joab and then David, the wise woman's glowing words in praise of David's wisdom appear ironic. Twice she compares him to an "angel of God": "My lord the king is like an angel of God in discerning good and evil. May the LORD your God be with you" (14:17). And again: "My lord has wisdom like that of an angel of God—he knows everything that happens in the land" (vs. 20).

Polzin (*David*, 141) notes that these warm words of commendation are bracketed in the author's story by two other speeches commending David's godlike qualities. Earlier, Achish had testified to David's integrity: "I know that you are as blameless in my sight as an angel of God" (1 Sam. 29:9, NRSV). Later, Mephibosheth will exclaim: "My lord the king is like the angel of God; do therefore what seems good to you" (2 Sam. 19:27, NRSV). Just how mistaken Achish was about David's integrity is revealed in 1 Samuel 27:8–12. And Mephibosheth's statement comes in the context of David's unpredictable decisions about Saul's property: all given to Mephibosheth (2 Sam. 9), then impulsively all given back to Ziba (2 Sam. 16), then on the spur of the moment again, half given back to Mephibosheth (2 Sam. 19). And the wise woman's own comments about David's wisdom come on the heels of David's sin and the LORD's promised punishment in chapters 11 and 12.

In short, in all three instances, what first appears to be praise turns out to be something like mocking irony. Just as Job's friends said fine things about God, only to learn that they were wrong, so Achish, the wise woman of Tekoa, and Mephibosheth all spoke words of high praise for David. They may have meant them honestly. But the author has put all three examples in settings that allow us to see how foolish it can be to multiply words in honor of sinful human beings.

The chapter concludes with a number of concise statements about Absalom and his return. While noting that the returned exile is forbidden to see the king, the author records some popular lore about him: "In all Israel there was not a man so highly praised for his handsome appearance as Absalom. From the top of his head to the sole of his foot there was no blemish in him" (14:25). We also learn that he had a marvelous head of hair and that his family included three (unnamed) sons and a "beautiful" daughter, Tamar (vs. 27).

But after two years, Absalom was chafing over the fact that he had not yet had an audience with the king. Joab apparently was ignoring him—until Absalom deliberately set fire to Joab's barley (vss. 30, 31).

When the two got together, Absalom declared that he would be better off as an exile in Geshur. "Now then, I want to see the king's face, and if I am guilty of anything, let him put me to death" (vs. 32). His bold stroke paid off, and Joab arranged the meeting with David. Absalom bowed low. David kissed him—a kiss that gave Absalom the momentum he needed to mastermind a rebellion against his father.

Revolt (15:1-12)

Chapter 15 opens with a vivid picture of Absalom's brash arrogance. "He provided himself with a chariot and horses and with fifty men to run ahead of him" (vs. 1). If the silence of Scripture means anything, even King David himself didn't have a chariot with horses! More serious, however, was the way Absalom "stole the hearts of the men of Israel" (vs. 6). He was energetic about it, too, rising early in the morning to greet visitors to the city. If anyone had a complaint, Absalom affirmed it as "valid and proper" (vs. 3). The king simply hadn't provided the proper personnel to give justice: "If only I were appointed judge in the land! Then everyone who has a complaint or case could come to me and I would see that he gets justice" (vs. 4).

Absalom didn't campaign to be king. He just wanted to be a judge, that's all. . . . He also may have been the original role model for baby-kissing politicians, for he made a special point of greeting anyone who came near to do him honor: "Absalom would reach out his hand, take hold of him and kiss him" (vs. 5).

Polzin uses the word *flagrant* to describe Absalom's disregard for Israel's law code (*David*, 150). He notes that in the history stretching from Deuteronomy through 2 Kings, the verbal form of the root *ts-d-k*, interpreting and applying the ideas of "justice" and "righteousness," appears only here in 2 Samuel 15 and in two other contexts—Deuteronomy 25 and 1 Kings 8. In Deuteronomy 25:1-3, the judge is assigned the responsibility for "acquitting the innocent and condemning the guilty." Absalom's half brother Solomon makes the same point in his prayer, calling upon the LORD to condemn the guilty and declare the innocent not guilty (1 Kings 8:32). Whether or not Solomon practiced what he preached is another matter, but at least he preached (or prayed!) it right.

By contrast, Absalom stole the hearts of the people by declaring everyone's case "valid and proper" (2 Sam. 15:3). He never knew a guilty person, for everyone he talked to was innocent! Thus what might appear at first glance as a sincere attempt to shore up his father's system of justice was actually a serious departure from the very foundation of Israel's heritage. Polzin's version of Absalom's claim in 15:4 accurately translates the Hebrew: "Then *every man* with a suit or cause might come to me, and *I would declare him righteous [ts-d-k]*" (*David*, 151, emphasis his). That's not justice. It's bribery and theft.

After four years of stealing hearts, Absalom was ready to wrest the kingdom from his father. In the name of a vow to the LORD taken while in exile, he asked David for permission to go worship the LORD in Hebron (vss. 7, 8). The LORD's name doesn't often appear in chapters 13 to 20, but when it does, it often is on the lips of questionable people or in questionable circumstances. Here, it is both. But David gave his permission: "Go in peace," he said (vs. 9).

So Absalom went in peace. But not really. His heart was set on war.

Remarkably, Absalom was able to work covertly with some and overtly with others. On the one hand, he sent messengers "throughout the tribes of Israel" (vs. 10), telling them to declare their allegiance to him at the sound of the trumpet—perhaps a series of trumpets would carry the message through the land at the designated blast from Hebron. On the other hand, the two hundred men accompanying him to Hebron from Jerusalem did so "quite innocently, knowing nothing about the matter" (vs. 11).

The strength of Absalom's support is reflected in the fact that he could actually spearhead his revolt from Hebron, the very place where his father had first been anointed king over Judah (2:4). How long it took for the revolt to break into the open is not entirely clear. The mention of the two hundred unsuspecting men from Jerusalem (15:11) might suggest a quick public announcement. And if Absalom himself was indeed offering sacrifices—the Hebrew of 15:12 is not clear whether he (NIV and NRSV) or Ahithophel (REB) was offering them—it would represent a full break with his father. But the last sentence of 15:12 suggests a more gradual and subtle build-up of power: "And so the conspiracy gained strength, and Absalom's following kept on increasing."

Fugitive King (15:13–16:14)

When the seriousness of the threat finally became evident at the palace, David himself described its potential in stark terms. Absalom could "bring ruin upon us and put the city to the sword" (15:14). So the king set out with his entire household following him. Curiously, however, he left ten concubines to care for the palace (vs. 16). Was he tempting Absalom?

As presented by the author, the escape from Jerusalem was a drawn-out, almost tedious affair, and heavily weighted with religious symbolism. At some distance from the city, the procession stopped so that David's men could pass in review before him (vss. 17, 18). The narrative that follows records five significant encounters with people who play a part in the ongoing story—Ittai the Gittite with his six hundred men from Gath, the priests Zadok and Abiathar with the ark, David's friend Hushai the Arkite, Mephibosheth's steward Ziba, and the cursing Benjamite, Shimei.

Before the chapter is over, David will have climbed to the top of

the Mount of Olives—head covered, barefoot, weeping all the way
(vss. 30-32). Everyone with him also had their heads covered and
wept as they went up (vs. 30). His first goal seems to have been the
summit, "where God was worshiped," the author tells us (vs. 32,
NRSV). The NIV translation, putting such worship of God in the
past ("where people used to worship God"), claims more than can
be proven from the Hebrew. The whole mournful journey suggests
a religious event. And if the NIV reading of 15:24 is correct (the
Hebrew is debated and debatable), the religious aspect assumes an
even higher profile, for it states that the Levites set down the ark at
a strategic point, and "Abiathar offered sacrifices until all the people
had finished leaving the city."

It is also of interest to note here that many commentators have
called attention to the fact that the Gospel writers seem to mirror
David's experience when they describe Jesus' way to the cross. Similarly, Judas's death recalls the suicide of Ahithophel (17:23), David's
friend and counselor, who defected to Absalom.

As for David's encounters along the way, the first was with Ittai
the Gittite, leader of the six hundred men who followed David from
Gath. David was amazed and grateful at Ittai's loyalty. His commitment to both David and the LORD is one of the few bright spots in
chapters 13 to 20: "As surely as the LORD lives, and as my lord the
king lives, wherever my lord the king may be, whether it means life
or death, there will your servant be" (15:21). Ittai brought with him
something of a crowd, too, for his six hundred Gittite warriors had
their families with them.

David next addressed Zadok the priest who was accompanied by
Abiathar and the Levites bearing the ark. The priests and the ark
must go back to Jerusalem, David said. He recognized that the ark
was a symbol that transcended his own personal interests. The return of Zadok, whose name denotes "justice" or "righteousness,"
could also symbolize David's hope that justice and righteousness
might one day reign again in Jerusalem.

At an earthier level, Zadok's son Ahimaaz and Abiathar's son
Jonathan were also to return to Jerusalem to assist with espionage.
They must keep David posted on events in the city (vss. 35, 36). It

would be a special challenge for the priestly contingent to appear supportive of Absalom while retaining loyalty to David.

David's encounter with his friend Hushai the Arkite is reported by the author as the concluding event in a significant three-part sequence: (1) The report to David that Ahithophel was among the conspirators; (2) David's prayer: "O LORD, turn Ahithophel's counsel into foolishness"; (3) David's arrival at the summit, where Hushai, with robe torn and dust on his head, is there to meet him (vss. 31, 32).

In chapters 13 to 20, David's only recorded conversation with the LORD occurs at this geographic high point of his journey and this psychological low point in his life. As commentators have often noted, no sooner prayed than done—Hushai appeared as the answer to David's prayer. He would, in fact, be the LORD's instrument to "frustrate the good advice of Ahithophel" (17:14). David sent Hushai back to Jerusalem to serve as counselor to Absalom. He was to swear loyalty to the rebel while maintaining his allegiance to David and furthering the exiled king's interests in Jerusalem (15:32-37).

Scripture is straightforward in reporting the royal mandate to Hushai. Does David's use of lies for the purpose of defeating the rebel Absalom show that "the end justifies the means"? *Brewer's Dictionary of Phrase and Fable* (14th ed., 1989) says that the dictum "the end justifies the means" is "a false doctrine frequently condemned by various popes, which teaches that evil means may be employed to produce a good result." *Brewer's* balances that comment with a verse from "Hans Carvel," by the English poet Matthew Prior (1664–1721):

> The End must justifie the means:
> He only sins who Ill intends;
> Since therefore 'tis to combat Evil;
> 'Tis lawful to employ the Devil.

In at least two passages, the author of 1 and 2 Samuel has linked the LORD with human efforts to use misleading words to accomplish the LORD's ends. In 1 Samuel 16:2, the LORD counseled Samuel to mislead Saul by telling a partial truth. Here in 2 Samuel 15 to 17, the deception goes a step farther and includes bold-faced lies. In both cases, the one deceived was no longer serving the "good." Indeed, both Saul and Absalom were seeking to destroy the "innocent" in support of their own personal aspirations after power and position. In the Old Testament, "self-interest" and "intention" are crucial for understanding truth telling.

That significance of intention is underscored in Deuteronomy 19:16-19, where the penalty for "giving false testimony" is described in reciprocal terms: Whatever the "malicious witness . . . intended to do to his brother" becomes the penalty. Thus intention becomes crucial for a correct understanding and application of the command against bearing false testimony (Exod. 20:16; Deut. 5:20).

But the story of David itself must give serious pause to anyone tempted to tell lies for a seemingly good purpose. His story is a wrenching biblical illustration of the slippery slope, of the one sin that leads to another, of the one lie that leads to another lie, and of the abundant heartache that follows.

From the three encounters with faithful friends and supporters, David moved on to two that were more troublesome: an ambiguous one with Mephibosheth's steward Ziba and one with the cursing Shimei that is just plain ugly. In a curious sort of way, David's encounters seem to start at the moral high ground and run downhill from there. First, the loyal but now-twice-exiled Gittites are most admirable, at least in one sense, for they are foreigners who follow David by extraordinary choice. Second are the faithful priests who go back to Jerusalem at some risk—but they are only doing their job. Third is the faithful Hushai, whose fierce loyalty to David emboldens him to stride into the lions' den for the king's sake—and to stain his soul with brazen lies for the same good cause. Fourth is Ziba, who graciously comes with food and pack animals for David (2 Sam. 16:1-4) but who (we learn later) may be telling lies about Mephibosheth for personal gain (19:27). Fifth and finally is the cursing, stone-throwing Shimei, certainly no friend of the king, but who just might be speaking on behalf of the LORD. In fact, a depressed David says the LORD Himself told Shimei to curse (16:11).

These last two encounters once again bring up the troubling spec-
ter of Saul's house. As David moved beyond the summit, Ziba met
him with a generous gift and gracious words: "The donkeys are for
the king's household to ride on, the bread and fruit are for the men
to eat, and the wine is to refresh those who become exhausted in the
desert" (vs. 2).

Traces of Saul's long shadow appear in David's words to Ziba, for
he addressed him not as Mephibosheth's steward but as Saul's:
"Where is your master's grandson?" David asked (vs. 3).

Ziba's response shatters our mental image of a grateful little
crippled boy: "He is staying in Jerusalem, because he thinks, 'Today
the house of Israel will give me back my grandfather's kingdom' "
(vs. 3).

With no sign of hesitation, David signed Mephibosheth's entire
estate over to Ziba (vs. 4), who gratefully accepted without murmur
or complaint. But one quick decision led to another. Just as hastily,
David would later revise his edict on Mephibosheth's property, dividing the estate in half (19:29). In both instances, a wise counselor
might have pointed the king to a pertinent passage in Deuteronomy:
"One witness is not enough to convict a man accused of any crime
or offense he may have committed. A matter must be established by
the testimony of two or three witnesses" (Deut. 19:15).

In the history of David's dealings with Mephibosheth, we recognize a painful irony: the same decisiveness that enabled him to grasp
and express spontaneously the principles of good government also
tempted him to make bad decisions under pressure. At Ziklag, when
his men were reluctant to share the recovered spoil, David laid down
the enduring principle of "share and share alike" (1 Samuel 30:24,
25). His decisions about Mephibosheth's estate were almost as memorable, not because they were good and enduring, but because they
were bad and short-lived. Similarly, the impulsive openness that led
David to confess immediately to Abigail how close he had come to a
massacre of Nabal's household was a near cousin to the volatile emotions that had triggered the call to arms against Nabal in the first
place. And that same volatility haunts his great sin, for in response
to Nathan's "you-are-the-man" speech, David quickly confessed his

sin—just as quickly, perhaps, as he had fallen into sin when he glimpsed the beautiful woman from his rooftop.

The fifth encounter, the confrontation with Shimei, brings into the open what the conversation with Ziba showed was lurking in the shadows of David's mind: the potential threat from the house of Saul. After David had queried Ziba about his gifts, he immediately asked about Mephibosheth (2 Sam. 16:3). Crippled feet might disqualify Mephibosheth himself from being king, but his son Mica, now close to twenty years of age, just might be a viable candidate.

Shimei's cursing shows how easily the friction between the house of David and the house of Saul could flare up. Here, the LORD's name again appeared on the lips of a scoundrel as Shimei trumpeted his explanation of David's distress: "The LORD has repaid you for all the blood you shed in the household of Saul, in whose place you have reigned. The LORD has handed the kingdom over to your son Absalom. You have come to ruin because you are a man of blood!" (vs. 8).

How much blood from Saul's house was actually on David's hands? Possibly a fair bit, at least in the popular mind. Though the chronological placement of the story is uncertain, the Gibeonite revenge on Saul's house (24:1-14) was likely already history, and King David had given the command to make it happen (21:6). The deaths of Abner (3:22-39) and Ish-Bosheth (4:1-12) could also be charged to David's account, even though the author goes to some lengths to show that David was not a party to either crime. Finally, at one step farther removed, a cynic could argue that David was also responsible for the deaths of Saul and his sons on Mt. Gilboa. Though David did not fight on either side in the conflict, his failure to fight with Saul's troops could leave David open to criticism. Even more significantly, since David was a formal ally of the Philistines, it could be said that he contributed to Israel's defeat by supporting the enemy.

Besides that list of bloody deeds, the names of Michal and Mephibosheth could be added to the list of potential complaints against the house of David. Michal, Saul's childless daughter, was back under David's control. And Saul's grandson Mephibosheth was also sequestered in the royal palace under David's watchful eye.

So Shimei had some grounds for cursing, and David was willing to let him rumble on, even in the name of the LORD. The stones and dirt that Shimei threw were more likely insulting rather than endangering (16:6, 13). But however much danger was involved, "Abishai son of Zeruiah" (note the full name!) finally had had enough. "Let me go over and cut off his head," he said to David (vs. 9). David said No. In David's view, the LORD could speak through this "dead dog," to use Abishai's term for Shimei. "It may be that the LORD will see my distress and repay me with good for the cursing I am receiving today" (vs. 12).

So Shimei kept up the cursing, stone throwing, and mud slinging. David and his people finally arrived at an unnamed destination exhausted. "And there he refreshed himself" (vs. 14).

■ Applying the Word

1. *Passion Control.* **How can a relationship with God help me to control my passions so that they don't ride rough-shod over the needs and rights of others? What instances in my life can I recall when I, like Amnon, have let passion hurt my family? What instances when I, like Absalom, have taken "justice" into my own hands, thus hurting myself and my family?**

2. *Ambition.* **Am I tempted by personal ambition to use other people to gain my own ends, perhaps even making impossible promises, as Absalom did to the people of Israel? How can I avoid such behavior?**

3. *Honesty.* **Am I more tempted to play fast and loose with the truth or to be too rigid, insisting on full, absolute, and truthful disclosure at all times? Have there been occasions when I should have been more honest? When I have hurt people with the "truth"? Was it a helpful hurt or a damaging one? Is a lie ever justified? Can the truth be a lie? Give reasons for your answers.**

4. *Tentative or Decisive?* **Do I tend to get into trouble by my**

impulsiveness or by lack of decisiveness? What examples in David's life could help me with my particular problem? How?

5. *Generosity.* When have I (like Ziba, perhaps) been generous for the wrong motives? Should I wait to be generous until I am sure that my motives are pure? Why or why not?

■ Researching the Word

1. *Sexual Morality.* The question of sexual morality is a very modern topic and a very ancient one. One way to study the biblical perspective is to use a concordance to discover the major contexts (especially the stories and the laws) by checking out key words (*rape, virgin, adultery, prostitute,* etc.). A Bible dictionary can often be helpful in identifying major and/or unusual passages that are important. The article "Sex and Sexuality," by Tikva Frymer-Kensky in *The Anchor Bible Dictionary* (5:1144-1146) provides a brief survey. Compare the legal codes with the actual practices as illustrated in the biblical stories, especially in 1 and 2 Samuel. Write out summaries and conclusions to help you clarify your own thinking. Comparing New Testament views with those of the Old Testament and with modern attitudes can also be helpful.

2. *Joab.* One of the most dominant, helpful, and troubling figures in David's court was his sister's son, Joab. Using a concordance, develop a list of all the contexts in which Joab appears. Analyze each passage for the purpose of developing a character sketch of the man. As a last step in your study, write out your conclusions about Joab: his character, his role in the kingdom, his effect on David's rule, and his standing before God.

■ Further Study of the Word

See at the end of chapter 11.

CHAPTER ELEVEN

Rape and Revenge,
Revolt and Return—Part II

2 Samuel 18–20

While King David flees for his life, his son Absalom is making himself at home in Jerusalem. A hard road lies ahead for both men. David will eventually return and rule once more from Jerusalem. But before that happens, his son Absalom will die at the hands of Joab. The sword is still taking its toll, just as Nathan said it would.

■ Getting Into the Word

2 Samuel 18–20

In the continuing saga of Absalom's revolt and David's return in 2 Samuel 18-20, we pick up the same questions that focused our thinking in chapters 13 to 17. The key items are repeated briefly here. For fuller descriptions, see "Getting Into the Word" at the beginning of chapter 10.

1. *Discipline.* Who should have disciplined whom? Summarize the consequences of failed discipline.
2. *Characters.* Note the strengths and weaknesses of key people: David, Absalom, Joab, and Abishai. Don't forget 1 Kings 1, 2 for David and Joab.
3. *The LORD.* Who talks about the LORD and when? Look for patterns, and summarize your conclusions.
4. *Places.* Note the role of key places in the story.

261

5. *Truth.* Update the "truth" section of your notebook.
6. *House of Saul.* Update your notebook. Evaluate David's handling of Saul's people.
7. *Exile and Return.* Compare David's flight from Jerusalem (15:13–16:14) and his return (19:9–20:3). Look for patterns in his actions and thoughts.
8. *Exilic Perspective.* Imagine yourself in exile as you read: No Jerusalem, no temple, no monarchy. What would be your thoughts?

■ Exploring the Word

Good Counsel for a Bad Rebel (16:15–17:29)

The tussle between Hushai and Ahithophel for control of Absalom's mind begins the moment Absalom arrives in Jerusalem. According to 15:37, Hushai arrived in Jerusalem "as Absalom was entering the city." The story resumes in 16:15 with the notice that Absalom arrived with "all the men of Israel," accompanied by Ahithophel. Hushai accosts Absalom with a double "Long live the king!" (vs. 16).

A double greeting from a double tongue! The reader knows which king Hushai is *really* referring to! Absalom does not, or at least he isn't sure. "Is this the love [*chesed*] you show your friend [meaning David]?" Absalom retorts, using the same term for covenant loyalty that marked the bond between David and Jonathan.

As the ongoing narrative reveals, Absalom accepts Hushai. His answer to Absalom as to why he did not go with David apparently was convincing, even if the written version reverberates with potential double meanings: "No, the one chosen by the LORD, by these people, and by all the men of Israel—his I will be, and I will remain with him. Furthermore, whom should I serve? Should I not serve the son? Just as I served your father, so I will serve you" (vss. 18, 19).

Hushai's rival, Ahithophel, seems to be first in counsel and is impressively endorsed by the author a few lines later: "Now in those days the advice Ahithophel gave was like that of one who inquires of

God. That was how both David and Absalom regarded all of Ahithophel's advice" (vs. 23).

Is it significant that Ahithophel's counsel is "like" someone who inquires of God? That same curious circumlocution is used by each of David's "admirers" who praise him for being "like an angel of God"—Achish (1 Sam. 29:9), the wise Tekoan woman (2 Sam. 14:17, 20), and Mephibosheth (2 Sam. 19:27). But as noted earlier, those seemingly resounding affirmations have a hollow ring to them in the larger context of 1 and 2 Samuel. If the author indeed uses their praise in ways that are ironic, does he do so here also? Probably. Speaking "like" God is not the same as speaking for Him. In fact, it's not at all clear that those who are "like" God in 1 and 2 Samuel are so described because they have any kind of contact with God. In short, wise counsel from someone who is "like God" may be very good counsel, but it's not necessarily God's counsel.

Based on his study of word distribution, Polzin puts a negative cast on the business of "seeking counsel" from wise human beings. He argues that from 2 Samuel 5, when David establishes his throne in Jerusalem, through 1 Kings 12, when Rehoboam loses the northern tribes to Jeroboam, no king of Judah—including David, Solomon, Rehoboam, or the royal pretenders Absalom and Adonijah—ever "asks of" (sha'al) or "seeks after" (darash) God "in their quest for future intelligence." He concludes that three generations of the house of David seem to have abandoned the ancient practice of inquiring of the LORD "through priests and prophets," replacing it with "merely human consultation." Even when Nathan conspires with Bathsheba to place Solomon on the throne, "the prophet uses language that befits this foreign or rationalistic phase in the monarchic history" (compare 1 Kings 1:12; Polzin, David, 175).

Absalom was definitely into seeking human counsel, and turned to Ahithophel, though the plural word forms suggest that he was addressing a group of counselors: "Give [plural] us your [plural] advice. What should we do?" (2 Sam. 16:20). Even if Absalom addressed a group, however, it still was Ahithophel who responded, and with a two-part agenda: First, make "yourself a stench in your father's nostrils" by sleeping with his concubines "in the sight of all Israel" (vss.

21, 22). And that's what happened—in a tent pitched on the palace roof (vs. 22). David knew about that roof. Now it was Absalom's turn. And sure enough, as Nathan had said, David's secret foray was matched by one "in broad daylight before all Israel" (12:12). Call it a fulfilled prophecy or your blood returning upon your own head or—to be more pointed—your sins of passion coming back upon your own roof.

Ahithophel's second piece of counsel was to track down David immediately. Send out a small force, and target the king only. Bring everyone else back safely (17:1-3).

Even though the plan sounded "good" to Absalom and the elders (vs. 4), they decided to ask a second opinion from Hushai. He just happened to have a counterproposal, one calling for a massive mobilization of "all Israel" and annihilation of David and all his men (vs. 13). He supported his suggestion with striking descriptions of a man far too dangerous to tackle with a small force. The exiled king was "as fierce as a wild bear robbed of her cubs" (vs. 8).

Without explaining the basis of their decision, Absalom and "all the men of Israel" opted for Hushai's plan. But if the author does not explain the human rationale behind the decision, he does interpret the mind of God for us: "The LORD had determined to frustrate the good advice of Ahithophel in order to bring disaster on Absalom" (vs. 14).

If Absalom did not fully adopt Hushai's counsel, he was even farther removed from Ahithophel's quick-strike plan. And when Ahithophel saw that his advice was not followed, he went home, put his affairs in order, and hanged himself (vs. 23). The fact that he was buried in his ancestral tomb suggests that suicide did not carry the stigma then that it does now.

In connection with Ahithophel's counsel, it can also be noted that if immediate action was required to implement a quick-strike plan, his other counsel to Absalom, namely, to sleep with David's concubines (16:21, 22), could well have been a hindrance.

Hushai himself seems to have been unsure about Absalom's intentions. Would he strike immediately (as per Ahithophel) or assemble a massive force (as per Hushai)? To be safe, Hushai explained both options to the priests, telling them to get an urgent message to David: The exiles must cross the Jordan without delay, "or the king and all the people with him will be swallowed up" (17:16). The comment in 17:24 that "Absalom crossed the Jordan with all the men of Israel" implies that the rebel was indeed hot on David's trail, whether or not he had "all Israel" with him at that point. But however the final plan shaped up, Hushai had somehow succeeded in turning "Ahithophel's counsel into foolishness," as David had prayed (15:31). Ahithophel, of course, saw it that way and took his own life (17:23).

Getting the word to David presented its own challenges. The two sons of the priests, Jonathan and Ahimaaz, were staying south of Jerusalem at En Rogel. Since it was too dangerous for them to enter the city, a servant girl was to pass messages on to them to be relayed to David (vs. 17). A young man spotted them, however, and told Absalom. Quickly taking refuge at a man's house in Bahurim— Shimei's hometown, no less—Ahimaaz and Jonathan climbed into a well in the courtyard. The man's wife put a covering on the well and scattered grain on it. Scripture says that "no one knew anything about it" (vs. 19). Anderson, however, interprets the Hebrew text as suggesting a more thorough camouflage: a well covered with sand "so that nothing (of it) could be noticed" (Anderson, 210, 215).

In any event, it was a close call, for Absalom's men came to that very house and asked the whereabouts of Ahimaaz and Jonathan. Whatever she told them is not clear to us (in the Hebrew), but it was to them. The men continued their search elsewhere and eventually returned to Jerusalem empty-handed (vs. 20).

The two young men climbed out of the well and carried the message to David. They were in time, for Scripture says that "by daybreak, no one was left who had not crossed the Jordan" (vs. 22). The multiple elements of deception in this incident again raise the question of the end justifying the means. The author of 1 and 2 Samuel might say it depends on what end and what means.

David and his people made their way to Mahanaim, some thirty miles (fifty kilometers) from the Jordan fords (vs. 24). Though the size of David's mercenary army would certainly help to "inspire" a cordial reception, it is remarkable that David took refuge in the very city that had been the capital of Saul's family under Ish-Bosheth and Abner (2:8). Polzin (*David*, 183) notes that David's arrival in Mahanaim is even more striking, since it represents the reversal of roles from 2 Samuel 2, where David was in Hebron as king over Judah, and Ish-Bosheth was in Mahanaim as king over Israel. Now, Absalom has gone to Hebron (2 Sam. 15) and David to Mahanaim (2 Sam. 17). How the mighty have fallen, or at least changed places!

Scripture names Shobi, Makir, and Barzillai as three Transjordanians who generously supplied the exiles with food and supplies. All three must have been both wealthy and influential. And they are notable for other reasons too. Shobi, for example, is identified as the "son of Nahash from Rabbah of the Ammonites" (17:27). Possibly he was the brother of Hanun, the Ammonite king who insulted David's men by halving their beards and garments (10:4). The war with Hanun that followed was the one bracketing David's affair with Bathsheba. While David was on his roof in Jerusalem, Joab "destroyed the Ammonites and besieged Rabbah" (11:1), the same siege that would take the life of Uriah the Hittite (vs. 17). David eventually joined Joab and led out in the final capture of Rabbah. He took much plunder, including the king's crown, and consigned the Ammonite people to forced labor (12:26-31). But in spite of all that, Shobi, son of Nahash, an Ammonite from Rabbah, voluntarily and generously came to the aid of David.

The second in the list of generous Transjordanians, Makir "son of Ammiel from Lo Debar" (17:27), had been Mephibosheth's host before David decided to show "kindness" (*chesed*) to the house of Saul for Jonathan's sake (9:1, 4). The third, Barzillai "the Gileadite from Rogelim," especially warmed the heart of David, not only for his generosity when the exiles first arrived, but also because he accompanied David partway on the return trip to Jerusalem (19:31-39). David actually invited Barzillai to join him at the palace in Jerusalem. "I will provide for you," he promised (vs. 33). But Barzillai begged off because of advanced age. In his final charge to Solomon, David singled out three people for Solomon to "remember": Joab and Shimei for execution (1 Kings 2:5, 6, 8, 9), but the sons of Barzillai for special "kindness" (*chesed*): "Let them be among those who eat at your table. They stood by me when I fled from your brother Absalom" (1 Kings 2:7). Barzillai the Gileadite joins Ittai the Gittite as one of the two really "good" people in chapters 13 to 20.

The Tree (18:1-18)

The battle with Absalom was joined in the forest of Ephraim, and it was a brutal scene. Without explaining why, the author says that "the forest claimed more lives that day than the sword" (vs. 8). David's men took the field against "Israel" (vs. 6), a reference that could suggest that the battle was once again between Judah in the south and Israel in the north—in other words, between David's supporters and Saul's.

Through circumstances related to David's return, those tensions would soon erupt again. But the situation during Absalom's actual revolt was much more complex. David, for example, was now in Mahanaim, territory formerly controlled by the house of Saul, and Absalom's power base was in Hebron and Jerusalem, David's former power base. On balance, it appears that Absalom hadn't stolen just the hearts of the people in the north; his influence had permeated every part of David's kingdom (15:6, 10).

Initially, David divided his troops into three companies, headed by the two sons of Zeruiah, Joab and Abishai, and by Ittai the Gittite (18:2). When David declared his intentions to march into battle with them, his men protested. The king meekly acquiesced to their wishes (vss. 2-4).

David was struggling with his emotions. As his troops passed in review before him, he told his three commanders, "Be gentle with the young man Absalom for my sake." The author notes that everyone heard those instructions (vs. 5). David had put his loyal people in an impossible situation. They were going into battle against the king's son who was seeking the king's life. And the king had just told them all to be nice to him.

According to Scripture, Absalom's end came when his head (not hair) got caught in the branches of an oak tree (vs. 9). His mule kept on going, and Absalom was left hanging in midair. Joab mocked the soldier who reported Absalom's predicament but refused to touch the king's son. The author reports the soldier's defense in some detail, including the repetition of David's words to the commanders, which "all" the troops had heard (vss. 12, 13).

Joab did not hesitate. Taking three javelins, he thrust them into Absalom. Ten of Joab's bodyguards surrounded the king's son and killed him (vss. 14, 15). Joab immediately sounded the trumpet, signaling the end of hostilities against "Israel," just as he had done once before at the beginning of David's reign (2:28). Joab and his men buried Absalom right there in the forest under a heap of stones. The author then states that all the Israelites fled to their homes (18:17), a clue to the fact that even with the rebel gone, the task of rebuilding the kingdom would be a daunting one.

The reference to Absalom's monument and his lack of sons is a forlorn note at the end of the battle account (vs. 18). According to 14:27, Absalom had three sons. Scripture does not tell us their fate. But the fate of Absalom, the rebel who died hanging from a tree, would give pause for thought to anyone steeped in Scripture. Deuteronomy 21:23 states that a person "who is hung on a tree is under God's curse," a comment that Polzin interprets to mean that "to be hung up" is a "fate worse than death" (*David*, 186). What would such a curse signify for the rebel and for the kingdom that had supported him?

One day another Son of David would hang from another tree, but in such a way as to transform the curse into a blessing. Jesus' followers boldly proclaimed His death as God's way to redemption, announcing to the world that God Himself had taken on human flesh, hanging from a tree in order to become "a curse for us" (Gal. 3:13).

But Absalom's death had no such redeeming value. For a while, he could be remembered by his monument in the King's Valley (2 Sam. 18:18) and by a pile of stones in the forest of Ephraim (vs. 17). But I'm not sure anyone knows where those monuments are now. All we have left is a stark picture, drawn for us by the words of 2 Samuel 18, of one of humanity's finest specimens hanging from a tree with three javelins thrust into his body.

Who Will Tell the King? (18:19–19:8)

With Absalom dead—contrary to David's wishes and at the hand of the king's own commander in chief—Joab, who was that commander in chief, faced the dilemma of how to tell David. Ahimaaz volunteered. But Joab said No, possibly because he didn't want to send a "good" man with the "bad" news that the king's son was dead (18:20). A "good" man implies good news, and this news was likely to be something less than good for the king.

So Joab called on a Cushite, a foreigner and a neutral figure, to be the official runner. He set off to tell the king (vs. 21). But Ahimaaz persisted, and when Joab finally let him run, too, he overtook the Cushite and sprinted into David's view first.

The narrator takes plenty of time to lead up to the formal announcement. The watchman reported to David no less than three times: once when Ahimaaz was first sighted, once more when the Cushite appeared on the horizon, and once again when Ahimaaz got close enough to be recognized (vss. 24-27). With each call from the watchman, David found a way to interpret the news as good. A single runner meant good news, he told the watchman; and since both men were running alone, each must be bringing good news. And again when Ahimaaz got close enough to be identified, David declared him to be a good man and hence a messenger of good tidings (vs. 27).

When within earshot of the king, Ahimaaz announced the victory. But David's first question was about Absalom, a question Ahimaaz didn't know how to handle, just as Joab had suspected. Did he fear a reprisal for bringing bad news? Joab had told him specifically that the king's son was dead (vs. 20). But for some inexplicable reason, Ahimaaz couldn't tell the king.

When the Cushite came, David pressed the same question and this time got the answer: "May the enemies of my lord the king and all who rise up to harm you be like that young man" (vs. 32).

Stunned, the king went up to the room above the gateway and wept. The author tells us what he said as he went: "O my son Absalom! My son, my son Absalom! If only I had died instead of you—O Absalom, my son, my son!" (vs. 33). Count them: "my son," five times.

Everyone could hear David weeping. The author says that the troops were slinking back into the city "as men steal in who are ashamed when they flee from battle" (19:3). Then he focuses once more on David: "The king covered his face and cried aloud, 'O my son Absalom! O Absalom, my son, my son!' " (vs. 4). Count them: "my son," three more times, for a total of eight.

That's when Joab came storming in, cutting loose with an incredible tirade. Let's note some of the more stinging lines. Remember, this is Joab talking to the king, no less:

"You have humiliated all your men" (vs. 5).

"You love those who hate you and hate those who love you" (vs. 6).

"You would be pleased if Absalom were alive today and all of us were dead" (vs. 6).

Swearing by the LORD, he concluded by saying that if David didn't go out and "encourage" his men, not a single one would be left with him by nightfall. "This will be worse for you than all the calamities that have come upon you from your youth till now" (vs. 7).

That is a mouthful, Joab. A real mouthful.

But it worked. In the words of Scripture: "The king got up and took his seat in the gateway. When the men were told, 'The king is sitting in the gateway,' they all came before him" (vs. 8).

The king's body is there, but the author tells us nothing about his emotions. We surmise that David has dried his tears. But has he found reason enough to look grateful?

At the risk of diminishing the author's intended effect from the powerful narrative, we should at least ask what his purpose was for including this intense drama of David's sorrow and Joab's anger. Was it to show us that in spite of everything, David was still a caring parent? Was it to show us how difficult it was to be a parent and a king at the same time? Or was it to show us that David's emotional trauma made it impossible for him to be king?

For a Christian, David's anguished cry, "My son Absalom! If only I had died instead of you" (18:33), immediately calls to mind the picture of One who did die in the place of His wayward children. And the swirling emotions of familial ties present us with a rich potential for exploring the mind and heart of God. What does it mean for God to clothe Himself in human flesh so that the Father dies in the Son—and thus God dies on our behalf and in our place?

"Anyone who has seen me has seen the Father," declared Jesus (John 14:9). And the Father He revealed to us is not one who angrily demands the death of sinners. Sin itself has already taken care of that. Our God has provided a sacrifice so that sinners might live. The inexorable law of sin, reflected in that vivid Old Testament dictum, "Your blood be upon your own head," is as true now as it was then and equally deadly. Sin punishes itself. That message is clear enough in the life of David and his family.

But how in the world do we keep sin from simply leaving a sobbing father over the city gate and a pile of stones over a beautiful body somewhere in the forest? There has to be a better way. God had to come and die in our place. And He had to live again. Or we are all forever under a pile of stones somewhere in the forest.

The story of David and Absalom is not the answer. But it is the question. And in the question we begin to sense that answer that is our hope.

For me, the drama of Absalom's death and David's sorrow has become so powerful that I have difficulty imagining what it might have meant for the author and his readers as they stumbled about in the ruins of Jerusalem. One thing they would have known for sure, however, is that every human king is also a very fragile human being. The implications of that insight are perhaps best reflected in David's own words, recorded in the last chapter 2 Samuel. It's another of his passionate outbursts, but this is one that still speaks with great power: "Let us fall into the hands of the LORD, for his mercy is great; but do not let me fall into the hands of men" (24:14).

I can't imagine anyone in their right mind wanting to fall into the hands of David. He might take your wife or your life. If somebody hurts you, he might come to your aid. But he might just get angry and leave it at that. Or he might tell you lies. But then again, he might wine and dine you at the palace for the rest of your life and his. The problem with David was that you never knew what to expect. So he spoke a great truth when he said he would rather fall into the hands of the LORD than into the hands of men. He knew what he was talking about. And after hearing his story, we do too.

Going Home (19:9–20:26)

After the high drama of Absalom's death, David's tears, and Joab's anger, the continuing narrative returns to the more mundane business of rebuilding the kingdom. If David's manners were bad and his emotions out of control when he heard the news of Absalom's death, the ongoing narrative suggests that his politics were also scrambled. Instead of seeking to bring the shattered fragments of his kingdom together, he threatened further fragmentation by pitting his own tribe, Judah, against the northern tribes, Israel.

Polzin notes that from 19:9b to the end of chapter 20, the term *Israel* refers "almost always to the northern tribes in contrast to Judah" (*David*, 181). That represents a significant shift in perspective, for in the chapters presenting Absalom's revolt (15:1–18:17), Polzin states that where *Israel* or *all Israel* (in various forms) is used, "it appears to refer to the whole nation, not just its northern part" (*David*, 181).

That analysis suggests that the tensions between north and south emerged with a vengeance after Absalom was gone and David returned to Jerusalem. While Absalom seems to have drawn strength from "all Israel," David inexplicably wanted to be recalled first by Judah. Having heard rumors that Israel was about to ask him to be king again, David sent a hasty message to the elders of Judah, one that missed the opportunity to bring healing: "Why should you be the last to bring the king back to his palace, since what is being said throughout Israel has reached the king at his quarters? You are my brothers, my own flesh and blood. So why should you be the last to bring back the king?" (19:11, 12).

David also sent word that he was appointing Amasa as commander of the army in place of Joab. Did David tell Joab before he told Amasa? Scripture doesn't say. Typically, Joab had no difficulty confronting the king, but David could not confront Joab—the sons of

Zeruiah (especially Joab!) were too much for him (3:39). But even if we don't know whether or how David broke the news to Joab, his words to Amasa throb with emotion: "Are you not my own flesh and blood? May God deal with me, be it ever so severely, if from now on you are not the commander of my army in place of Joab" (19:13).

David had hit all the right buttons as far as Judah was concerned: "He won over the hearts of all the men of Judah as though they were one man" (vs. 14). And so Judah invited David to return as king. Israel would be something else again. But Judah, at least, was now solidly in David's camp.

We can only surmise the complex blend of politics, justice, and revenge that led to the invitation from Judah and the appointment of Amasa in place of Joab. Amasa had been Absalom's commander in chief, "appointed in place of Joab" (17:25). But his pedigree is a jumble. Depending on whether one reads from the Septuagint or the Hebrew text of 2 Samuel 17:25 or from 1 Chronicles 2:17, Amasa's father was either an Israelite, Jezreelite, or an Ishmaelite. Most scholars favor Ishmaelite. The Chronicler identifies Amasa's mother as Abigail, David's sister, but with Jether the Ishmaelite (not Jesse) as his father. In any event, it would appear that Amasa and Joab were cousins and both were David's nephews. David appeals to the blood tie as a reason why Amasa should be commander of David's army.

It must have been a daring act for David to name Absalom's army commander as his own. But it may have been a key point in the negotiations with the elders of Judah. Was Joab demoted because he killed Absalom? Scripture doesn't say.

The narrative shows that David's return to Jerusalem was by no means automatic. He had to be invited, or "brought back," to use the language of both Israel (19:10) and David (vss. 11, 12). After he had the invitation from Judah in hand, David went as far as the Jordan, but waited there for the elders of Judah to "bring him across the Jordan" (vs. 15). Since the return to Jerusalem was a kind of ritual retracing of the steps he took when he fled the city, the act of crossing the Jordan was of particular significance—how, with whom, and when.

Gilgal was also prominent in the "return" itinerary. The elders of

Judah assembled there before going to meet the king (vs. 15) and it was David's immediate destination after crossing the Jordan (vs. 40). God's people had good reasons for remembering Gilgal. It was Israel's first stop after crossing the Jordan and the place where Joshua had set up the twelve stones taken from the river (Josh. 4:19, 20). Gilgal was also a place for the making and breaking of kings. Samuel had summoned the people to Gilgal to "reaffirm the kingship" under Saul (1 Sam. 11:14, 15). But Gilgal was also the place where Saul had forfeited the kingdom for failing to wait for Samuel (1 Sam. 13:4-15). And at Gilgal, Samuel confronted Saul for his failure to destroy Amalek: "You have rejected the word of the LORD, and the LORD has rejected you as king over Israel!" (1 Sam. 15:26). And from there we hear one of the most striking statements in Scripture: "Samuel hewed Agag in pieces before the LORD in Gilgal" (1 Sam. 15:33, NRSV).

Yes, Gilgal was a place for making and breaking kings, for anointing and rejecting them, and for hewing them in pieces before the LORD. On his way back to Jerusalem, David would go to Gilgal.

While the return to Jerusalem bears the external marks of a ritual reenactment of David's departure, explicitly religious references have faded almost completely. From 19:8b to the end of chapter 20, "God" is mentioned twice and the "Lord" twice, but each reference is only incidental and peripheral. David swears to Amasa in the name of God (19:13), and Mephibosheth (ironically?) compares David to an "angel of God" (vs. 27). Abishai wants to execute Shimei for cursing "the LORD's anointed" (vs. 21) and the wise woman of Abel asks Joab why he wants to "swallow up the LORD's inheritance" (20:19). Otherwise, no priests or prophets appear. There are no offerings, sacrifices, prayers, or praise. It's all power politics. In spite of the rich possibilities suggested by the visits to Gilgal and the "crossing of the Jordan" theme, it's all politics.

On the return journey, the king once more encountered Shimei and Ziba, and then Mephibosheth, each one an important link with the house of Saul. Shimei and Ziba were eager to please, willing to do whatever the king wished (19:18). Shimei, in particular, was profuse in his apologies. He confessed his sin and asked the king to put the matter "out of his mind" (vs. 19). Not insignificantly, he had brought with him a thousand Benjamites, and he noted for David's benefit that he was "the first of the whole house of Joseph to come down and meet my lord the king" (vs. 20).

But Abishai was ready to make Shimei pay the price for cursing "the LORD's anointed." Although Abishai was the son of Zeruiah that David could handle, the king still threw a jab at the "sons of Zeruiah" in the plural, declaring that they had become "adversaries" (*satan*) to him that day (vs. 22). "Do I not know that today I am king over Israel?" David exclaimed—perhaps protesting too much (vs. 22). "You shall not die," he told Shimei, confirming it with an oath (vs. 23).

But David would remember Shimei's curse against "the LORD's anointed" and in his final charge to Solomon would ask him to bring Shimei's "gray head down to the grave in blood" (1 Kings 2:9). Apparently David intended his oath to be interpreted narrowly, i.e., that David himself would not put Shimei to death. But since cursing "the LORD's anointed" was still a sin worthy of death, it was appropriate to pass the responsibility on to Solomon.

The author records no conversation between David and Saul's servant Ziba. But Ziba looms in the background as David "confronted" Mephibosheth: "Why didn't you go with me, Mephibosheth?" David asked (19:25). The disheveled son of Jonathan protested his innocence, claiming that Ziba had slandered him (vs. 27). Apparently David wasn't convinced. Perhaps his decision to give back only half of the estate (vs. 29) indicated a desire to reward Ziba for his assistance to the exiled king. But on any interpretation, the episode leaves question marks over both Ziba and Mephibosheth and further discredits the house of Saul.

But then a bright spot illumines the narrative: the farewell encounter with Barzillai. He accompanied David across the Jordan for a short way, and David treated him with great warmth and cordiality. Barzillai declined the invitation to stay at the palace with David, claiming he was too old; but he would send Kimham in his place. After David kissed Barzillai and gave him his blessing, the old man returned home (vs. 39).

With the personal encounters out of the way, the narrative erupts into conflict between Israel and Judah. Each side wanted to claim credit for restoring the king to power. Israel claimed numerical superiority; Judah claimed blood ties (vss. 41, 42).

The uproar allowed a Benjamite "troublemaker," Sheba son of Bicri, to rebel. He sounded the trumpet and called for Israel to abandon their claim to David (20:1). They did. Before David ever reached the city, "all the men of Israel" deserted him to follow Sheba. The men of Judah stayed by and ushered David back to Jerusalem (vs. 2).

David's first priority in Jerusalem was to put his violated concubines under house arrest. He would care for their basic needs but have no more sexual relations with them (vs. 3).

His second priority was to quell the rebellion. Calling Amasa, he asked him to bring the men of Judah to David within three days (vs. 4). Some scholars suggest that David set an impossible time frame just so that he could have an excuse to get rid of Amasa. In any event, when Amasa didn't show up on time, David called Abishai: "Sheba son of Bicri will do us more harm than Absalom did. Take your master's men and pursue him, or he will find fortified cities and escape from us" (vs. 6).

So the king had turned to Abishai, not Joab! Yet Joab kept on fighting for and with David's men as if he were still in good graces. Abishai might be in charge, but Joab was right behind him—maybe even in front! So when Amasa finally showed up, Joab gave him a cordial greeting—and plunged a dagger deep into Amasa's belly (vss. 9, 10).

Not only was the death ugly and lingering, but Joab seemed to be in charge again, for one of his men stood by the dying Amasa and pointed north: "Whoever favors Joab, and whoever is for David, let him follow Joab!" (vs. 11). But the troops didn't start moving again until Amasa's body was moved to the side and covered up.

Scripture says nothing about David's reaction to Joab's murder of Amasa. But that's not unexpected. David couldn't discipline Joab for the death of Abner or Amnon for the rape of Tamar, and his handling of the rebel Absalom puzzled everyone. In his final charge to Solomon, however, David would add Amasa's murder to the indictment against Joab. He commanded Solomon not to let Joab's "gray head go down to the grave in peace" (1 Kings 2:6).

As for Sheba, even though "all the men of Israel" had turned away from David to follow him (2 Sam. 20:2), his route and final destination suggest that no one particularly wanted to take him in. He ended up in Abel Beth Maacah, far to the north. And that was where Joab and his troops caught up with him.

As David's men began preparations for demolishing the city, a wise woman called to Joab from the wall, claiming that the city was "peaceful and faithful in Israel" (vs. 19). Just give me Sheba, said Joab, and I'll withdraw (vs. 21). The woman promised Sheba's head; after consulting with her fellow citizens, she delivered (vss. 21, 22).

Joab sounded the trumpet. The war was over. "And Joab went back to the king in Jerusalem" (vs. 22). The narrative closes with a list of David's officials like the one in 8:16-18. Once again, just as in that earlier list, Joab son of Zeruiah is commander of the army. That earlier list, however, is prefaced by an admiring statement: "David reigned over all Israel, doing what was just and right for all his people" (8:15). No such glowing preface appears in chapter 20.

Two other changes in the list are also worth noting. First, David's sons are no longer named as priests (8:18); their place has been taken by Ira the Jairite (20:26). Second, and perhaps more ominously, an officer is now in charge of "forced labor" (vs. 24). In Hebrew, his name is Adoram, though the NIV follows some Septuagint manuscripts and reads Adoniram, the man who was in charge of forced labor under Solomon (1 Kings 4:6 and 5:14).

Given David's glorious reputation as remembered in later years—encouraged, no doubt, by the Chronicler's "good news" perspective—it may be surprising that the story in chapter 20 ends with a whimper instead of a shout. The "succession" narrative will continue in 1 Kings 1 and 2 with an account of David's last days and his final charge to Solomon. The conclusion of 2 Samuel, however, is a carefully constructed appendix consisting of two striking narratives in which the LORD "plagues" Israel and her king, two military-style lists singing David's praises, and two hymns that David sings. The chronology of the events in chapters 21 to 24 cannot be determined, but their message is important for understanding the author's purpose.

Summary: Rape and Revenge, Revolt and Return

Chapters 13 to 20 show how David was punished for his sin. His women are publicly violated by his own son; the sword continues to devour, son against son, nephew against son, and nephew against nephew. That's what Nathan said would happen.

Maybe the LORD had told Shimei to curse after all (16:11).

Yet the LORD is rarely mentioned in these chapters. Warriors and wise men and women, all quite human, dominate the stage. And the house of David, like the house of Saul, grows weaker and weaker, even as it stands on the verge of its greatest external glory, the reign of Solomon.

For the exiled readers of 2 Samuel, David's exile and return would be particularly thought-provoking. When David fled, the ark went back to Jerusalem. But it is not mentioned again. And David's anguish at his departure is not matched at his return by a corresponding intensity, either emotionally or spiritually. But maybe that is the best that can be done with a king as human as David. And maybe a human king isn't such a good idea after all.

■ Applying the Word

2 Samuel 18–20 (13–20)

1. *The Tree.* **What does it mean to me that God took on human flesh and died for His children, just as David wished he could have done for Absalom?**
2. *Good and Evil Tidings.* **To what extent am I like Ahimaaz, capable of sharing only the good news? How can I prepare myself to share both good news and bad news with those who need to hear it?**
3. *Confrontation.* **On what occasions in my life has someone**

jarred me back to reality after a traumatic event, as Joab did
for David following the death of Absalom? How did I react?
Did I appreciate it or resent it? Have there been occasions
when I should have intervened as Joab did? Or do I think
Joab did more damage than good? Why or why not?

4. *Counsel.* Do I know how and when to seek counsel from the
LORD? How does seeking God's counsel relate to my readiness to seek good counsel from Christian brothers and sisters? Could a non-Christian counselor ever be a help to me
as a Christian? Why or why not?

■ Researching the Word

1. *Comparing Samuel/Kings With Chronicles.* One of the most
helpful ways to discover the purpose of one person's writing
is to compare it with someone else's work covering the same
topic. Within the Old Testament, the books of 1 and
2 Chronicles offer an ideal opportunity to place another version of the history of the monarchy alongside that found in
Samuel and Kings and to study the differences. An important idea to keep in mind (and to test continually along the
way) is the difference in the historical circumstances surrounding the writing of each history.

   Samuel-Kings interprets Israel's history in the immediate wake of the destruction of Jerusalem, the loss of the
monarchy, and the beginning of the Babylonian exile. Thus
a vivid realism about the deadly effect of idolatry and disobedience permeates these books. Chronicles, on the other
hand, interprets the same history to readers who were
threatened by discouragement over their sinful past. Hence
the emphasis is on the good news of God's leading and the
opportunities that still remain open to God's people.

   Pictured in practical terms, think of one story (Samuel/
Kings) being told to children who have been very naughty
and maybe don't even realize it yet. Then think of another
story (Chronicles) being told to children who have been

punished so much—maybe even for things they didn't do—that they are in danger of giving up.

Using chapter headings in the Bible to guide you, develop an outline of the story of David from 2 Samuel (and 1 Kings 1, 2). Then do the same for the story of David as found in 1 Chronicles. By comparing the two, discover the major additions and deletions in both accounts, and summarize your conclusions. The same kind of comparison can be done at a more detailed level when the same story is told in both histories. The whole process shows how God has used different messengers at different times to help different people with different needs—but using the same story.

2. *Vengeance and Redemption.* Does violent sin require violent redemption? The imagery of the *go'el* suggests that it does. Through the use of the language helps in your exhaustive concordance, do a word study of *go'el*, the kinsman avenger (traditionally translated as "redeemer"), and then pursue topics related to it. Include the gentle side of the story, as found in the book of Ruth, where Boaz is the *go'el* who "redeems" Ruth. But look at the violent side, too, as found in the provisions for the blood avenger (Num. 35:6-28). What does Scripture mean when it says that God "redeems" Israel, using the same root verb with all its "violent" overtones (Exod. 6:6)? Does a weeping David, wishing that he could have died for his son (2 Sam. 18:33), belong to the same story? What about Micah's reference to the sacrifice of the firstborn as a payment for sin (Mic. 6:7)? And where does the death of God's Son fit into the picture? There's an eternity of study here.

■ Further Study of the Word

1. For general comment, see E. G. White, *Patriarchs and Prophets*, 727-745.
2. For those interested in a broader and deeper study of 1 and 2 Samuel, two survey articles explaining and illustrating his-

torical trends in the study of 1 and 2 Samuel are found in D. N. Freedman, ed., *The Anchor Bible Dictionary* (1992). The first one, "Text, Composition, and Content," by J. W. Flanagan (5:957-965), shows how scholars have analyzed manuscripts, sources, and the editing process in an attempt to understand the books and their message. Flanagan's article describes and illustrates the more typical approach of so-called critical commentaries in the last century.

The second article, "Narrative and Theology," by W. Brueggemann (5:965-973), explores recent trends that emphasize coherence and meaning from a more literary perspective.

CHAPTER TWELVE

Falling Into the Hands
of a Merciful LORD

2 Samuel 21–24

At the close of 2 Samuel 20, David is again on the throne in Jerusalem. But unanswered questions remain: With the death of the Benjamite rebel Sheba and the return of Joab to Jerusalem, what was the status of the northern tribes? Did they eagerly, reluctantly, or sullenly return to David's fold? And what kind of king was David now that he was back in Jerusalem?

The author of 1 and 2 Samuel never answers those questions. And when the chronological sequence of events resumes in 1 Kings 1, David is old and bedridden, unable to keep warm even with many blankets. And Scripture doesn't say whether the innovative solution of sending a beautiful virgin to bed with him generated enough heat. The young Abishag cared for him, however, and Scripture is clear that David had no intimate relations with her (1 Kings 1:4).

In any event, from the bedside of a feeble David, we watch the final events of his reign: Adonijah's revolt, Solomon's succession, David's charge to his son, and Solomon's obedient execution of the details.

As an interlude between Joab's return in 2 Samuel 20 and David's bedridden appearance in 1 Kings 1, the author inserts an appendix of six diverse items, three pairs organized as a chiasm. Two plague accounts from an unknown time in David's reign act like bookends holding together the author's last word in 2 Samuel. His organization and the chiastic relationship between the six parts are easily illustrated in outline form:

Plague against Israel for the sins of Saul (21:1-14)
Exploits of David's mighty men (21:15-22)
David's psalm of thanksgiving to the LORD (22:1-51)
The LORD's oracle in praise of David (23:1-7)
Exploits of David's mighty men (23:8-39)
Plague against Israel for the sins of David (24:1-25)

Once again we sense both the agony and the ecstasy of David's reign. At the heart of the appendix is a celebration of human greatness and divine goodness. But the first and last scenes reveal a painful world of pride, punishment, and expiation—with God's mercy finding its way back as the author's very last word in 2 Samuel: "Then the LORD answered prayer in behalf of the land, and the plague on Israel was stopped" (2 Samuel 24:25).

■ Getting Into the Word

2 Samuel 21–24

For an overview, read quickly through 2 Samuel 21 to 24, the chapters that comprise the final "appendix" to 2 Samuel. Then read the appropriate portions again as suggested by the points noted below.

1. *Troublesome Story.* As you read 2 Samuel 21:1-14, list the aspects of the story that are troublesome to you, noting briefly in each case the reason why.
2. *House of Saul.* Review the entries in your notebook under "house of Saul"; then try to read chapters 21 and 22 from the perspective of a member of his family. Summarize what you think your feelings might have been. Then write a final summary for your notebook.
3. *Psalms of Praise.* Read chapters 22 and 23 from the perspective of your own worship experience. List those features that would nourish your spiritual life and those that might be difficult for you. Briefly summarize the view of David presented there, comparing and contrasting it with the view of

David as revealed in the story of his life.
4. *Census.* Read chapter 24 and its parallel in 1 Chronicles 21, noting the primary differences between the two accounts. Identify those features of the story that are troublesome for you as well as those parts that are helpful.
5. *Two Plague Stories.* Compare the themes and major elements in the two plague stories in chapters 21 and 24, making a list of similarities and differences between the two accounts.

■ Exploring the Word

Paying for Saul's Sins (21:1-14)

The violent story in 2 Samuel 21, like the story of the dismembered concubine in Judges 19 to 21, is one that many gentle readers would just as soon skip. And we're in good company, for Ellen White skipped it too, at least in her writings. In the "Scripture Index" found in the first volume of her three-volume *Index,* references to 1 and 2 Samuel abound, with every single chapter represented—except this one. The generous sprinkling of references runs right up through 2 Samuel 20 and uncannily resumes again with 2 Samuel 22. But chapter 21 doesn't earn the slightest squiggle of ink.

To summarize the story briefly: God sent a famine to punish Israel because King Saul had tried to destroy the Gibeonites, ignoring Israel's oath of protection, which the Gibeonites had gained by deception (Josh. 9). In response to the king's inquiry, the Gibeonites demanded seven of Saul's male descendants. David handed them over, and the Gibeonites executed them "before the LORD" (2 Sam. 21:6). Then Saul's concubine Rizpah maintained a lonely vigil over the bodies until David gave them a proper burial. "After that, God answered prayer in behalf of the land" (vs. 14).

The only way I can explain the story as part of God's larger plan for His people is to accept the premise that God condescends to work within the framework of a limited human understanding of right and wrong. Because sin continually distorts our ability to know God and His ways, He has to nudge us step by step toward enlightenment and truth. In the meantime, while He continues the task of refining our thinking, He asks us to be faithful to our conscience, however much it may be conditioned by the culture in which we live.

For us, the troublesome features of the story involve those acts of God that seem to fly in the face of *our* sense of right and wrong. They can be summarized under four main headings:

1. *Corporate punishment.* The nation paid for the king's sin, and his descendants paid for Saul's. Our individualistic culture demands that children *not* pay for the sins of their parents (compare Ezek. 18). And we do not want to hear that God visits the father's sins upon the children even to the fourth generation (Exod. 34:7).

Because the Old Testament so often describes God's hand as directly meting out punishment, it is easy to overlook the obvious truth of David's life that the parents' sins are visited upon the children *quite naturally*! Kings and leaders dramatically affect the lives of their people. If we have a say in choosing our leaders, we would do well to remember the lessons of 2 Samuel 21.

2. *Enforcing an oath procured under false pretenses.* To our modern way of thinking, contracts or oaths gained through deceit are not considered binding. In the Old Testament, where finely nuanced qualifiers were less likely to be realistic, an oath was binding regardless of the methods that put it into place.

3. *Sacrificing human life as expiation for sin.* Jesus' words are pertinent here: "You have heard that it was said, 'Eye for eye, and tooth for tooth.' But I tell you, Do not resist an evil person. If someone strikes you on the right cheek, turn to him the other also" (Matt. 5:38, 39). For the Gibeonites to claim blood for blood could hardly be called "Christian." Yet David went along with it in the name of the LORD. The cause may have been just. But we would likely consider the punishment excessive.

At the same time, however, if the story testifies to some innate human sense that blood demands blood, then the necessity of the death of Christ looms larger on the horizon. Abraham was ready to sacrifice his son at God's command (Gen. 22:12); the prophet Micah records the impulse to "offer my firstborn for my transgression, the

fruit of my body for the sin of my soul" (Mic. 6:7); and here in
2 Samuel 21, God honors the demand that blood be expiated by
blood. All the more reason to recognize the power of Paul's words
that "we have peace with God through our Lord Jesus Christ," because "while we were still sinners, Christ died for us" (Rom. 5:1, 8).

4. *Ritual requirements valued more than human life.* The famine
continued to plague the nation until David had given the members
of the former royal family a proper burial. Even though the people
of Jabesh Gilead had already buried Saul and his sons (1 Sam. 31:11-
13), God did not answer prayers on behalf of the land until the deceased members of Saul's house were buried in their ancestral tomb.

Again our modern age tends to rob us of any sense of the sacred.
Ritual becomes "mere" ritual instead of being an integral part of our
life. In David's case, if societal norms demanded reverent treatment
for the human remains of "the LORD's anointed," then serious steps
had to be taken to see that the "right" thing be done. And that is
what happened in 2 Samuel 21.

To sum up, I would simply say that however one might view the
origin of the customs involved or whether or not they were appropriate for God's people, the narrative is clear about what David and
his people considered to be right at that time. Until God reveals a
clearer and better way, He expects His people to be faithful to their
own standards of right and wrong. Thus Saul sinned when he broke
the oath to the Gibeonites because he "knew better." And only when
David, his royal successor, had put things right could the LORD be
satisfied that "justice" had been done.

Similarly, only when the proper burial rites for royalty had been
performed would God respond to prayer on behalf of the land (21:14).
God was the guarantor of justice and held David responsible for
practicing justice according to the accepted norms of his day.

Moving beyond that catalog of uneasy customs, we must ask how
this story fits the author's purpose. Some scholars have suggested
that it was intended to refute Shimei's claim that David was responsible for shedding the blood of the house of Saul (16:5-8). Others
suggest just the opposite, that the story subtly implicates David in
the massacre of Saul's house. But however one might see David's

role in the affair, the message that Saul's sin had been brought back on his own head, i.e., upon his descendants, would be a clear signal that Saul's house deserved to be judged.

Philistine Giants (21:15-22)

While seeming to sing David's praises, this brief account of his mighty men battling four Philistine giants actually pushes him into the background. Against Ishbi-Benob, a weary David was rescued by Abishai son of Zeruiah. David's men then insisted that the king no longer risk his life by going out to battle with them (vs. 17).

The reference to the killing of Goliath the Gittite (vs. 19) is also of interest, since here the credit goes to Elhanan, son of Jaare-Oregim the Bethlehemite, instead of to David (1 Samuel 17). In 1 Chronicles 20:5, however, Elhanan (described as son of Jair) is said to have killed Goliath's brother Lahmi instead of Goliath himself.

These differences have been explained in various ways. Some scholars propose that Elhanan was just another name for David, an explanation already proposed in Jewish tradition (Anderson, 255). Another explanation is that the Chronicler was attempting to solve the problem in 1 and 2 Samuel by "creating" a brother for Goliath (Anderson, 255). That more radical and "liberal" explanation was dressed up in "conservative" attire by the translators of the King James Version, who introduced the Chronicler's solution into the text of 2 Samuel 21:19: Elhanan "slew *the brother of* Goliath the Gittite."

Though the KJV translators were "honest" in what they had done, using italics to show that *"the brother of"* is not in the original text, their harmonizing tendency would later fuel the debate between liberals and conservatives, for when the American Revised Version of 1901 returned to the straightforward reading of the Hebrew text of 2 Samuel 21:19, i.e., that Elhanan killed Goliath, the discrepancy that then seemed to come to light was bandied about by liberals as one of many "errors" in Scripture. Thus the opening salvo in B. G. Wilkinson's *Our Authorized Bible Vindicated* referred to two articles in *The Literary Digest*, one entitled "Who Killed Goliath?" (29 December 1928), the other, "The Dispute About Goliath" (9 March 1929). Wilkinson threw down the gauntlet, using the Goliath incident as the entering wedge in his defense of the KJV as the only true Bible (Wilkinson, 1, 2).

I know of no easy solution to such discrepancies, at least not at the "micro" level. And they are not at all unusual in the parallel lists appearing in Samuel/Kings and Chronicles. If such details are an obstacle to faith, then it would be safer to avoid close study of Scripture, a subconscious solution adopted by many believers. At the "macro" level, however, it would be more helpful if we could somehow break the vice grip of the all-or-nothing mentality evident on both sides of the debate. The fact that Scripture is sacred text somehow makes it vulnerable to impossible demands. Even the Enlightenment philosopher G. E. Lessing (1729-1781) noted the phenomenon and regretted it. Referring to the differences between the various Gospel accounts, he said: "If we are likely to treat Livy and Dionysius and Polybius and Tacitus so respectfully and nobly that we do not put them on the rack for a single syllable, why not also Matthew, Mark, Luke and John?" (cited in Kuitert, 279).

As for the author's purpose for including this list of military heroes, he may have intended to portray David as a more ordinary mortal while praising David's men. Or is it possible that he is playing with irony again, presenting a weakened and vulnerable David just before the psalm in which David declares himself virtually invincible in the LORD?

Thanksgiving (22:1–23:7)

With only minor differences, 2 Samuel 22 parallels Psalm 18. In both contexts, the heading ascribes the psalm to David, indicating that it was a "song when the LORD delivered him from the hand of all his enemies and from the hand of Saul" (vs. 1). In vivid language, the psalm describes David's near-fatal encounter with death (*she'ol*, vss. 5, 6) and his successful cry to the LORD. Indeed, the LORD's response reverberates through heaven and earth (vss. 8-16). As Baldwin comments, "The concept of God and nature moving in concert to answer prayer for one man is bold almost beyond belief, if it were not affirmed in Scripture" (Baldwin, 288).

After describing how the LORD delivered him from his foes (vss. 17-20), the psalmist declares his purity and innocence in words that contrast sharply with the narrative of David's life: "The LORD has dealt with me according to my righteousness; according to the cleanness of my hands he has rewarded me" (vs. 21). "I have been blameless before him and have kept myself from sin" (vs. 24).

A brief word of praise for God is followed by a detailed description of how God had given him victory over his foes: "I pursued my enemies and crushed them; I did not turn back till they were destroyed" (vs. 38). "They cried for help, but there was no one to save them—to the LORD, but he did not answer. I beat them as fine as the dust of the earth; I pounded and trampled them like mud in the streets" (vss. 42, 43).

The psalm concludes with more praise of God and an application to "his anointed, to David and his descendants forever" (vs. 51).

The "last words of David" (23:1) follow immediately in 23:1-7, a shorter piece described as an "oracle of David" (vs. 1). And here the words are even more glowing: "When one rules over men in righteousness, when he rules in the fear of God, he is like the light of morning at sunrise on a cloudless morning, like the brightness [*nogah*] after rain that brings the grass from the earth" (vss. 3, 4).

In the words of Polzin (*David*, 205): "David basks in the reflected glory of God's favor. The brightness (*nogah*) he ascribed to God in 22:13, he now openly appropriates to himself in 23:4." Polzin notes that the "solar language" that David here applies to himself is found elsewhere in the Old Testament only in Psalm 84:11, where it is applied to God Himself: "For the LORD God is a sun and shield; the LORD bestows favor and honor" (*David*, 204).

If these hymns that praise God's glory and its reflection in David's own experience were independent of their narrative context, they could be more readily accepted simply as glorious expressions of thanksgiving. In worship, "the sweet psalmist of Israel" (23:1, KJV) can more easily be forgiven the language of superlative, exaggeration, and hyperbole, for that has always been the language of believers when they celebrate God's goodness—the world was so very dark until He intervened with a burst of glorious light.

When applied to the historical David, however, the contrast between the realities of flesh and blood and the glories of divinity stands out with striking clarity. In a sense, the Christian practice of applying the psalms to a truer "Son of David" rather than to the real David in the flesh is spiritually perceptive. The real David of history did not approach the blameless, all-powerful, and glorious image announced in these psalms. Though Polzin (*David*, 202-207) presses the contrast too far, he is right in calling attention to the note of realism sounded in the preceding military annals. Hardly the all-conquering warrior-king, David grows "exhausted" in battle and has to be rescued by Abishai. Then his men tell him that he cannot go out to battle anymore lest the "lamp of Israel" be "extinguished" (21:15-17). That contrast between the exhaustion of real life and the exuberance of real worship is "like the difference between a flickering lamp and the blazing sun," to borrow Polzin's phrase (*David*, 205).

Writing in view of the ruins of David's kingdom, the author of 1 and 2 Samuel may have wanted his readers to ponder the contrast between the David of history and the David of the psalms. Was David too quick to declare in song that God had exalted him over his adversaries (22:49)? He could and did sing a more self-effacing line, declaring of the LORD: "You save the humble, but your eyes are on the haughty to bring them low" (vs. 28). But humility is always at risk in the aftermath of a great deliverance. And that may have been David's problem.

In the poetry at the beginning of 1 Samuel, Hannah faced the same problem, exclaiming, "My mouth boasts over my enemies" (2:1). But then she says: "Do not keep talking so proudly or let your mouth speak such arrogance" (vs. 3). In short, the exuberance of deliverance may lead to an arrogance that must again be humbled through distress, a dilemma believers constantly face in real life. And Hannah knew that the LORD could act on both sides, for "the LORD brings death and makes alive; he brings down to the grave and raises up. The LORD sends poverty and wealth; he humbles and he exalts" (vss. 6, 7).

For Hannah, for David, and for us, Polzin's concluding words come close to the truth: "David's mistake, foreshadowed by Hannah and documented throughout the History, was to move too quickly from exaltation to exultation" (*David*, 207).

More Mighty Men (23:8-39)

Immediately following the two glorious hymns in praise of God and David, the author inserts another list of David's military heroes, a cushion between the glories of the psalms and the deadly agony of the plague account that follows. The parallel list is found in 1 Chronicles 11:10-47, with enough variations to make comparisons interesting.

The annalist seems intrigued with the number 3 and its multiples, using "three" ten times, "thirty" three times, "three hundred" once—and if one tinkers with the Chronicler's parallel passage, yet another three hundred can be garnered from 1 Chronicles 11:11, a replacement for the eight hundred of 2 Samuel 23:8. The number 3 also crops up elsewhere in the appendix: three years of famine (21:1); Ishbi-Benob's spear, weighing three hundred shekels (vs. 16); three months of flight from David's enemies and three days of pestilence (24:13). Extend the author's interest in numbers to 7, as in the seven members of Saul's family who die in 21:9 and the seventy thousand Israelites who die in 24:15, and you have quite an interest in "ideal" numbers. Conceivably, such an interest could explain the explicit statement at the end of the list that "there were thirty-seven in all" (thirty plus seven?; 23:39), even though the list includes only thirty-six names. It is also possible, of course, that a name has fallen out, perhaps "Zabad son of Ahlai," who appears in the Chronicler's list (1 Chron. 11:41; Anderson, 277).

In spite of the author's attraction for numbers, however, it must be said that he did not seem particularly interested in using them with the kind of precision we might desire. Attempting to sort out how all the threes relate to each other and to the thirty is no simple task. And the Chronicler doesn't help us much, either. He uses some alternate names, adds and deletes, and because he inserts a whole cluster of names at the end, he understandably omits any reference to a total of thirty-seven.

In terms of content, the list in 2 Samuel includes some narrative expansion in 23:8-23. The longest note involves a picture of David's reverential awe at his warriors' gift of water from the well in Bethlehem, water that he poured on the ground as an offering to the LORD (vs. 16). "Is it not the blood of men who went at the risk of their lives?" David said (vs. 17).

Aside from the obvious symmetry that the list provides in the chiasm, balancing out the previous list of exploits against the Philistines (21:15-22), it is more difficult to asses the author's purpose for the list here. Having said that, however, the name with which he concludes the list is a startling one: Uriah the Hittite. Most of the other names are not prominent in the story of David's life. But Uriah we know. We have met him somewhere before. And his is the last name before the plague story in chapter 24.

In the Hands of the LORD (24:1-25)

The last story in 2 Samuel is another jarring one. Scripture says: "Again the anger of the LORD burned against Israel, and he incited David against them, saying, 'Go and take a census of Israel and Judah' " (vs. 1). The word *again* harks back to the beginning of the appendix and the story of blood guilt for Saul in chapter 21. Here, once again, is royal culpability, the suffering of innocent people, sacrifice, and the mercy of the LORD.

The parallel account in 1 Chronicles 21 reveals several striking differences: Samuel records eight hundred thousand fighting men in Israel; the Chronicler has one million, one hundred thousand (2 Sam. 24:9; 1 Chron. 21:5). Samuel has five hundred thousand in Judah; the Chronicler gives four hundred and seventy thousand, noting that the total does not include Benjamin or Levi (2 Sam. 24:9; 1 Chron. 21:5, 6). In Samuel, David pays fifty shekels of silver for "the threshing floor and the oxen"; in Chronicles, he pays "six hundred shekels of gold for the site" (2 Sam. 24:24; 1 Chron. 21:25).

In Samuel, the owner's name is consistently Araunah; in Chronicles, it is consistently Ornan (2 Sam. 24:16; 1 Chron. 21:15, see note to vs. 15 in NIV margin).

Of all the variants between the parallel accounts, however, the most intriguing one is the contrast between the LORD inciting David in Samuel 24:1 and Satan doing it in Chronicles 21:1. In a comment remarkable for an evangelical scholar, Baldwin notes: "The parallel account in 1 Chronicles 21 shows how theological thought had developed over the years, and attributed to 'Satan' or 'an adversary' what was earlier attributed to *the Lord*" (Baldwin, 294).

From our perspective, the account in 2 Samuel is puzzling for two reasons: (1) the author never explains why it was wrong to take a census (the Chronicler doesn't explain it, either); (2) the LORD incites David to an act for which He subsequently punishes him.

The solution to the first puzzle may be in connection with David's supposed "pride" in the size of his army. Some scholars have noted Exodus 30:12 as a legal passage that implies some kind of risk or culpability in census taking. But no explanation appears quite convincing. Let it be said, however, that even if we cannot grasp why it was wrong to number the people, the crusty Joab could, and he challenged the king. Yet Joab doesn't tell us why it was wrong, either (2 Sam. 24:3). In any event, the king overruled Joab, and the census went ahead.

The second puzzle is more ours than the Old Testament's. In the Old Testament, since the LORD was known to be just, He was free to punish and reward as He saw fit. In some ways, this story is similar to the one in 1 Kings 22, where the LORD seeks counsel from His heavenly court on how to make Ahab fall at Ramoth Gilead: "Who will entice Ahab into attacking Ramoth Gilead and going to his death there?" (vs. 20). Again there is no debate over whether Ahab deserved to die. The only question was the manner of his death. Likewise, in 2 Samuel 24, there is no debate over whether it was right or wrong to number the people. Joab, and soon David, too, knew that it was wrong. The only question was how the sin was to be punished.

When David finally came to his senses, he was "conscience-stricken" (vs. 10). The prophet Gad came with three choices of punishment. David's response is one of the most moving testimonies in Scripture to a believer's confidence in the LORD: "Let us fall into the hands of the LORD, for his mercy is great; but do not let me fall into the hands of men" (vs. 14).

The same story reveals a crack in the solid wall of the idea of corporate solidarity. As David pondered all the people who were suffering because of his sin, he cried out, "I am the one who has sinned and done wrong. These are but sheep. What have they done? Let your hand fall upon me and my family" (vs. 17). Remarkably, David's protest came *after* the LORD had already ordered the angel to stop the calamity.

For David, of course, the sword had already been unleashed on him and his family, and it would continue to wreak havoc. But the author's audience, hearing the story in the setting of a Jerusalem in ruins, might realize that David wasn't the only guilty one. They, too, shared in the blame. After all, who was it who had asked for a king in the first place?

The scene at the threshing floor is significant for the future worship experience of Israel. In 2 Chronicles 3:1, the place is also identified with Mt. Moriah, the place where Abraham sacrificed Isaac (Gen. 22:2, 14). While dickering over price, David expressed an important principle of gift giving: "I will not sacrifice to the LORD my God burnt offerings that cost me nothing" (2 Sam. 24:24). In the end, commitment to the LORD is costly, even though His mercy and grace are free and everlasting.

The last scene in 2 Samuel is of David building an altar and sacrificing to the LORD. Only twice does our author record such an event for David: when he brought the ark to Jerusalem (2 Sam. 6:13, 17) and here, when the plague was stopped.

Summary: The Appendix in Perspective

The last story in 2 Samuel reveals enough glimpses of mercy that it could serve both as a message of judgment (2 Samuel) and as a message of hope (1 Chronicles): the staying of the destructive sword

(24:16), David's confession about the LORD's great mercy (vs. 14), and the final word: "The LORD answered prayer in behalf of the land, and the plague on Israel was stopped" (vs. 25).

But the disturbing elements stand out more vividly when the story is seen as the counterpart to the other plague story in 2 Samuel 21. If, in connection with the first plague, Saul's house was effectively destroyed, in connection with the second David's house remained alive. Was continued existence good news? Given the assurance that the sword would never depart from David's house (12:10), the promise of an enduring house may not have been all that encouraging.

Perhaps more sobering, however, is the fact that in the first plague story, seven people died, while seventy thousand died in the second. Saul's sin cost seven lives; David's cost seventy thousand; and now the people themselves may have been implicated, for the account begins with the statement that the anger of the LORD was kindled against Israel (24:1). In spite of David's disclaimer, the people were being punished, not just David, a powerful message to those who witnessed the end of the monarchy. Their kings had failed. But so had the people. And now they had fallen into the hands of men.

If only they could fall into the hands of the LORD. . . .

■ Applying the Word

1. *Troublesome Stories.* **When I read troublesome stories in Scripture, do I find it encouraging or distressing to think that God is reaching other people where they are? How does it affect my view of God to find Him involved in situations that are not in harmony with my ideas of right and wrong? How does it affect my view of Scripture and of truth?**

2. *Promises.* **How does the story of blood guilt for Saul tell me that I should take all my promises more seriously? What kinds of promises am I inclined to forget? Why?**

3. *A Powerful God.* **Am I able to appreciate violent psalms that speak of God's power and might? Why or why not? If not, can I think of people who might find them helpful?**

4. *Innocence.* Are there times in my life when I, like David, have felt so buoyed up by God's presence and power that I can virtually claim to be without sin (2 Sam. 22:21-25)? What does that mean for me as a Christian who might be more inclined to model my life after the publican rather than the Pharisee (Luke 18:9-14)? Or am I in danger of making claims like the Pharisee?

5. *Domino Effect.* What instances in my life can I recall when my sin has caused others to suffer? When have I suffered as a result of others' sins? How can I avoid hurting others by my sin and be able to grant forgiveness to those who have hurt me by their sins?

6. *Into the Hands of a Merciful God.* How can I develop such trust in God that I am more willing to commit myself into His hands than into the hands of human beings, even when I have committed great sins?

■ Researching the Word

1. *Wrath of God.* Using a concordance, compile a list of key passages that help define what the term *wrath of God* means. It may be helpful to carry out two separate studies, one based on the Old Testament and another based on the New Testament. When you have completed both the Old and New Testament aspects of your study, compare your conclusions for each part and construct a synthesis position. Compare your findings with those in a good Bible dictionary.

2. *Psalms of Guilt, Psalms of Innocence.* In 2 Samuel 22:21-25, David boldly claims innocence and righteousness before God, a sharp contrast with Psalm 51, for example, where he sees himself as an unworthy sinner. Expand your study of the psalms of guilt and the psalms of innocence by reading Psalm 17 and Psalm 18 (the parallel to 2 Samuel 22), on the one hand, and Psalm 38 and Psalm 69, on the other. For each psalm, list the various emotions expressed; then characterize the thrust of each psalm as a whole. Imagine pray-

ing these psalms yourself, asking when, where, and how you would be able to pray like that. As you have time, add other psalms to your study and prayer list for similar reflection.

∎ Further Study of the Word

1. For general comments, see E. G. White, *Patriarchs and Prophets*, 746-749.
2. For a discussion of the role of Satan in the Old Testament, see A. Thompson, *Who's Afraid?*, 43-70.
3. For a discussion of the violent prayers in Scripture, including the imprecatory psalms, see A. Thompson, *Who's Afraid?*, 158-168. For an alternative view, see A. M. Rodriguez, "Inspiration and the Imprecatory Psalms," in *Journal of the Adventist Theological Society* 5:1, 40-67.